ITALY COOKS

page 81

page 155

page 181

page 29

page 21

page 125

RISTORANTE

page 113

page 73

page 30

page 50

page 81

ITALY COOKS

BY JUDY ZEIDLER

The photographs of the people and places in this book were taken by Judy Zeidler

Illustrated by Suzanne Dunaway

Book Design by Marcie Rozalsky

Ciao Cindy,
Buon Appetito!!
Judy Zeidler

MOSTARDA PRESS | LOS ANGELES

Also by Judy Zeidler:
THE GOURMET JEWISH COOK
MASTER CHEFS COOK KOSHER
THE 30-MINUTE KOSHER COOK
JUDY ZEIDLER'S INTERNATIONAL DELI COOKBOOK

Co-Authored:
MICHEL RICHARD'S HOME COOKING WITH A FRENCH CHEF
FARMERS MARKET COOKBOOK
DISNEYLAND COOKBOOK
KNOTT'S BERRY FARM COOKBOOK

Library of Congress Control Number 2011922249

ISBN 978-0-615-41913-8

Printed in the United States of America

First Edition

10 9 8 7 6 5 4 3 2 1

Book Design by Marcie Rozalsky
www.rozegraphics.com

www.judyzeidler.com & www.mostardapress.com

For Marvino

and

to my children and their spouses: Susan and Leo, Marc and Amy,
Kathy and Steve, Paul and Amber, Zeke and Jay. And to our grandchildren:
Aaron and Amanda, Normandie, Giamaica, Zane, Ariella, Melina, and Quest.

I hope that the Italian friends we have made over the years will also be your friends.

Mille Grazie!

Thank you, first of all, to my husband, Marvino, without whom I would never have met these wonderful Italian friends. I thank him also for the fun we had cooking all of these marvelous recipes together.

To Pam Hunter, my good friend. Thank you for getting this book off the ground. *If only you could see this now! I miss you.*

My sincere thanks to Marcie Rozalsky for loving my stories as much as I do. I couldn't have done this without you.

Suzanne Dunaway...thank you for adding another dimension to my book with your beautiful illustrations.

My thanks to Angela Rinaldi for her efforts on my behalf.

My sincere thanks to Ricardo Febbrari for translating the recipes of his father, Mauro, from Italian into English. Thanks to my dear friends, Daniela Pironti and Gessica Guidi, for their perfect translations of the recipes.

My daughter Susan and my good friend Florine Sikking for their eagle eye proofreading.

Special thanks to my daughters, Susan and Kathy, daughter-in-law, Amy, and friends Diane Bokor Sargisian, Sue Cheldon, and Lou and Marcia Liuzzi for their expert recipe testing.

Dan Kacvinski, your professional photographs of my recipes help my book shine.

Kathy, Steve, Aaron, Amanda, Zeke and Jay...your glorious pictures have given life to my recipes.

A special note of thanks for the inspiration derived from our friends in Italy.

page 60

page 130

page 143

page 179

page 31

page 96

page 149

page 117

page 35

page 164

page 83

page 68

page 39

page 178

page 126

page 115

page 147

page 94

page 113

page 31

page 105

SCHIACCIATA

page 171

page 60

page 175

TABLE OF CONTENTS

TABLE OF CONTENTS

True to the nature of all of my cookbooks, the recipes
you will find in Italy Cooks have been adapted for a kosher kitchen.

On a personal note, as you read about my culinary travels, I hope you will feel as though you and I are friends.
It is my desire to try to make you feel as though I am telling you of my experiences first-hand—
as though we were chatting about them together, over espresso and biscotti.
To preserve this intimacy, I have written my manuscript in a conversational tone that I know you will enjoy.

INTRODUCTION

After Susan, our first child, was born, Marvino and I discovered a small, family-owned Italian restaurant in our Los Angeles neighborhood. Children were welcome. At that time, I assumed that spaghetti with meatballs in tomato sauce was the ultimate authentic Italian cuisine.

On our first trip to Italy a few years later, I learned that spaghetti with meatballs was not all that easy to find. Nor did Italians consider it particularly authentic. I quickly discovered that Italian cuisine is not characterized by any single dish, but includes a stunning variety of approaches and ingredients.

It has now been thirty-five years since Marvino and I traveled to Italy on that first business trip. At the time, I was the mother of five young children, and my husband owned several men's clothing stores in Los Angeles.

Italy has been a second home to us ever since. Our love affair with Northern Italian cuisine and the gifted individuals involved in developing and preserving its foods and wines have changed our lives. We spend several months there each year, visiting restaurants and food and wine purveyors, collecting new recipe ideas and culinary inspiration.

The Northern Italy I write about in this book is the visitor-friendly Italy of villages, local markets and seasonal produce, of family-run restaurants, wineries and hotels. It is a place where we have made lifelong friends, attended family weddings and holiday celebrations, and have come to cherish the people, and the food. My purpose in writing this book is to share with you information that will enhance your own Italian culinary adventures and perhaps your choices of where to travel, as well.

If you are reading this book you may already know that Northern Italy is home to some of the most extraordinary cooking in all of Europe. My goal is not simply to produce yet another restaurant guide. What I have aimed to do here is offer an insider's perspective to the restaurants in these regions, the extraordinary chefs who run them, and to introduce you to the close friends we've made along the way.

My greatest pride in this book is to offer you authentic recipes created by such legendary figures as Dario Cecchini, the youngest in a long line of master butchers in Panzano; Angelo Gaja, one of the best-known Piemontese vintners; and Romano Levi, creator of a distinctive and personalized *grappa*, an Italian elixir.

This book features their stories, among many others, as well as over one hundred fifty tested recipes. Each chapter includes a personal narrative that describes my connection with the people and the place: how we came to the area, what foods we tasted and learned to make ourselves, and the locally-grown produce and markets we discovered. Many of the recipes are unique family gems that have never before been published. Some are recipes I created, based on dishes we were served by our Italian friends. These are the heart of my book, and I hope they will offer you as much delight and inspiration as they have given me and my family.

I'm excited about sharing the enormous variations in ingredients and cooking techniques involved in preparing classic dishes from region to region and even village to village. During our years of travel, I've come to appreciate the extent to which Italy is made up of small towns where the farmers work the land and are sustained by the food that they grow or trade with their neighbors.

In Thiene, for example, near Venezia, we found restaurants that specialize in quail and pigeon roasted on an open spit with fried potatoes on a shelf below, so that the juices from the birds drip down to flavor the potatoes.

In Lombardia, on the shores of Lago Maggiore, fish from the lake is one of the specialties of Il Sole Ristorante, where Chef Davide Brovelli continually creates new dishes using local ingredients. Peach orchards are close by, and when the chefs are not preparing a dessert of fresh white peaches, they make peach preserves to serve guests for breakfast.

Piemonte offers substantial peasant-type fare. In the fall and winter, fragrant white truffles and porcini mushrooms are abundant.

In the Province of Liguria, on the northwest border of the Italian coast, most restaurants specialize in fresh fish, and seafood is featured in *antipasti*, soups, pasta and main courses. The Ligurians take pride in their light extra-virgin olive oil from small producers, as well as the aromatic basil that they turn into pesto sauce.

For the freshest ingredients from the Italian countryside, there is no place like Toscana, whose rolling hills are filled with olive groves and grapevines. Their simple, pure cuisine relies on the best of what the land produces, and unsalted Tuscan bread is like no other.

In all the regions of Northern Italy, the characteristic foods have an intimate relationship to the local geography, climate, soil, and family traditions. I also have seen firsthand how those unique recipes have, over time, been passed down through generations, revised and revisited, and, ultimately, become commonplace not only in Italy but around the world. An example is *Tortelli di Zucca*, ravioli with pumpkin filling. When we first tasted this sweet and savory ravioli, at dal Pescatore Ristorante, it was a distinctive specialty of the Po Valley; today, thirty-five years later, it is served throughout Italy and is widely available in America as well.

Italy has always been known as an agricultural country. In the areas with vineyards and olive trees they make their own wine and prepare most of their dishes with olive oil.

Depending on the climate, olive oil from the north of Italy is lighter in color and flavor than the olive oil from the sunny south. If dairy cows or sheep are prominent in a region, they make cheese and prepare most of their dishes with butter. These variations within the country enable a visitor to experience an astonishing variety of flavors and specialty products.

In every village there is a farmers' market at least once a week that offers the freshest vegetables, fruits, fish and meats. A visitor walking through one of these markets has only to look at what the vendors are selling to know what will be featured on the menus of the best restaurants in the area. Many of these villages are only about a 30 minute drive apart, and you often see the same people shopping at markets in different villages, wandering among the tables piled high with fruits and vegetables, comparing the offerings of various vendors, choosing what most appeals to them. Market days also offer opportunities for meeting friends and talking about the weather, the family, and what they are making for lunch or dinner.

I cannot end this introductory note without mentioning the inspirational family life that is common among the Italians we have come to know through our travels. In many of the restaurants I describe here, you will notice that the chefs we met thirty-five years ago have now passed their skills and dedication down to their sons and daughters—and sometimes to grandsons and granddaughters who are the cutting-edge chefs of the new generation. The children of people in the restaurant world seem to delight in picking up the torch passed down by their elders and creating their own culinary masterpieces in the contemporary food world. There is a harmony and generosity of spirit in these families that has been deeply touching for us to witness, and it is no wonder we have come to know and love several generations of master chefs and their helpers in these exceptional establishments.

Looking back on our experiences over the last 35 years, we consider ourselves lucky beyond our wildest dreams. It is my hope that this book will allow you to share in the excitement, high spirits and good eating that we have been so privileged to enjoy.

Judy Zeidler

Los Angeles, California , 2011

THE VENETO

VICENZA
Nino and Vicki Maule: *Our Adventures Begin*

Our culinary adventures in Italy began in 1975. My husband, Marvino, owned Zeidler & Zeidler, a chain of men's clothing stores in California, and we attended fashion shows in Paris twice a year. When styles shifted to Italy, we traveled to Milan and Florence as well as other parts of the country where Marvino would design menswear and contract for the clothing to be made and shipped to Los Angeles.

An Italian friend, Romeo Palmesano, who was born near Fano on the Adriatic coast, would often travel with us. His skills as a translator and business negotiator were invaluable to Marvino. As a bonus for both Marvino and me, he was a food lover. We always consulted with Romeo about where to eat, what to eat and what the locals were eating. Through Romeo, we learned the history of the food we were served, which enhanced our enjoyment of every meal. Like many Italian men, Romeo didn't cook much, but if you asked him about a dish–any dish–he knew exactly what was in it and how it should taste.

Between appointments, we would always search out good places to eat, checking guide books, asking the locals where we could eat a great lunch or dinner, often driving for hours to get there. In those days there was a small group of *ristoranti* called "*Buon Ricordo*" (the "good memory"). When you ordered the restaurant's specialty, at the end of the meal you were presented with a handcrafted ceramic plate that commemorated the dish. At one of these establishments, I had my heart set on getting a plate, but the dish–octopus baked in its own ink–was not to Romeo's taste, and he didn't think we would enjoy it. Always a gentleman, he ordered it "for the table," didn't eat it, and gave me his *Buon Ricordo* dish as a souvenir.

On those first visits to Italy, we stopped at many clothing factories, from Veneto to Lombardia. On one occasion we were scheduled to visit a factory in Thiene, northwest of Venice. The owner, Nino Maule, and his wife, Vicki, were old friends of Romeo's. Before our visit to their factory, the Maules, accompanied by their son and two daughters, picked us up at our hotel and took us to one of their favorite restaurants in Vicenza. Nino, a tall, slender man who had once been a university history professor, spoke excellent English. Vicki, a statuesque blond, didn't speak English, but as we got to know each other we managed to communicate and even gossip in both languages. I later observed that she really ran the household as well as helped with the business.

When the Maules discovered that we loved food, they wined and dined us for four days, inviting us to their tennis club for lunch, their family home for dinner, and to a picnic at their country house. We ate in a fish restaurant on the Veneto Canal and dined with Nino's fraternity friends, one of whom lived in a 17th century villa. After a dinner at a

Upon our departure from a wonderful evening, the women were serenaded by our own personal Italian quartet, with a verse of "Goodnight Ladies."

Above: "Ribs are meant to be eaten with your hands," Romeo, who now resides in New York, explained to Vicki. Vicki replied, "But Italians don't eat with their hands!" At right: Alessandro & Nadia on their wedding day.

restaurant, we were all invited back to their villa, where we continued to eat, drink, laugh and tell stories late into the night.

But still we did no business.

Again and again during this parade of gourmet lunches and dinners we asked when we could visit Nino's factory. Again and again he said, "We're having such a good time–why work? The next time you're in Italy call us and we'll have a meal together."

We left Vicenza without writing an order.

A week later, still in Italy, we called Nino to thank him for his hospitality and asked when we could get together again. He said, "Come back, there's another great restaurant here where we can eat lunch." We drove three hours back to meet him. After lunch at a local *trattoria* he finally agreed to take us to his factory, where we wrote a large order. When we asked about extra terms or a letter of credit, Nino said, "It's really not necessary, because now we're friends."

Twice a year, when business took us back to Italy, we would return to visit our new Italian friends, Nino and Vicki. We enjoyed many meals with them and their family, often in their home. One year we cooked a traditional American dinner for their family and friends: barbecued beef ribs and fried chicken, coleslaw, potato salad, and apple and lemon meringue pies.

Ron Rossi, who traveled with us, collaborating with Marvino on fabric choices and designs for the clothing stores, said he was a master at preparing ribs and took charge of that part of the menu. It was a challenge, because the local butcher had no idea what we wanted. But we were finally able to buy something close to the ribs familiar to us in the States. Ron first boiled them, then brushed them with his homemade barbecue sauce and finished them on the grill. Marvino fried the chicken, and I prepared the coleslaw and potato salad. Then I rolled out pie crusts and made two pies: apple and lemon meringue.

The Maules had a great time watching us and asked endless questions about the dishes we were preparing. Once the meal was served, we noticed that our friends resisted eating anything with their hands, including the ribs and chicken. Even though they cut everything with a knife and fork, they were good sports, and the food we prepared met with their hearty approval.

When the Maules's son, Alessandro, was married we were among the guests invited to the ceremony in a beautiful 16th century church. The ceremony began promptly at 4:30 p.m. on a lovely sunny day. A large red banner with the names "Alessandro & Nadia" hung from one of the church pillars. The bride and groom–both in their twenties–were seated in front of the altar, flanked by their witnesses. The bride wore a long white wedding gown with layers and layers of organdy, embroidered with pearls and rhinestones. Her tiara was trimmed with pearls, and streamers of pearls flowed from her upswept jet-black hair.

Just before the bride and groom signed their marriage certificate, they were given a silver plate containing the key to their home, two roses, a basket with a round loaf of bread, a cluster of grapes and a bottle of wine. All of these items had spiritual meaning for the newly wedded pair, symbolizing a long and happy life together. After emerging

Alessandro e Nadia · 6 settembre 1986

aperitivi

cascata di prosciutto crudo con fichi
voul-au-vent ai funghi porcini
barchette con gamberetti in salsa rosa
coppa ghiacciata di melone
crostini di salmone

risotto ai funghi di bosco
gnocchetti alla parigina

branzino in crosta di pane

sorbetto al limone

sella di vitello all' Orloff

contorni di stagione

macedonia di frutti di bosco

torta nuziale

caffè

from the church, the guests followed the newly married couple to a private villa for the reception and wedding feast.

On our arrival at the villa, we were served strawberry, apricot and orange champagne punch. Large bowls of green and black olives filled a long buffet table. Fried olives and fried sage were delicious new taste experiences.

Then we moved into the colorful, secluded garden of the villa, where a large red-and-white-striped tent protected the antipasti buffet table. The tables were decorated with carvings of fish and mushrooms made out of chilled butter, resting on ice. A large ceramic bowl was filled with melon balls marinated in wine, a traditional local dish. Also on one of the tables was a huge tiered platter draped with salami and figs in the shape of a wedding cake–a magnificent sight. We sampled an assortment of puff pastries filled with tuna, caviar, olive paste and smoked salmon, and toasted the happy couple with abundant white wine and champagne.

Dinner was served inside the villa. A menu rolled and tied with a thin silver ribbon lay on each plate. The *risotto*, my favorite, made with porcini mushrooms, broth, and cheese, was cooked to perfection, *al dente*. The *gnocchi*, (*Gnocchetti alla Parigina*), were not prepared in the usual manner; using no potatoes, they consisted only of milk, eggs and flour and were served with a creamy cheese sauce. Next, large platters appeared with poached whole fish encased in a bread crust that was carefully spooned onto guests' plates and garnished with fresh herbs.

After refreshing our palates with lemon sorbet served in a champagne glass, we were presented with the main course: a whole rack of veal carried in on the shoulders of two waiters. The veal was sliced and served with perfectly cooked vegetables of the season, including tiny,

A small selection from my collection of over one hundred-fifty *Buon Ricordi* (Good memory) plates,

tender asparagus. A salad of arugula, radicchio, mache and endives with an olive oil vinaigrette offered a refreshing contrast.

Once dinner was over, the bride and groom were photographed cutting the wedding cake. The cake was even more elaborate than I had anticipated, piled high with layers of *genoise* alternating with layers of flaky pastry filled with rum-flavored custard. Surrounding the entire cake, for a final exotic touch, were tiny cream puffs filled with chocolate cream, glazed with caramel and decorated with pastel flowers. A bell-shaped nougatine ornament graced the top of the cake.

As the guests left, well fed and happy, each one was presented with a gift from the bride and groom: a gilded box containing traditional homemade candy-coated almonds in a little tulle bag decorated with tiny pink flowers, and a beautiful blown-glass vase hand-painted with the same pink flowers.

Because of the amount of wine consumed, many of the guests probably didn't remember how they got home, but memories of the wedding will always be with us.

The natural generosity of the Maule's never ceased to amaze us. Each time we visited they would greet me with a big smile, holding out a beautifully wrapped gift. On one occasion their gift was two Venetian hand-blown glass decanters with colorful floral tops. On another, the Maules could hardly wait until we entered their home to hand me an antique pasta maker equipped with discs that processed the dough into many shapes. They had observed how fascinated I always was with the varieties of pasta served when we dined with them. We did have a small problem bringing this antique pasta maker through customs, since it resembled a rocket launcher. But once we unwrapped it and explained what it was, the suspicious customs agents could see that it was basically harmless.

On another occasion, while dining in one of the Maules's favorite restaurants, the waiter grated the Parmesan cheese with a hand-held sterling silver grater. One part of the grater gripped the cheese like a vise while the other had a handle for shredding it. "What a wonderful object!" I exclaimed. When we arrived home in Los Angeles, it was waiting in our mailbox.

Vicki's Fried Olives
(*Cicchetti*)

The first time we were served fried olives was in a villa outside of Vicenza, at the wedding of Nino and Vicki's son Alessandro. Their crisp saltiness makes them an especially appealing complement to champagne or *prosecco*.

Makes 36

36 pitted green olives
1 cup flour
2 eggs, beaten
1 cup fine dry bread crumbs
Olive oil for deep frying

Place the olives in a bowl, cover with water, and allow them to soak for at least 15 minutes, to remove some of the salt. Rinse the olives and dry them well.

Roll the olives lightly in flour, then dip in beaten egg, and roll them in bread crumbs to coat. Transfer to a paper-towel lined plate and refrigerate for one hour.

In a skillet or deep fryer, heat 2 to 3-inches of oil over high heat. Place the olives in the oil and fry them, rolling them around to brown evenly.

Remove the olives with a slotted spoon and spread on paper towels to drain. Serve hot. They can be held for a few hours, then reheated in a 250°F oven.

Vicki's Roasted Peppers with Anchovies
(*Peperoni Arrosti con Acciughe*)

On our first trip to Italy we discovered how satisfying roasted peppers can be. Once back in Los Angeles, I adapted the technique for this recipe from a family recipe for the locally available Anaheim chilies. This is a simple, foolproof method. If I am not planning to serve the peppers immediately, I cover them with oil and garlic and store them in a bowl in the refrigerator to serve as an appetizer or to garnish a salad. The olive oil serves as a preservative and the garlic actually brings out their flavor.

Although some people suggest substituting jarred roasted peppers, these cannot compare with peppers prepared at home.

When selecting peppers, choose smooth and shiny ones without punctures or soft spots. They should be crisp and firm to the touch.

To serve this dish as a festive appetizer, arrange the sliced roasted peppers on a large platter or shallow serving dish, garnished with anchovy fillets, olives and parsley or watercress. Or serve as a side dish to a main course.

Serves 8

4 to 6 firm, crisp red,
yellow or purple bell
peppers (or a combination)
2 to 3 garlic cloves, minced
Olive oil
1 (2 ounce) can or jar
anchovy fillets, packed in oil
Parsley sprigs for garnish

Preheat the oven to 450°F. Place a large sheet of foil on the lower rack of the oven. Place the peppers on the rack above, in the middle of the oven. Bake 20-25 minutes or until the skin has puffed and darkened slightly on top. Turn each pepper over and continue baking for 10 to 15 minutes longer.

Remove the peppers from the oven, and very carefully peel off the skins while they are still warm. Pull out the stems and discard the seeds. Cut the peppers into segments that follow their natural ridges. Remove the peppers from the juices and layer them in a bowl, with garlic, and enough oil to cover. Cover with plastic wrap and refrigerate. Be sure to let them warm to room temperature before serving because the oil congeals when refrigerated. When ready to serve, arrange the peppers on a serving dish and garnish with anchovies and parsley springs.

Variation: To use as a Roasted Pepper Sauce, place peppers in a food processor or blender with a little olive oil and purée until smooth.

Radicchio on the Grill
(Radicchio alla Griglia)

There are two varieties of red radicchio: one is a small round cabbage shape, the other has elongated leaves and is called trevigiano, after Treviso, the town near Venice where it is grown.

Many people use radicchio only to give a salad a little bit of crimson to break up the monotony of a pale green mix. In Italy, radicchio is cooked almost as often as it is served raw.

Radicchio is used in *risotto* and pasta dishes, spread on pizza, sautéed and grilled, as well as being served in a salad. My favorite way to serve it is grilled, as a separate course. The delicately bitter flavor of radicchio takes on a different dimension when it is grilled.

The first time I was served radicchio—up in the hills in the Veneto area—it was placed on an open grill with a brick on top. Recently, a chef served us grilled romaine lettuce—an excellent substitute—with a Caesar dressing.

Serves 4

2 heads treviso radicchio or
   romaine lettuce
1/2 cup olive oil
Salt
Freshly ground black pepper
1/2 cup grated Parmesan
   cheese

Trim each radicchio by cutting off a little of the core, leaving enough to hold the leaves together. Cut in half lengthwise and brush with olive oil, place on a hot grill or frying pan and sprinkle with salt and pepper to taste. Place a heavy weight on top of the radicchio and grill or sauté it until lightly browned, then turn it over and repeat the same procedure. Just before serving sprinkle with Parmesan cheese.

Vicki's Risotto with Wild Berries
(Risotto al Frutti di Bosco)

Our first taste of this unusual *risotto* was in Pisa. When we were visiting Vicki Maule I asked her about it, and she was happy to share her recipe. The berries produce a surprisingly savory dish; like fruit vinegar, they add flavor with just a hint of sweetness. Either fresh or frozen berries work beautifully in this dish.

Serves 8 to 10

1/2 cup unsalted butter
1 onion, minced
2-1/2 cups arborio rice
8 to 10 cups vegetable stock
   or water, heated

In a heavy 4-quart pot, heat 4 tablespoons of the butter, add onion and sauté for 2 minutes, until it begins to soften, being careful not to brown.

Add rice, using a wooden spoon, stir for 1 minute, making sure the grains are well coated. Add 1 or 2 ladles of stock, or enough to cover the rice. Cook, stirring constantly, as the stock is absorbed. Continue

1/2 cup blueberries*
1/2 cup strawberries,* hulled
  and sliced
1/2 cup whole raspberries,*
  cut in half
1 cup grated Parmesan cheese
1/3 cup cream

adding stock a little at a time, until the rice is just tender, 10 to 15 minutes.

Add the berries and continue cooking, add additional stock as needed. Add remaining butter, Parmesan and cream. Mix well.

Spoon into shallow bowls and serve immediately. Serves 8 to 10.

* This dish is especially good when prepared with wild berries.

Vicki's Risotto with Mushrooms
(Risotto con Funghi)

This adaptation of a recipe I got from Vicki is my favorite version of the classic mushroom *risotto*. Fresh shiitake mushrooms combined with the dried porcini give it a deep, rich flavor. I store dried porcini mushrooms in the freezer so I always have them on hand for this dish. Here, as with all *risottos*, the secret is in the timing. In the finished product the rice should be cooked *al dente*, bound together with a velvety sauce. I always keep a spoon close by to taste it as it comes to a finish.

Serves 8 to 10

6 tablespoons unsalted butter
1/2 cup thinly sliced fresh
  shiitake mushrooms
1/2 cup sliced dried porcini
  mushrooms, soaked in water
  for 30 minutes
1 onion, finely chopped
2-1/2 cups arborio rice
6 to 8 cups hot vegetable stock
1/4 cup minced parsley
1/2 to 1 cup cream
1 cup freshly grated
  Parmesan cheese
Salt
Freshly ground black pepper

In a small skillet, melt 1 tablespoon of the butter and sauté the shiitake mushrooms until soft. Set aside.

With a slotted spoon, transfer the porcini mushrooms from their soaking liquid to a bowl. Strain the soaking liquid into a small saucepan; bring to a boil and simmer for 5 to 10 minutes, until it thickens and the flavor intensifies. Set aside.

In a large heavy skillet, melt 4 tablespoons of the remaining butter until foamy. Add the onion and sauté over medium heat until soft.

Add the rice and mix well with a wooden spoon. Add 1 or 2 ladles of stock, or enough to cover the rice. Cook, stirring constantly, as the stock is absorbed. Continue adding stock a little at a time, until the rice is just tender, 10 to 15 minutes.

Add the sautéed mushrooms, porcini, parsley and cream to the rice mixture. Mix well and cook 3 to 4 minutes longer. When the rice is tender but firm to the bite, blend in 1/2 cup of the Parmesan cheese and the remaining 1 tablespoon of butter. Season to taste with salt and pepper.

Serve immediately in heated shallow bowls. Garnish each serving with the reduced porcini liquid. Serve the remaining Parmesan in a bowl, to be passed separately.

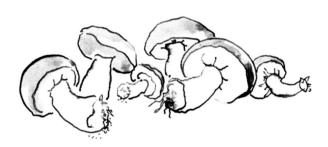

VENICE
Marie and Brandino Brandolini
A Gifted French Artist and an Italian Wine Maker

Above: Marie and Brandino Brandolini. Left: Lele, owner of Busa-Alla-Torre da Lele a wonderful restaurant on Murano.

We met Marie and Brandino Brandolini in 1999 at a summer solstice festival and charity auction lunch at Capezzana winery, home of Count Ugo and Contessa Lisa Bonacossi, just outside of Florence.

I sat next to Marie, a beautiful woman with long red hair. Born in France, her mother was part of the Rothschild family. Marie and Brandino have a *palazzo* in Venice, where she designs a wonderful line of Venetian glasses, vases, dishes, and jewelry. She looked so fabulous in her sleeveless black dress, you could hardly tell she was five months pregnant with her third child. We became instant friends.

After the party at Capezzana, we left for a three-day adventure with food writer, Faith Willinger, where we were guests of Brandino, Marie's husband, and his father, Count Brandolini in their family home, located near their winery, "Vistorta." Brandino

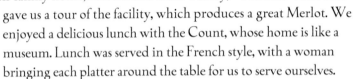

gave us a tour of the facility, which produces a great Merlot. We enjoyed a delicious lunch with the Count, whose home is like a museum. Lunch was served in the French style, with a woman bringing each platter around the table for us to serve ourselves.

The next day, we visited Marie at her *palazzo* in Venice, saw a display of her Venetian glassware, and visited the factory on the island of Murano, where she oversees its production.

One of her collections is designed in a tradition that goes back hundreds of years. It is common after a day's work for the glass blowers to collect all the leftover glass pieces to make colorful drinking glasses for their families. Little goes to waste in Italy, and Marie uses these many-colored odd pieces to create a distinctive line of glassware.

After our visit with Marie, she invited us to lunch. We went by private water taxi to a restaurant on Murano, Busa-Alla-Torre da Lele, which is within walking distance of many glass shops. The restaurant, which is open only for lunch, specializes in seafood. It is a place for the locals, and few Americans know about it. We were seated at a table on the *piazza*, which I prefer to the two interior rooms. The owner, Lele, a large man with a long red beard and twinkling eyes, is the prototype of a rotund and jolly chef. He sat with us and offered suggestions for our lunch as he took our order. We were served two seafood courses: a seafood salad was brought to us in a large ceramic shell, and a seafood *risotto*. For dessert we had *sgroppino*, a combination of lemon *gelato* and *prosecco* blended together until foamy.

The following year, when we visited Marie and met her new baby—a

WHEN YOU GO, YOU SHOULD KNOW:

Laguna B (Handblown Glass)
Marie Brandolini
Dorsoduro 3228
30123 Venezia – Italy
Tel: (041) 5233035
Fax: (041) 5224527
www.lagunab.com

Busa-Alla-Torre da Lele
Piazza Santo Stefano 3
30141 Murano, Venezia – Italy
Tel: (041) 739662

Ristorante da Fiore
S.Polo – Calle del Scaleter, 2002
30125 Venezia – Italy
Tel: (041) 721308
Fax: (041) 721343
www.dafiore.net

Ristorante al Covo
Castello, 3968
30122 Venezia – Italy
(041) 5223812
www.ristorantealcovo.com

third boy, she invited us to dinner at da Fiore, a well-known restaurant where reservations are difficult to get. Located in the inner core of the city near the Rialto Bridge, it has for decades been the place where Venice offered its most exquisite tastes to its most exclusive patrons. In my opinion this is the best restaurant in Venice.

We ordered the six-course tasting menu, and every dish was creative and delicious. I especially enjoyed the roasted snapper flavored with a hint of orange zest, coated with fresh herb breadcrumbs and roasted. The sweet cherry tomatoes served with it made a perfect counterpoint.

Peach Drink
(Bellini)

At San Marcos you can take a private motorboat to the Cipriani Hotel, a luxury inn on Torcello Island, a 25-minute ride. Sit at one of the small round tables in their garden area and order their famous Bellini. Ripe, sweet peaches and tangy raspberries mimic the colors of a Venetian sunset.

Makes 2 Servings

2 ounces peach juice
  (or peach nectar)
3 slices of a fresh peach
1 or 2 ice cubes
12 raspberries, pureéd
Champagne

In a blender, purée peach juice, 1 slice of peach and ice cubes. Pour the mixture into a small glass measuring cup and set aside. Rinse out blender, purée raspberries and divide evenly between two flute glasses. Add about 1 ounce of peach mixture to each glass and fill glasses with Champagne. Garnish with remaining 2 slices of fresh peach and serve.

Variation: add 3 ounces Prosecco sparkling wine to 2 ounces fresh white peach purée for one cocktail.

Spaghetti with Snapper Ragu
(Spaghetti con Ragu di Triglie)

I was inspired to create this spaghetti dish by a seafood pasta we were served at da Fiore while dining with Marie Brandolini.

Serves 8 to 10

1/2 pound string beans,
  ends trimmed
Coarse salt
1/2 cup olive oil
2 garlic cloves, minced
10 anchovy fillets, mashed
2 tomatoes, peeled, seeded
  and chopped
1/2 cup dry white wine
1 pound snapper fillets,
  cut into 1-inch pieces
1 tablespoon minced parsley
Salt and freshly ground
  black pepper, to taste
1 pound of spaghetti

Drop string beans into a large pot of boiling, salted water and simmer until tender. Drain, reserving water for pasta, and set aside.

In a large skillet, heat olive oil and garlic over medium-high heat and add anchovies. Lower heat to medium-low and cook, stirring until smooth, about a minute. Add the string beans and tomatoes and cook, stirring until tomatoes soften, about 5 to 10 minutes. Add wine and simmer until alcohol evaporates. Add snapper and cook for another 3 to 4 minutes. Add water, if necessary, to keep sauce moist. Stir in parsley and salt and pepper to taste.

Add spaghetti to reserved water and boil until tender but firm. Add drained spaghetti to sauce in skillet and toss to coat. Serve immediately.

Lemon Gelato and Prosecco Foam
(*Sgroppino*)

In the Veneto they use vodka as the spirit of choice, but you could use *grappa* or *limoncello* if you prefer. Italian lemon *gelato* is like a *sorbet* but denser; it includes no dairy products. A good *Sgroppino* is basically a lemon slushie for adults. It makes a perfect pre-dinner cocktail or a refreshing substitute for dessert at any time of year.

Serves 4

 2 cups lemon *gelato*,
   slightly softened
1 tablespoon *limoncello*
4 tablespoons vodka
   (Absolut Citron)
1 cup *Prosecco*, chilled
Zest of one lemon

Chill 4 champagne flutes. In a shaker, combine *gelato*, *limoncello* and vodka; add *Prosecco* and stir. Serve immediately in chilled flutes. Sprinkle lemon zest on top.

LOMBARDIA

LOMBARDIA

CANNETO SULL'OGLIO
Nadia and Antonio Santini
dal Pescatore: The Best Restaurant in Italy

One of our first food adventures in Italy occurred during a business trip Marvino and I took in the late 70s.. It was nine in the morning when we arrived at a clothing factory in the small village of Gambera, just south of Brescia in the Po Valley. We worked all morning selecting fabrics for slacks and suits, and we were close to finalizing the order when the owner suddenly said, "It's twelve o'clock, we must eat. There's a great restaurant close by that I think that you'd like. We'll finish our business after lunch."

Top: Three-star restaurant, dal Pescatore, shines both indoors and out. Above left to right: Valentina, Giovanni, Alberto, Bruna, Antonio and Nadia Santini.

Leaving Marvino to attend to some last-minute details at the factory, I got into a car with one of the owners and we drove for thirty or forty minutes, mostly on a narrow dirt road surrounded by fields of wheat and corn, stopping finally in front of a lovely stone building covered with ivy. I got out of the car and breathed in the smell of cows and hay.

We were just outside the village of Canneto sull'Oglio, a few miles west of Mantova, and the restaurant in the ivy-covered building was dal Pescatore. Originally a stop for the men who fished on the Olgio River behind the restaurant, dal Pescatore had been in the Santini family for three generations. In those early days the fishermen were served

lunch and dinner on wooden tables and benches. There were no tablecloths, only a fabric-covered lamp overhead for illumination.

When Antonio and Nadia Santini got married, after finishing college, they decided to work with Antonio's mother, Bruna, and his father, Giovanni, in the restaurant. Antonio became the maitre d' in charge of the dining room, while Nadia trained under Bruna in the kitchen. A quick learner, Nadia soon developed a passion for cooking, continually reading cookbooks and food magazines, always experimenting with new dishes. From the beginning, Antonio helped create the menu and did most of the food shopping in Milan, although many local purveyors still come to the restaurant to sell them special fish, meats, cheeses and other products.

On this first visit, we entered a room with a small bar and fireplace and were greeted at the door by Antonio. We saw Nadia and Antonio's three-year-old Giovanni, Jr., a cherub with huge brown eyes like his father's, playing with his mini cars in the middle of the entryway.

During lunch Nadia came out of the kitchen to greet us. An unpretentious dark-haired woman with a lovely shy smile, she was at that time the only one in the family who spoke English, and we became instant friends. Her passion for cooking was evident even then, and she obviously enjoyed answering the many questions I asked about the dishes she and Bruna had prepared for us that day. Although it was rare for Bruna or Nadia to come out of the kitchen during the meal, Nadia would often come into the dining room after she finished cooking, ready to answer any questions her guests might have.

Lunch that first day started with a selection of Bruna and Nadia's *antipasti* specialties: *agrodolce* (a sweet and sour mixture made with red bell peppers), a tiny slice of *frittata* (a mixture of eggs, green onions, asparagus or spinach and Parmesan), cubes of *polenta*, thinly sliced salami, and chunks of Parmigiano-Reggiano cheese. All this was accompanied by *Mostarda di Cremona* (a spicy mixture of fruits candied in a thick mustard syrup–usually pears or watermelon rind).

After this came a plate of Bruna's famous *Tortelli di Zucca*. We had never eaten these pumpkin-filled ravioli–a traditional regional dish few Americans knew about at that time, though it is now a standard on most Italian restaurant menus. Bruna's *Tortelli di Zucca* were not made in the familiar square ravioli shape, but twisted to resemble bonbons. She prepared each order individually, lightly boiling the tortelli, then tossing them in brown butter and grated Parmesan cheese and arranging them on a serving plate.

Bruna's *tortelli* was dal Pescatore's special *Buon Ricordo* dish–the one that entitled the diner to take home a special plate commemorating the restaurant and its specialty. I still have that original plate, along with a dozen or so others that represent dal Pescatore *Buon Ricordo*

Top: A very young Alberto displays early affection for fine foods. Above: Antonio and Nadia in the early years of their restaurant. At right: Giovanni, at about 5 years old, making *grissini* (breadsticks) with Grandma Bruna. Far right: Giovanni now surpasses Grandma Bruna's height!

dishes that accompanied the restaurant's changing specialties over the years.

Later, in the kitchen, I watched Bruna and Giovanni, Antonio's parents, rolling out the pasta, hanging it on a line to dry, cutting it, filling it, and shaping it to make those luscious *Tortelli di Zucca*. I also remember, on that first visit, watching three-year-old Giovanni Jr. help Bruna shape the dinner rolls. (Today Giovanni Jr., having finished college, stands in the same workspace making the pasta and rolls.)

On our first visit, as on so many later ones, Giovanni, Antonio's father, selected a local live fish from the pond in the garden and grilled it on the open fireplace that was then in a corner of the kitchen. All the fish caught in the Oglio River behind the restaurant were put into the pond until the time came to grill them. Another regional traditional dish on dal Pescatore's original menu was horsemeat, which was marinated for several days in red wine, then roasted until tender.

Bruna offered one of her regional cake recipes for our dessert during that memorable first visit. To prepare it, she would pour the batter into a heavy cast-iron covered pot that she placed in the fireplace on top of hot coals. She then raked hot coals over the lid of the pot to bake the cake, which she served with a rich *zabaglione* sauce spooned over the top.

Over the decades since that first visit, we have eaten at dal Pescatore four or five times a year, and have now become part of the Santini family. We have always accepted their invitation to come on Monday or Tuesday, when the restaurant is closed, to have lunch with them, even if that meant we had to drive for two hours. When we have lunch with the family, Bruna always serves us her traditional *risotto* with porcini, fresh peas, and *pesto* because she knows how much we love it. When he was still alive, Papa Giovanni often prepared his special marinated barbecued chicken cooked over an open fire and served with a fresh parsley-olive oil sauce that Mama Bruna made.

Each time we return we notice the changes Nadia and Antonio have made to the restaurant and the new menu items they have added. No longer a rustic stop for local fishermen, dal Pescatore currently welcomes its guests into an elegant sitting room with saffron-colored walls and comfortable upholstered chairs in place of the original wooden tables and benches. Visitors drive into a grassy parking area at the rear of the ivy-covered building and enter the restaurant through a lush garden. The kitchen has remained basically the same, except that the open fireplace where Bruna's traditional cake was once baked has now been replaced with a modern oven.

Nowadays there are several young chefs apprenticing in the kitchen that once contained only the family: Bruna, Giovanni Sr., and Nadia. The Santini family is always generous about sharing their expertise, and chefs from all over the world have spent time in their kitchen, observing their cooking techniques and learning to prepare the regional specialties.

In the early days, our dinners at dal Pescatore usually ended after midnight, and because there were no hotels in the area, we were often invited to stay overnight in great-grandmother's room. Several years ago the Hotel Margot opened close by, and when you make your reservation at dal Pescatore they can reserve a room for you. You can also stay in a contemporary hotel, Hotel delle Arti in Cremona, a short drive from dal Pescatore. This hotel is right in the center of Cremona, a wonderful small village to walk in and have a look in the windows of the small shops to see what Cremona is famous for—violin making.

Over the years we have been visiting the Santinis, I remember a time we came to dal Pescatore when Nadia was pregnant, though still working in the kitchen. The following year we met her chubby red-cheeked baby, Alberto. He slept in a large baby buggy in the middle of the kitchen and *Nonna* Bruna gently rocked him while stirring *risotto*. Alberto is now 6 feet, 2 inches tall, attends college in Parma, and works in the front of the restaurant with Antonio.

Dal Pescatore is now a three star Michelin Restaurant as well as a *Relais Chateaux.* Nadia is the chef in charge of the kitchen, but she insists that Mama Bruna taught her everything she knows about cooking. Giovanni Jr., who was three years old when we first visited, has now finished college and is apprenticing to be a chef. He has the same passion for food as his parents and is eager to continue the family restaurant tradition.

Giovanni Santini and Valentina Tanzi Get Married

In 2010, we received a very special invitation to the wedding of Giovanni Santini and Valentina Tanzi. We had known Giovanni since he was 3 years old, and we were thrilled and immediately made arrangements to attend.

Prior to the wedding, there was a lovely reception in Valentina and Giovanni's new home, where champagne and appetizers were served. Everyone then drove to an intimate 17th century church where Giovanni and his mother, Nadia arrived in a horse-drawn carriage.

The ceremony was beautiful, as was the bride. She wore a white satin gown decorated with pearls in both the front and back. Everyone left the church and returned to their house, where a bus took us to the Antica Osteria della Pesa in Cado, which is owned by friends of the bride and groom.

While the newly married couple stopped by the Oglio River at sunset for a photoshoot, we enjoyed scrumptious appetizers and Ca' del Bosco sparkling wine.

After the reception, everyone went upstairs to a private room, where dinner was served. Every dish was delicate and delicious.

We were delightfully honored to sit at the table with Antonio and Nadia.

Just before dessert, everyone returned to the garden and watched a spectacular fireworks display.

For dessert, and as a gift to the married couple, famous pastry chef and good friend, Giancarlo Perbellini, of Ristorante Perbellini, prepared an array of pastries that covered no less than eight long tables, with the wedding cake in the center of the room. It was beyond any dessert presentation we had ever seen.

The bus returned us to our cozy accommodations at Hotel Palazzo Quaranta in the village of Isola Dovarese at 4:00am.

The next day, Antonio and Nadia invited us to have lunch with the *new* Mr. and Mrs. Santini, and their parents. Grandma Bruna prepared a delicious lunch of fried mushrooms, Parmesan *risotto*, and sea bass (*branzino*) with cherry tomatoes baked in aluminum foil. Dessert was cake and homemade ice cream.

Left page: There's simply no denying the beauty of dal Pescatore. Left, middle: A casual "family" photo, during a recent visit. Left, bottom: The Santini family personalizes their new cookbook for me. This page, above: The lovely "just married" couple make their first public appearance as Mr. and Mrs. Giovanni Santini.

**WHEN YOU GO,
YOU SHOULD KNOW:**

dal Pescatore
Proprietors: Antonio and
   Nadia Santini
Località Runate
46013 Canneto sull'Oglio
Mantova, Italy
Tel: (0376) 723001
Fax: (0376) 70304
email: santini@dalpescatore.com
www.dalpescatore.com

Hotel Margot
Via Tazzoli
46013 Canneto sull'Oglio
Mantova, Italy
Tel: (0376) 709011
Fax: (0376) 723961
email: info@hotelmargot.it
www.hotelmargot.it

Hotel delle Arti
Via Geremia Bonomelli, 8
Cremona, Italy
Tel: (0372) 23131
Fax: (0372) 21654
email: info@dellearti.com
www.hoteldellearti.com

Nadia's Rosemary Potato Chips
(Tuiles di Patata e Rosmarino)

Chef Nadia calls these elegant potato crisps *tuiles* of potatoes and rosemary. After dinner, when all the guests had left, I complimented her on the paper-thin delicacies, and her typically generous response was to invite me into the kitchen and teach me to prepare them.

Makes 3 or 4 dozen

1 small Idaho potato
1 tablespoon unsalted butter
2 tablespoons thinly sliced
  green onions
1 tablespoon minced
  fresh rosemary
1-1/2 cups flour
1 cup cold water
1 teaspoon salt
2 tablespoons olive oil

Peel and dice potato, place in water to cover, bring to a boil and simmer until soft. Transfer to a shallow bowl and mash until smooth. Set aside.

In a skillet, heat butter and sauté onions, stirring with a wooden spoon until soft. Add rosemary and continue cooking for 2 minutes. Add 3 tablespoons of the mashed potato and mix well. Set aside.

In a large bowl, using a wooden spoon, add the flour, water, salt, and olive oil, and mix to combine. Add the potato mixture and stir well. Mixture should have an elastic consistency.

Preheat the oven to 325°F.

Line a baking sheet with a Silpat or aluminum foil and brush with olive oil. Using a tablespoon, place small amounts of the potato mixture on the prepared baking sheet and spread into paper-thin oval shapes. Bake for 15 to 20 minutes or until golden brown. They crisp up as they cool. Continue with remaining potato mixture.

Nadia's Parmesan Crisps
(Schegge di Parmigiano)

The first time I saw Nadia experimenting with these thin Parmesan wafers, I could not imagine what she was cooking up. She had only a bowl of grated Parmesan cheese, a spoon and an iron skillet. I was sure the cheese was going to burn, but the next thing I saw was her lifting the sheer, lacey cheese crisps from the skillet and placing them atop bowls of hot onion soup.

For Nadia, these cheese curls are a signature appetizer. She often welcomes her guests with a glass of sparkling wine and a platter of cheese crisps.

Makes about 20 crisps, depending on size

3 tablespoons unsalted butter
1 cup finely grated Parmesan
  (if lumpy, press through
  a strainer)

Brush a large nonstick frying pan with butter and heat over medium-high heat until butter begins to bubble. Spoon 2-3 teaspoons of grated Parmesan in the center of the frying pan. Fry over medium heat until Parmesan melts and browns on bottom. Use a small metal spatula to loosen Parmesan crisp around edges and transfer to a paper towel to absorb excess oil.

Serve on a paper-doily lined plate. They will still be soft when removed from the pan, but will crisp up immediately.

Bruna's Ravioli with Five Cheeses
(*Ravioli ai Cinque Formaggi*)

The Santini family at dal Pescatore is famous for starting trends, and this is one of them. Make your own pasta, fill squares with the 5-cheese mixture, and shape them into ravioli or tortellini. They are as light and melt-in-your-mouth as you can get.

When a customer orders Bruna's Ravioli, Bruna melts butter in a frying pan, adds grated Parmesan cheese, tosses the ravioli in the sauce, spoons it onto a plate and *voilà*!

Serves 6 to 8

12 ounces Parmesan cheese*
1/2 pound ricotta, drained
6 ounces Romano cheese*
6 ounces Emmenthal cheese*
6 ounces Gruyere cheese*
1 cup whipping cream
1/2 cup butter, melted
2 eggs
3 tablespoons grated onion
2 tablespoons minced parsley
1/4 teaspoon nutmeg
Salt
Freshly ground black pepper
1 recipe fresh pasta
   (see recipe, page 168)

1/2 cup unsalted butter, diced
Parmesan cheese*

In a large bowl, combine the 5 cheeses, cream, butter, eggs, grated onion, parsley, nutmeg, salt and pepper and mix well.

Prepare the fresh pasta and roll it out in long wide sheets. Place a teaspoon of filling every 2 to 2-1/2 inches on one sheet of prepared pasta. With pastry brush or fingers dipped in water, moisten all sides and between cheese mounds. Carefully place second sheet of pasta over cheese-filled sheet. Using fingers gently press sheets together to seal firmly at edges and between mounds of filling. With ravioli cutter or small sharp knife, cut ravioli into individual squares. Place squares on a clean, lightly floured cotton towel and let rest 1 hour, if possible. Repeat with remaining dough and filling.

Butter a large serving dish. Bring a large pot of water to a boil. Cook 8 to 10 ravioli at a time. Remove with slotted spoon to prepared serving dish. Repeat until all ravioli are cooked.

Toss generously with the diced butter and the Parmesan. Serve immediately.

* Freshly grated

Bruna's Pumpkin-Filled Pasta
(*Tortelli di Zucca*)

This pasta has a distinctive spicy-sweet pumpkin filling. It originated in northern Italy, where it can be found in many country restaurants. We ate it for the first time many years ago at dal Pescatore, where the Santinis serve it with a simple butter sauce.

No two Italian families cut and shape stuffed pastas such as tortelli, ravioli or cappelletti the same way. The directions here are for *tortelli* the way the Santini family has prepared it for four generations.

You can find jars of *mostarda*, a mustard-scented compote, in most Italian delis or specialty markets; if you don't find it, try substituting fruit chutney.

Makes about 78 tortelli

2 cups pumpkin purée
   (or Hubbard or banana
   squash purée)
2/3 cup crushed amaretti
   (Italian imported cookies)

In a large bowl, combine the pumpkin purée with the amaretti and bread crumbs and blend well. Add the eggs, *mostarda*, cheese, nutmeg, salt and blend well. Cover with plastic wrap and refrigerate until ready to use.

Prepare the pasta as directed in the basic recipe on page 168 and roll it out to a medium thickness. Cut it into rectangles, 3-inches by

1/2 cup bread crumbs

2 eggs

4 tablespoons *mostarda* (recipe follows) or fruit chutney, optional

1 cup freshly grated Parmesan cheese

1/4 teaspoon of freshly grated nutmeg

Salt

1 recipe Pasta Dough (see page 168)

1-1/2 cups unsalted butter

1/2 cup freshly grated Parmesan

4-inches. Place a generous spoonful of pumpkin filling in the center; lift one corner and fold it on an angle over the filling, then continue folding to completely enclose the filling. With your index fingers, press down firmly on either side of the filling to seal it in, giving the tortelli a bon-bon shape.

As the tortelli are finished, place them on lightly floured kitchen towels and let them dry for at least 15 minutes, until ready to cook and serve.

If you want to store them in the freezer, place the towel with *tortelli* on a baking sheet, then cover with another towel and place in the freezer. When the tortelli are frozen peel them off the towels and place in a plastic bag; return to the freezer. When ready to cook, remove from the plastic bags and defrost on towels, 1/2 inch apart. (Do not let the tortelli touch each other or they will stick together.) To cook the tortelli, drop them into lightly salted boiling water and boil until tender, 5 to 10 minutes. While the tortelli are cooking, melt the butter in a large skillet. Drain the *tortelli* well and gently transfer them into the hot melted butter, sprinkling them with Parmesan cheese and tossing to coat thoroughly.

Nadia's Fruit Preserved in Sweet Mustard Sauce
(*Mostarda*)

This sweet-spicy preparation, usually made with whole fruit, is an essential ingredient in Bruna's classic pumpkin-filled *tortelli*. It also makes a delicious accompaniment to a simple dish of roast chicken or grilled fish. My adaptation of Nadia's recipe for this Italian specialty substitutes a combination of powdered mustard and white wine for the mustard essence that can be difficult to find outside of Italy.

Makes about 5 cups

4 pounds pears, pitted apricots, peaches (or a mixture of some or all of these fruits)

4 cups sugar

10-16 drops of *essenze de senape* liquid (OR 4 tablespoons dry mustard and 4 tablespoons white wine)

Peel and wash fruit of choice and cut into thin slices. In a stainless steel pot layer fruit with sugar and let sit for 24 hours. Liquid will accumulate from the sugar and fruit. Bring the liquid and fruit to a boil and simmer for 5 minutes. Cover and let sit overnight. Repeat two more times (three times in all).

Using a slotted spoon, transfer the fruit to a wax paper-lined baking pan. Meanwhile, bring sugar mixture to a boil and simmer until reduced by one-third. If using *essenze de senape* liquid, add it now, OR in a small pot, whisk the mustard and wine together and cook for 3 minutes until well-blended. Add to sugar mixture and mix well.

Return fruit to the sugar mixture, bring to a boil and simmer for 5 minutes. Cool and transfer to sterilized jars.

Bruna's Pesto, Porcini and Fresh Pea Risotto
(*Risotto ai Piselli Freschi Funghe e Pesto*)

On Tuesday, when dal Pescatore is closed, we often enjoy having lunch in the garden with the Santini family. Bruna prepares this *risotto*, which she knows is our favorite, and I always find my way into the kitchen to watch her. The care and attention she devotes to the dish makes it clear that it's a labor of love. She combines the *risotto* with fresh peas from their garden, behind the restaurant and adds the pesto at the last minute for color and flavor.

Serves about 10-12

Pesto (recipe follows)
8 cups vegetable broth or water
5 tablespoons unsalted butter
1 medium onion, diced
2-1/2 cups arborio or
    carnaroli rice
1 cup fresh or frozen peas
3 or 4 large porcini or shitake
    mushrooms, cut in large slices
1/2 cup dried porcini mushrooms,
    soaked in water
1/2 cup grated Parmesan
1/4 cup cream

Prepare the pesto and set aside.

In a large pot, heat vegetable broth and keep warm.

In another large pot, heat 3 tablespoons of the butter and sauté onion over medium heat until soft. Add rice and mix well with a wooden spoon, coating with butter mixture.

Add 1 or 2 ladles of stock or enough to cover the rice. Cook, stirring constantly, as the stock is absorbed. Continue adding stock a little at a time, adding peas and then porcini (fresh and dried) and additional broth from porcini, and mix until the rice is just tender, 10 to 15 minutes. Add pesto to *risotto* at the last minute with salt and pepper to taste. Add grated Parmesan, the remaining butter and the cream.

Pesto

1 cup basil leaves
3 tablespoons olive oil

In a food processor chop basil and add olive oil in a thin stream.

Giovanni's Barbecued Chicken with Green Sauce
(*Pollo Arrostito Intero con Salsa Verde*)

We love sharing Sunday lunch with the Santinis. The menu never varies: grilled home-raised chicken with a salsa verde, scented with garlic. This cherished recipe has been in their family for generations and was the responsibility of Papa Giovanni to prepare, usually on a wood fire grill, while Bruna was busy in the kitchen vigorously whisking the salsa verde to accompany the chicken. Note that the chicken must marinate twenty-four hours.

Serves 4-6

2 cups olive oil
Juice of 2 lemons
1/2 cup white wine vinegar
4 cloves garlic, crushed and
    thinly sliced
1/2 cup minced fresh parsley
Pinch sugar
Salt
Freshly ground black pepper
2 small frying chickens (2-1/2 to
    3 pounds each), cut into pieces
    Salsa Verde (recipe follows)

In a large, shallow glass bowl or pan, combine olive oil, lemon juice, vinegar, garlic, parsley, and sugar. Season with salt and pepper to taste. Arrange chicken pieces in the pan and turn to coat evenly with olive oil mixture. Cover pan with aluminum foil and marinate chicken for 24 hours in the refrigerator, turning pieces occasionally.

Prepare Salsa Verde and chill.

Prepare coals for grilling or preheat the broiler. To barbecue, arrange chicken on a 2-sided grilling basket and enclose the chicken pieces securely. Grill until the chickens are cooked through, about 20 minutes.

To broil, place chicken pieces under a hot broiler, skin side down. Turn and broil until brown and crisp on both sides. Serve with a bowl of cold *Salsa Verde*.

Green Sauce
(*Salsa Verde*)

Makes about 2 cups

2-1/2 cups tightly packed
　fresh parsley sprigs
3 cloves garlic, crushed and
　thinly sliced
3 tablespoons lemon juice
1 cup olive oil
Salt
Freshly ground black pepper

In the bowl of a food processor, blend parsley, garlic and lemon juice. Continue processing, adding olive oil in a thin stream. Season with salt and pepper to taste. Pour into a smaller bowl, cover with plastic wrap, and chill.

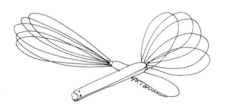

Nadia's Cheese with Honey or Balsamic Vinegar
(*Formaggi con Miele e Aceto Balsamico*)

Our first introduction to chestnut honey with Gorgonzola was when Nadia served it to us just before dessert. We found the combination such a delicious surprise that we have been serving it to our guests ever since.

A variety of cheeses can be served with honey, balsamic vinegar or marmalade. Parmesan goes well with balsamic vinegar; Gorgonzola or ricotta is perfect with honey. These offer an option for the guest who says, "I never eat dessert."

Gorgonzola and Honey
Makes 8 servings

1/2 pound Gorgonzola,
　cut in chunks
1/2 cup honey,
　preferably chestnut

Arrange chunks of Gorgonzola cheese on serving plates and drizzle with honey. Serves 8.

Parmesan and Balsamic Vinegar
Makes 8 servings

1/2 pound Parmesan cheese,
　cut in chunks
4 tablespoons Balsamic vinegar

Arrange chunks of Parmesan on serving plates and drizzle with balsamic vinegar.

Ricotta and Honey
Makes 8 servings

1 pound fresh ricotta
　(see recipe page 117)
1 cup castagne (chestnut) honey

Spoon fresh ricotta into serving plates and spoon honey on top.

Polenta Crisps
(Sfogliatine di Mais)

At dal Pescatore, Nadia places these light and crunchy chips in bowls, in the center of the tables. They serve a dual purpose as both a "welcome" snack and lovely centerpiece.

Makes about 24

1-1/2 cups water
2 tablespoons of olive oil
1/2 teaspoon salt
1/2 cup instant cornmeal
  or polenta

Preheat the oven to 350°F.

In a non-stick pot, mix the water, oil and salt. Bring to a boil. Add polenta little by little. Continue to mix with whisk. Cook for 6-8 minutes, adding additional water as needed for a smooth, soft consistency.

Place a Silpat on a cookie sheet and spoon 1/2 cup of polenta mixture in the center of the Silpat. Lightly brush a sheet of parchment or wax paper with water and place on top of the polenta. Using a rolling pin, gently roll out as thin as possible (wafer thin). Carefully peel off the paper. Bake 20-30 minutes or until brown and crisp. Remove from oven, transfer to a wooden board and cool. Break into pieces.

Bruna's Ricotta Cake with Zabaglione
(Torta di Ricotta e Zabaglione)

Bruna served this traditional cake of the region to us on our first visit. The batter was poured into a heavy iron pot, covered, and placed in the fireplace. Hot coals were raked over the pot to bake it. A large slice of cake was served with a rich *zabaglione* sauce spooned over the top.

Serves about 12

3/4 cup dried currants
Sweet wine
2 tablespoons melted
  unsalted butter
1/2 cup finely ground almonds
1 pound ricotta cheese,
  pressed through a strainer
2-1/4 cups sugar
5 eggs
3 3/4 cups flour
2 tablespoons rum
2 tablespoons olive oil
1 teaspoon vanilla
1 teaspoon baking powder
1 teaspoon baking soda
1/4 cup milk
Zabaglione Sauce
  (recipe follows)

Plump currants in sweet wine or warm water until soft, at least 2 hours or overnight in the refrigerator. Drain just before using and set aside.

Preheat the oven to 350°F.

Brush a 12-cup bundt pan with the melted butter and sprinkle with ground almonds. Set aside.

In the large bowl of an electric mixer, beat ricotta and sugar until creamy. Add eggs, beating after each addition, then flour. Blend plumped currants into flour mixture with rum and oil. Add vanilla, baking powder, baking soda and milk to soften batter and blend.

Spoon batter into prepared bundt pan. Bake in preheated oven for 50 minutes, or until a wood pick inserted in center comes out clean and sides begin to pull away from pan. Cool, loosen cake from cake pan and invert onto a platter. When ready to serve, slice and serve with *zabaglione*.

Zabaglione Sauce

Makes 1 cup

5 egg yolks
5 tablespoons sugar
5 tablespoons Marsala

Beat yolks and sugar until thick, creamy and light in color. Add Marsala and whisk well to combine. Cook over simmering water in a double boiler for 10 minutes, whisking constantly.

MALEO
Franco Colombani
The Most Important Italian in the Food World

During the 1970s we were fortunate enough to meet and become friends with Franco Colombani, who was known as the godfather to a new breed of young Italian restaurateurs. Our introduction to him came from his best friend, Antonio Santini, the owner of Ristorante dal Pescatore.

Franco had no formal training as a chef. His knowledge of food and cooking came from the kitchen of a farmhouse that had been his family's home for about six hundred years. Out of those first lessons came a knowledge and passion that eventually made Franco one of the leaders in a movement to renew Italian cuisine.

In the sixties, a select group of chefs came to feel that Italian cuisine had fallen into a rut. While wanting to keep faith with their classic culinary tradition, they were determined to find the way to present it in a modern fashion. Franco, an enthusiast for Lombardian cooking, had an almost evangelical zeal for producing authentic dishes in this regional style. During his lifetime he served as a generous mentor to dozens of today's most admired Italian chefs and *sommeliers*.

We first met Franco at Sole, his restaurant, in Maleo, halfway between Milan and Bologna. When we landed in Milan, the first stop on our trip, we would drive directly from the airport to Sole. Franco would call our mutual friend, Antonio, and in thirty minutes, the time our drive took, Antonio would be sitting with us at Franco's restaurant ready for lunch.

The high-beamed ceiling in the dining room of Sole gave the place a homey feeling, and guests felt so comfortable in this setting that they mingled around the large tables, making friends. The simply presented dishes featured the freshest local ingredients.

The most sought after place to sit was the large family table right next to the tiled oven. This communal table seated almost twenty diners, and each place setting had an engraved brass nameplate honoring one of Franco's friends. An ancient meat-slicing machine sat on the counter, and the kitchen hummed with the steady stirring of the *risotto* that would be served with Franco's braised veal.

Franco had foraged in the mountains that morning for dandelion leaves and lemon thyme that became our insalata *del giorno*, combined with curly endive and wild arugula. These tender mouthfuls of bitterness were topped with crumbled hardboiled egg, then dressed with crushed lemon thyme, garlic, oil and Colombani's own balsamic vinegar.

On Franco's property behind the restaurant was an old barn whose loft held a series of barrels made of different woods—juniper, myrtle, cherry, oak and chestnut. These barrels were the secret to the aging process of Franco's balsamic vinegar. While wine-making is a well-known art, knowledge of the intricacies of aging vinegar is much rarer. Franco was devoted to his balsamic, and it was a tradition of his to disappear after dinner through a trap door to the basement where he kept his special old balsamic. He would reappear with a dusty bottle of balsamic and a couple of teaspoons, then carefully pour this thick dark liquid for us to savor as both a digestive and a final taste treat.

In addition to his tireless efforts to inspire and educate up-and-coming chefs, Franco served as president of the Italian Association of Sommeliers and had a passion for introducing diners to the fine wines of Italy. His fascination with the history of cooking manifested itself in his signature dishes, many derived from a marvelous collection of recipes that were hundreds of years old.

He wrote and hand-printed his own cookbook, *Cucina d'Amore*, and presented this treasure to us on one of our visits. This white hardcover book with a coral jacket slides into a handcrafted box that was made especially for him.

Lunch with Antonio and Franco often lasted several hours and could make eating dinner a challenge. Arriving at Franco's one evening, we explained that we were not hungry and wanted only a salad for dinner. Franco looked devastated. With tears in his eyes he said, "A salad with a bottle of 30-year-old Barolo!" It turned out that when he learned we were coming that day he had taken a prize wine out of his cellar to share with us. Needless to say, it was impossible to have just a salad that night.

On another visit, we had made plans to stay for a couple of days, so when we arrived we were surprised to find the restaurant closed. Franco was alone in the kitchen cleaning up. Knowing that we would probably be hungry, he invited us for dinner and announced that he was going to cook his favorite dishes. The next thing we knew he was digging food out of the refrigerator and turning on the stove. That night I tasted the most marvelous dish of veal liver combined with fresh garden peas. We talked, stayed late, and helped clean up the pots and pans. When we asked for the check, Franco said that "maybe tomorrow" when we checked out he would add it to our bill. But the next day, as any friend of this generous man might have predicted, there was no charge for that delicious dinner.

His *Cantina* (wine cellar) was legendary. You entered through what appeared to be an ancient door in the dining room and descended a steep flight of steps into another world: shelves full of wine bottles gathering dust and cobwebs, stacks of bottles scattered here and there, and piles of unopened cases. If you looked closely in the dim light, you would see treasures from all over Europe. In those days, restaurants in Italy usually had a selection of local wines, but Franco introduced the concept of sourcing wine from all over Italy and beyond.

I could never figure out how he priced the wines he served us. There was no detail on the bill, and since we always let him select the wines we drank, it was an adventure. I think he made an assessment of how much we enjoyed whichever wine he chose, then just assigned a price. Whatever his system, the wine was always a bargain.

Devoted to the cuisine of Lombardia, a gifted teacher of chefs, and a thoughtful friend, Franco was, in his private life, a somber man who rarely smiled. After his wife of many years left him, he became despondent. About five years after her departure he took his own life. Even though his restaurant is long closed, we honor his memory and the great impact he made on the food world in Italy.

Whitefish Mousse
(*Spuma di Pesce*)

This dish was a favorite of Franco's, and he often served it to welcome guests as they arrived in his restaurant. Whitefish makes an excellent substitute for the San Pietro fish he used, and the capers and mustard perfectly complement the fish. We often serve it on top of an arugula and fennel salad as a first course.

Vegetable stock
(recipe follows)
1 pound whitefish or sea bass
1/4 cup mayonnaise
1 tablespoon Dijon mustard
2 tablespoons lemon juice
1 tablespoon capers, drained,
rinsed and finely chopped
Salt and freshly ground
black pepper, to taste
Thinly sliced toast

Serves 6 to 8

Prepare the vegetable stock and keep warm.

Simmer fish in vegetable stock for 15 to 20 minutes, or until cooked through. Cool and transfer to a large bowl and mash it with a fork.

In a small bowl, combine mayonnaise, mustard, lemon juice, capers, and mix well. Add the mayonnaise mixture to the fish and mix well. Season with salt and pepper to taste. Cover with plastic wrap and refrigerate. Serve on thin slices of toast or salad greens.

Vegetable Stock

Makes about 4 cups

2 tablespoons olive oil
1 onion, diced
1 celery stalk, diced
1 carrot, diced
Juice of ½ lemon
1/2 cup dry white wine
3 cups water
Salt and freshly ground
black pepper, to taste

In a pot, heat olive oil and sauté onion, celery and carrot until soft. Add lemon juice, wine, water and bring to a boil. Add salt and pepper and simmer for 20 to 30 minutes.

Franco's Soup of Dried Lentils
(*Zuppa di Lenticchie Secche*)

This hearty and healthy soup can stand alone as a substantial lunch or, with the addition of country bread and a green salad, as a simple and satisfying dinner. I find it especially appealing in cold weather.

1-1/2 cups dried lentils
2 bay leaves, crushed
4 tablespoons unsalted butter
or margarine
1 tablespoon olive oil

Serves 6 to 8

Soak the lentils in 4 cups of water for 6 hours or overnight.

Drain the lentils and place them in a large pot with 2 1/2 quarts of warm water and the bay leaves. Over high heat, bring the water to a boil, reduce the heat, partially cover, and simmer for 15 to 20 minutes, or until the lentils are tender.

In a large skillet, heat the butter and olive oil. Add the garlic, carrots,

3 garlic cloves, minced
4 medium carrots, peeled
  and finely chopped
1 medium parsnip, peeled
  and finely chopped
1 large onion, finely chopped
2 celery stalks, thinly sliced
1/2 cup minced fresh parsley
1 tablespoon fresh rosemary
  or 1 teaspoon dried
4 large tomatoes, peeled and
  finely chopped
Salt
Freshly ground black pepper
Grated Parmesan cheese
  (optional)

parsnip, onion, celery, and parsley. Sauté this mixture for 10 to 15 minutes, or until the vegetables are tender. Add the rosemary and tomatoes and simmer for 10 minutes.

Remove 2 cups of the cooked lentils and 1/2 cup of the liquid and purée in a processor or blender. Return the purée and the sautéed vegetable mixture to the soup pot. Mix well. Season to taste with salt and pepper. Over medium heat, bring to a boil, cover, reduce the heat, and simmer, covered, until the soup thickens, 30 to 40 minutes.

Ladle the soup into warm bowls and garnish with a sprinkle of Parmesan cheese, if you wish.

Franco's Venetian Style Liver
(*Fegato alla Veneziana*)

Franco prepared liver this way when we visited one year and it reminded us of the way they prepare liver in Venice, where mere liver and onions transcend the ordinary through careful cooking and seasoning.

Serves 6

1-1/2 pounds of calf's liver
4 tablespoons olive oil
3 pounds finely sliced onions
Salt
Freshly ground black pepper
1 teaspoon fresh sage leaves
  or 1/2 teaspoon dried
1 tablespoon dry white wine
1-1/2 tablespoons white
  wine vinegar

Trim liver of any sinews and cut into 1/4-inch slices. Cut the slices into pieces about 2 inches long. With paper towels, pat liver dry, place on a platter, cover and refrigerate until ready to use.

In a large, heavy skillet, heat oil and add onions; season with salt and pepper and cook over very low heat, stirring frequently, until the onions are golden and very tender, about 15 minutes. Remove onions from pan and place in a bowl, draining them well in order to leave as much oil as possible in the pan.

Increase heat to high and add liver, tossing in oil for about 3 minutes, until strips of liver lose their redness and are beginning to brown but are still very pink inside. Sprinkle with sage, wine and vinegar, season with salt and pepper to taste, and reduce heat to low.

Return onions to pan, mix to reheat and serve liver and onions moistened with pan juices at once.

Roast Veal
(Arrosto di Vitello)

Veal can be bland without perfectly balanced seasonings. Franco's Roast Veal is enhanced by garlic both inserted in the meat and roasted with vegetables placed around the roast as it cooks. Sage and rosemary add their own aromatic notes, and a wine-based sauce that marries all these flavors gives the dish an elegant finish.

Serves 8

1 (3-pound) boneless veal
   shoulder roast, tied
6 garlic cloves cut in half
3 tablespoons olive oil
3 garlic cloves, minced
1 tablespoon minced fresh sage
1 tablespoon minced rosemary
Salt
Freshly ground pepper
   black pepper
1 large carrot, diced
1 large celery rib, diced
1 large shallot, coarsely chopped
2 cups dry white wine

Preheat the oven to 400°F.

Set veal roast on a work surface, fat side up. Make 12 (1-inch) incisions over the top of the roast and insert a half clove of garlic in each one. In a small bowl combine one tablespoon of the olive oil, half of the minced garlic, sage, rosemary, and 1/4 teaspoon each salt and pepper. Rub the mixture over the roast.

In a large roaster that will hold the roast snugly, place the carrot, celery, shallot and sprinkle with the remaining minced garlic. Add the meat, fat side up, and drizzle with 2 tablespoons olive oil. Season with additional salt and pepper.

Cover the roaster and roast the meat for 1-1/2 hours, turning it every 30 minutes. The roast is done when an instant-read thermometer inserted in the thickest part registers 145°F to 150°F.

Transfer the roast to a carving board and let rest for 10 minutes. Place roaster over high heat, add wine and boil until the liquid has reduced to 1-1/4 cups, about 3 minutes. Strain through a coarse sieve, pressing the solids into the sauce. Skim off the fat and season with salt and pepper.

Carve the veal into 8 slices. Pour any accumulated meat juices into the sauce and serve at once.

Sweet Wine Sorbet
(Sorbetto al Vino)

Franco served this sorbet in a classic stemmed glass—sometimes as a palette refresher between courses, sometimes with *biscotti* for dessert.

Serves 6 to 8

Grated peel and juice of
   1 orange
2 cups dry red wine
1 cup sugar
1/8 teaspoon freshly ground
   black pepper

In a mixing bowl, combine the orange zest and juice with the wine, sugar and pepper. With a wire whisk, combine the mixture until completely blended.

Cover and refrigerate until cold. Transfer to an ice cream machine and freeze, following manufacturer's instructions. Store in freezer.

LAGO MAGGIORE
The Brovelli Family – *Il Sole di Ranco:*
Distinguished Cooking in a Distinctive Setting

A single vowel can change a perfect dining experience in Italy. "Ranco" is home to Itala and Carluccio Brovelli's Hotel-Ristorante, Il Sole. "Ronco" is another story. On our first visit to Il Sole, a misunderstanding about that slippery vowel sent us hours out of our way and very nearly caused us to miss years of friendship, good eating and adventures with this talented family.

It was over thirty years ago that we made our first Sunday lunch reservation at Il Sole di Ranco, at the suggestion of our friends Nadia and Antonio Santini of Ristorante dal Pescatore. The Santinis had told us about this exceptional restaurant close to the Malpensa Airport outside of Milan. Driving from Verona, we planned to arrive in the early afternoon. We drove northeast to Varese, stopped at a gas station, and in our best Italian asked how to get to "Ranco."

An hour later, driving in the mountains, we finally decided to stop and ask for directions again. Yes, we were told, this was "Ronco," but "Ranco" was more than forty kilometers away, with no short cut available. We had driven so far out of our way no one thought we could make it back to Ranco in time for lunch. But the villagers of Ronco had no clue about our sheer determination, peerless navigation skills and appetite for speed. Marvino and I made it to Ranco–and Il Sole–by three in the afternoon.

At Il Sole, a table on the terrace was set and still waiting for us. We sat down to feast our eyes on the garden below and Lago Maggiore beyond, a sight that has now welcomed us to Italy countless times. The outdoor dining area covered with vines and blossoms was crowded, a testament to the Brovellis' culinary talent.

Itala Brovelli, a striking woman with auburn hair and a sophisticated air about her welcomed us. A model of seemingly effortless chic, Itala always wears high heels, and when the restaurant serves outside she manages to walk back and forth from the kitchen over the loose cobblestones all day. In the early days of Il Sole Itala waited on tables, but now she moves among the tables making sure the diners are enjoying themselves and satisfied with the service and the food.

She is also one of Italy's few female *sommeliers*, having made the effort to educate herself about this complex subject. On our first visit, when Itala presented Marvino with the wine list and began suggesting wines to accompany our meal, we became immersed in a thirty-minute discussion of Italian wines. Thus began our long friendship with this amazing family.

At the end of that memorable lunch, when we were the only diners left in the restaurant, Carluccio emerged from the kitchen to greet us. A shy man who speaks French but no English and is easily bored with people, he was friendly to us from the beginning, perhaps

We managed to capture Carluccio and Itala Brovelli during a casual moment.

because of our strong ties with his friends the Santinis. Our admiration for his creativity with food has brought us even closer over the years, and he often pinches my cheek affectionately when we meet each other now.

When we parted that first afternoon, we made plans for the Brovellis' older son, Davide, to stay with us in Los Angeles, study English, and work at several restaurants to help broaden his kitchen experience. Davide came to Los Angeles a year later, accompanied by his mother. Itala stayed for about a week, during which time we introduced them to Los Angeles. After she left we enrolled Davide in a language school and asked friends who owned restaurants if he could work for them. At one point, while he was working at Michael's restaurant in Santa Monica, he was thrilled about an opportunity to take part in a major event for the American Institute of Food & Wine. Chefs from all over Los Angeles cooked for a thousand people, and it was all captured on video. Davide later developed his culinary skills further at Le Notre in Paris.

The routine of our trips to Italy has never changed. We board a flight in Los Angeles to Malpensa Airport, just outside Milan, where we pick up a rental car. Then we speed toward our first stop, an Autogrill on the Autostrada, with the reliable brilliance of the Italian *barristas* the only thing on our minds. When American coffee enthusiasts are served their first espresso or cappuccino with grilled *panini* from one of these remarkable highway snack bars, they often can't quite believe their good fortune. For us, that first delicious sip tells us we have arrived in the country we love.

Once fortified, we drive contentedly through the countryside to Lago Maggiore and Il Sole di Ranco. It's hard for us to imagine starting a trip in Italy without taking our first meal here and, if our schedule allows, spending a night or two enjoying the inimitable hospitality of another of our beloved "Italian families."

When we arrive at Il Sole, before we can even unload our car, we are met by the entire Brovelli family. They usher us into the garden where a bottle of champagne or a fresh-squeezed fruit drink serves as prelude to yet another delicious Italian holiday. On Tuesdays, when the restaurant is closed, the Brovellis' cousin Ginetta prepares her famous Gorgonzola Lasagne, made with the thinnest sheets of pasta imaginable.

On our first visit to Il Sole, it was only a restaurant. But by our next visit Itala had renovated the building where the restaurant was located and added nine contemporary hotel rooms. She took us to the neighboring property and told us of her plan to persuade the owners to sell it to her—which they finally did. By one of our subsequent visits she had remodeled the historic building, raised floors and ceilings, and generally transformed the structure to accommodate her vision: a large reception area, a breakfast room, and an elevator to six suites, each charmingly decorated with fabric-covered walls and matching bed linens and drapes. Each suite has a spectacular view of Lago Maggiore.

Recently the Brovellis leased the property along the lakefront where the ferry stops. There they built an octagon-shaped glass café-bar, Molo 203, where breakfast, lunch, and

Above: It's always hard to say *buona notte* after a wonderful meal with the Brovelli family. At right: Davide doing what he does best.

light dinner is served. Itala's latest projects are a pool-spa area in the shape of a woman's luscious red lips that overlooks the lake, and a newly installed helicopter pad.

The Brovellis' sons were small children when we discovered Il Sole di Ranco, and they have grown up to take major roles in the family business. Andrea–whose interests have evolved from introducing us to his hamster, "Arturo," to showing off his custom Harley-Davidson, which has won top awards in many European countries–now manages the hotel. Davide, with his shaved head and lively brown eyes, now presides over the kitchen, while his wife, Cristina, oversees the dining room.

We were among the invited guests to attend Davide and Cristina's wedding. The list included many of the famous chefs in Italy. They were married in the small village church, where Davide and Andrea were baptized, just a stone's throw from the restaurant.

In Italy, there is a saying that it is a sign of good luck for the couple when there is a storm with thunder and lightening during the wedding. And so it has been for Davide and Cristina. They now have two adorable children.

The reception took place along the lake in a beautiful old villa. The bride and groom were scheduled to arrive by boat, but the rain changed their plans.

The wedding cake had five individual tiers decorated with hundreds of slices of strawberries and kiwi. We learned later Itala had arranged them herself early that very morning, alternating strawberries and kiwi around each cake layer. Just in case there wasn't enough, six more individual cakes were decorated in the same manner.

Although Davide's culinary innovations have inspired imitations from chefs around the world, my personal favorite among his inventions is a large open *raviolo* with a thin sheet of green pasta on the bottom, a filling of mixed seafood in cream sauce, and a top sheet of thin "*tri-colore*" pasta striped in green, white, and red–the colors of the Italian flag. This alone would make anyone's trip to the Brovellis' magnificent Il Sole worthwhile.

It was 1997 when Il Sole introduced its guests to Ivano Antonini, then their new *sommelier*. Ivano has since become quite famous for his talents, having been crowned with many prestigious titles, including "Best Sommelier of Italy" in 2008. When at Il Sole, we enjoy leaving our wine selections in his care. His passion and knowledge of wines is unsurpassed.

On one of our visits, Andrea invited us to a neighborhood restaurant, Vecchia Capronno, in the village of Capronno di Angera. His girlfriend ordered a cheese dish served with grilled Pecorino cheese for her main course. Marmalade was served with it, and when I asked the waiter about it he said it was red onion marmalade that the chef had made. He brought me a bowl of it, and it was a delicious addition to my roast turkey entrée. If you are staying at Il Sole and are interested in exploring this restaurant, Andrea Brovelli would be happy to make a reservation for you.

WHEN YOU GO, YOU SHOULD KNOW:

Il Sole di Ranco
Hotel and Ristorante
Proprietors: Itala and
** Carluccio Brovelli**
Piazza Venezia N5
21020 Ranco (VA) Italy
Tel: (0331) 976507
Fax: (0331) 976620
email: info@ilsolediranco.it
www.ilsolediranco.it

Vecchia Capronno
Piazza Matteotti 17 - 21021
Capronno di Angera (VA)
Tel: (0331) 957313
email: info@vecchiacapronno.it
www.locandalacasetta.it

Davide's Fresh Figs with Smoked Salmon
(*Fichi e Salmone Affumicato*)

There are two fig trees below the outdoor restaurant, and in season they are laden with ripe figs. The smoked salmon creates a saltiness that balances the figs so well. This makes a perfect appetizer, served with a light sparkling wine.

Serves 4

8 fresh figs
4 slices smoked salmon
Garnish with grated lemon peel

Peel and slice each fig in half and arrange on small serving plates. Top with sliced smoked salmon and garnish with grated lemon peel.

Davide's Smoked Salmon Stacks
(*Fichi e Salmone Affumicato*)

Who knew potato salad was Italian? Chef Davide Brovelli created these *panini* (small Italian sandwiches) as an appetizer at Il Sole. You need to cut 2-inch rounds from smoked salmon slices with a cookie cutter. These small rounds of salmon replace the usual bread slices and are filled with Davide's delicious version of potato salad, made with new potatoes, green beans, diced red peppers, and peas. I sometimes replace the smoked salmon with slices of salami.

Makes 12 mini-sandwiches

Potato Salad Filling
  (recipe follows)
Mustard-Dill Sauce
  (recipe follows)
24 rounds of smoked salmon,
  2 inches in diameter
Julienne zucchini and diced
  tomatoes, for garnish

Prepare Potato Salad Filling and Mustard-Dill Sauce, cover with plastic wrap and chill.

   Place 1 round of salmon in the bottom of a 2-inch round cookie cutter and spoon in about 1 tablespoon potato salad until it reaches a height of 1 inch. Cover with a second salmon round. Press down gently and carefully remove cookie cutter. Repeat the process with the remaining rounds of salmon and potato salad. Garnish with "flowers" made of zucchini stems and diced tomato petals.

Potato Salad Filling

Makes 3 cups

4 small new potatoes (about
  1 pound), boiled and cut
  into 1/4-inch cubes
1/2 cup diced green beans,
  steamed
1/2 cup seeded and diced
  red bell pepper
1/2 cup fresh or frozen peas,
  cooked
1/2 cup mayonnaise
Salt
Freshly ground black pepper

In a large bowl, combine potatoes, green beans, bell peppers, and peas. Blend in mayonnaise, 1 tablespoon at a time. Gently mix until vegetables are moistened. Season with salt and pepper, to taste.

Mustard Dill Sauce

Makes about 1 cup

3 tablespoons Dijon-style
  mustard
1 teaspoon powdered mustard
2 tablespoons sugar
1 tablespoon white vinegar
1/3 cup olive oil
3 tablespoons fresh chopped
  (or snipped) dill

In a small, deep bowl, combine the mustard, powdered mustard, sugar and vinegar and blend well. With a wire whisk, slowly beat in the oil until it forms a thick mayonnaise. Stir in the chopped dill. Cover with plastic wrap and refrigerate until ready to serve.

Davide's Green Bean Salad with Orange Mayonnaise

(Insalata Gagiolini con Salsa Aurora)

This salad, brilliant in its simplicity, depends for its success on the quality and freshness of the beans. Chef Davide Brovelli at Il Sole on Lago Maggiore often serves this salad with chunks of poached fish from their lake.

Makes 4 servings

Orange Mayonnaise
  (recipe follows)
1 pound thin green beans
Salt
Freshly ground black pepper
Olive oil
Long thin strip of orange peel
  and orange sections for
  garnish

Prepare Orange Mayonnaise and set aside.

In a steamer basket set over a large saucepan of simmering water, steam the green beans, covered, for 5 to 10 minutes, until tender but still crunchy. Or plunge them into boiling salted water and boil for 3 to 4 minutes. Drain well.

Toss the beans with salt and peper to taste and a little olive oil. Place bunches of them on plates and top with fresh Orange Mayonnaise. Garnish with orange peels and surround with the orange sections.

Orange Mayonnaise

Mayonnaise is always easier to make if the ingredients are at room temperature. Warming the bowl before you start making the mayonnaise will help insure good results. Use your food processor to save time.

Makes about 1-1/2 cups

2 large egg yolks
1 tablespoon fresh orange juice
2 teaspoons fresh lemon juice
1 teaspoon Dijon-style mustard
1/4 teaspoon salt
1 cup olive oil
2 tablespoons grated
  orange zest
Freshly ground black pepper

Rinse a medium mixing bowl with hot water and dry it well. In the warm bowl, beat together the egg yolks, orange juice, lemon juice, mustard and salt. In a slow, thin stream, add 1/2 cup of the oil, beating constantly; as the mayonnaise begins to thicken, gradually add the remaining oil and the zest. Season to taste with additional salt and freshly ground pepper.

Salad Niçoise at Molo 203
(Insalata Niçoise al Molo 203)

The Brovelli Family built an octagon-shaped cafe, Molo 203, along the lake below their hotel/restaurant. Davide developed the menu, and people come by boat or car, or simply walk down from the hotel to have breakfast, lunch or dinner. This Salad *Niçoise* is perfect for lunch.

Serves 6

8 to 10 cups mixed salad greens
 (romaine, arugula)
1/2 pound cooked string beans,
 cut in pieces
1/2 red onion, thinly sliced
1/2 pound new potatoes, boiled
 and cut into 1/2-inch chunks
3 ripe tomatoes, quartered
1 (6 1/8 ounces) can tuna in oil
1/2 to 1 cup pitted black olives
12 (fillets or rolled) anchovies,
 washed free of salt
3 hard-boiled eggs, quartered
Olive oil
Wine vinegar
Salt and freshly ground black
 pepper, to taste

Tear greens into bite-size pieces and arrange them in large individual serving bowls. Arrange the beans, sliced onions, potatoes, tomatoes, tuna, olives, anchovies and hard-boiled eggs on top of greens. Serve with olive oil, wine vinegar, salt and pepper for guests to help themselves.

Davide's Cold Beet Soup
(Zuppa Fredda di Barbabietola)

Nothing could be easier and more refreshing than this elegant cold soup that Davide Brovelli, chef of Il Sole di Ranco, prepared for us. The fruit flavors add complexity without overwhelming the beets in this perfect summer first course.

Makes about 3-1/2 to 4 cups

3 large beets (1-1/2 pounds)
2 tablespoons lemon juice
1/3 cup orange juice
1/3 cup grapefruit juice
2 tablespoons sugar
Crème fraîche or sour cream
4 tablespoons minced chives

Place beets in a large pot, cover with water and bring to a boil. Simmer until a fork inserted in the beet is tender, about 1-1/2 hours, depending on the size of the beets.

Cool. Transfer to a bowl, peel and cut in quarters. Place in blender or food processor with 1/2 to 1 cup of the liquid from beets. Purée until smooth. Add juices and sugar to taste. Cover with plastic wrap and refrigerate until ready to serve. Ladle into soup bowls and garnish with a spoonful of crème fraiche and garnish with minced chives.

Ginette's Gorgonzola Lasagne
(Lasagne alla Gorgonzola)

Ginette, a cousin of the Brovelli family, often prepares this savory lasagne for the family on Tuesdays, when the restaurant is closed. When she knows we are visiting, Ginette always prepares it for us. It is one of the most mouth-watering dishes I have ever eaten. The sheets of paper-thin homemade pasta and the Gorgonzola make your palate stand up and salute.

Serves 8 to 10

1/2 pound Gorgonzola cheese
2 tablespoons of cream or milk
10 large (wafer thin) paper-thin
   sheets of pasta* (see recipe,
   page 168)
1/2 cup melted, unsalted butter
1 cup grated Parmesan cheese

Preheat the oven to 350°F. Brush a 9x12-inch baking dish with butter.

In a large bowl, using a fork, mix the cheese and cream until smooth, but still a little lumpy.

Pre-cook each sheet of pasta in boiling water until tender. Remove from the water and transfer to a tea towel. Cover the bottom of the prepared baking dish with thin sheets of pasta. Spread melted butter and then the Gorgonzola mixture over surface. Sprinkle with grated Parmesan. Cover with another layer of sheets of pasta, brush with melted butter, add the Gorgonzola mixture and the Parmesan. Repeat one more time. Then cover with sheets of pasta and brush with butter. Bake in preheated oven until the filling is melted; do not allow the lasagne to brown. Remove from oven and serve immediately.

* If using store-bought lasagne noodles, try to find the thinnest noodles available.

Davide's Barolo and Radicchio Risotto
(Risotto al Radicchio e Barolo)

This is another of Davide's distinctive dishes. Serve the *risotto* in a soup bowl or soufflé dish. Pour a spoonful of dry red wine into the dish and spoon the *risotto* on top. This creates a small rim of red wine around the *risotto*.

Serves 6 to 8

5 cups vegetable broth
2 tablespoons unsalted butter
1 tablespoon olive oil
1/2 cup finely minced onion
1-1/2 cups arborio rice
1/2 cup dry red wine
2 cups finely chopped
   radicchio leaves
1/4 cup cream
1/3 cup grated Parmesan cheese
Salt and pepper
Additional dry red wine,
   for garnish

In a saucepan, bring broth to a steady simmer. In a heavy 4-quart pot, heat butter and oil over moderate heat. Add onion and sauté for 1 to 2 minutes, until it begins to soften (do not brown).

Add the rice, using a wooden spoon, stir for 1 minute, to coat grains. Add wine and stir until completely absorbed. Add 1 cup of the radicchio and begin to add the simmering broth, 1/2 cup at a time, stirring frequently. Wait until each addition is almost completely absorbed before adding the next 1/2 cup, reserving about 1/4 cup to add at the end. Stir frequently to prevent sticking. After about 18 minutes, when rice is tender but still firm, add the remaining radicchio, reserved broth, cream, and Parmesan, and stir vigorously to combine with rice. Season with salt and pepper to taste.

To serve, pour a spoonful of the red wine into the dish and spoon the *risotto* on top. Serve immediately.

Red Onion Marmalade
(Marmellata di Cipolle Rosse)

Red Onion Marmalade is served with grilled pecorino cheese at Vecchia Capronno, a country restaurant in the village of Capronno di Angera that we were introduced to by Andrea Brovelli. I serve this delicious marmalade with chicken, turkey and meat.

Makes about 3 cups

2 cups sugar
1/2 cup water
4 medium-size red onions,
  thinly sliced (about 4 to 5 cups)
2 cups warm orange juice
Grated peel of 2 oranges

In a heavy saucepan place sugar and water and bring to a boil, stirring constantly until sugar dissolves. Reduce heat to medium-high and simmer until the sugar begins to turn golden. Add the onions, orange juice and peel, mixing vigorously until liquid and sugar are dissolved. Continue cooking on medium heat, mixing occasionally until the onions are soft and the liquid has reduced to a thick syrup, about 20 to 30 minutes. Cool.

Davide's Seafood Fillet with Fennel Sauce
(Pesce con Salsa ai Finocchio)

Davide prepared this for us one night. The anise liqueur and the fennel sauce were a perfect match for the delicately prepared halibut. A tablespoon of ground fennel seeds added to the bread crumbs is an alternative to the fennel flowers.

Serves 4 to 6

Fennel Sauce (recipe follows)
2 pounds halibut or sea bass,
  cut in cubes
1 cup bread crumbs or
  panko crumbs
Salt
Freshly ground black pepper
1 tablespoon fennel seeds
  or dried fennel flowers
1 cup anise liqueur
Olive oil for frying

Prepare the fennel sauce and keep warm.

In a bowl, combine bread or panko crumbs with salt, pepper, and fennel seeds or flowers. Dip the halibut cubes into anise liqueur and then into bread crumb mixture.

In a non-stick frying pan, heat oil and brown halibut cubes. Arrange on serving plates and top with Fennel Sauce.

Fennel Sauce

Makes about 1 cup

1 head of fresh fennel,
  trimmed and thinly sliced
1/4 cup cream (optional)
Salt
Freshly ground black pepper

In a saucepan place sliced fennel and enough water to cover. Bring to a boil and simmer until tender, about 30 minutes, adding additional water if needed. Transfer to a blender or food processor with a little of the cooking liquid and blend until smooth. Add cream if desired. Season with salt and pepper, to taste.

Espresso Cooked Cream
(Panna Cotta all'Espresso)

*P*anna Cotta is a dessert that you will find all over Italy. This espresso-accented *panna cotta* is delicious sprinkled with ground espresso coffee and served with a chocolate sauce. The first time we ate this dish was at Il Sole, where it was prepared by Davide Brovelli.

Makes 6 servings

1-1/2 cups cream
4 tablespoons coarsely ground
  espresso beans
3 tablespoons sugar
Grated peel of 1 orange
1 teaspoon powdered gelatin
1 teaspoon coffee flavoring

In a heavy saucepan place cream and espresso beans, sugar and orange peel; bring to a simmer over medium-low heat. Turn off heat and let steep for 5 to 10 minutes.

Add powdered gelatin and stir with a whisk over low heat to warm the mixture and dissolve the gelatin. Do not boil. Add coffee flavoring. Strain the mixture through a fine sieve, then pour into individual espresso cups. Cover with plastic wrap and refrigerate until set, about 1 hour. To speed up the process, place in freezer for 10 minutes.

Itala's Fresh Fruit Drink
(Bevanda alla Frutta)

*W*hen we arrive at Il Sole directly from the airport to stay overnight, it is usually in the morning. Itala and Carluccio Brovelli always greet us with either a bottle of champagne in an ice bucket with champagne glasses or a delicious fruit drink. This fruit drink is in a tall glass with a wooden skewer lying across the top spearing fresh fruit (strawberries, pineapple or peaches)

Serves 6

1-1/2 cups orange juice
2 quarts grapefruit juice
Soda water
Strawberries
Pineapple
White peaches
6 wooden skewers

Pour the orange juice into an ice cube tray. Freeze overnight. Fill six tall glasses halfway with 2 or 3 orange juice ice cubes and grapefruit juice. Just before serving, add soda water. Thread fresh strawberries, pineapple and peaches on skewers and place it across top of glass.

BERGAMO
Dottore Mauro and Floriana Febbrari
Physician by Profession, Food & Wine Expert by Passion

Three days before we were to leave for Italy, we received a call from our friend Antonio Santini of Ristorante dal Pescatore. Antonio told us that his friend Dr. Mauro Febbrari, who lives in Bergamo, would be in Los Angeles to visit his sons, who had just begun studies at Santa Monica College. He asked if Mauro could phone us when he arrived.

He did call us and, although we were leaving for Italy the next day, we invited him; his wife, Floriana; and sons, Ricardo and Nicolo, to our home.

When they arrived that evening we served sparkling wine and *bruschetta* with smoked salmon. Then we drove to a local restaurant, Capo, for dinner. Chef Ricky Moreno, came out and offered to make us a special dinner. The one he produced included a dish that Mauro and Floriana would most likely never experience in their home country: a pumpkin tamale sizzling in a cast iron skillet on a bed of banana leaves surrounded by tomato salsa. We all had a great time and, as usual, I had my camera with me and took many photos.

Mauro specializes in dietary habits that promote good health. Many of his patients are chefs and restaurateurs who he knows because he also writes restaurant reviews for a food magazine. When the evening was over, the Febbraris made us promise to call them when we were in Italy.

We left the next day as scheduled, and a couple of weeks into our trip, we made good on our promise. We phoned Mauro and he and Floriana immediately arranged to have dinner with us.

Mauro said he would make a reservation for us to stay in one of the six suites at the Hotel da Vittorio, in Brusaporto, just outside Bergamo. The hotel includes a 2-star Michelin Restaurant, also called da Vittorio, where they would meet us for dinner.

We arrived at the restaurant at noon during a rainstorm, wet and hungry. A staff member led us to an enormous room with a fireplace and a large corner window seat, and promised to bring us appetizers in five minutes. Trays of food soon arrived, more than enough for lunch, including glasses of sparkling wine, cups of porcini mushroom soup, homemade bread sticks, and spiral rollups of smoked salmon and creamy white cheese.

The parents of the hotel's proprietors, Bruna and Vittorio Cerea, had owned a famous restaurant in Bergamo for many years. When Vittorio died, their five children decided to open da Vittorio Hotel/Restaurant, named in his honor. Housed in a spectacular villa in Brusaporto, just outside Bergamo, the hotel is surrounded by several acres of green lawns and two small lakes.

Bruna and Vittorio's sons, Enrico and Roberto, are both chefs and manage the kitchen; the other son, Francesco, is the *sommelier* and responsible for the wine cellar and off-site catering. One of the daughters, Rosella, is responsible for hospitality in the restaurant and hotel, and the other daughter, Barbara, owns and manages a pastry shop in Bergamo Alta.

Mauro and Floriana joined us at 8 p.m., and the four of us drank sparkling wine and ate savory mini-cones filled with diced tomatoes and *crème fraîche* in the reception lobby of the hotel. On the way to our table, Floriana quietly asked me if we liked truffles. "Of course," I said, "we love truffles."

When we arrived at the table, there was a menu on our plates. It read: "To my friend Marvino: a truffle dinner." When each course arrived, the waiter came with a truffle slicer and covered the plate with truffles. The service ranked with the best we have ever had in a restaurant. And the "Il Tartufo" menu the chef selected was amazing. We began with a cup of thick and creamy potato soup (*Cappuccino di Patate*) and happily ate our way through a series of truffled delicacies to an unusual duck liver soufflé (*Soufflé di Fegato*), followed by dessert.

During the course of the meal, Bruna, the mother of these five children with food-related careers, made her way around the room and greeted everyone. You could see how proud she was of her talented brood.

The following year we again arranged to meet Mauro and Floriana in Italy. This time they made a reservation for us at Hotel L'Albereta in Erbrusco, which is located in the Franciacorta wine region. Our rooms were charming and overlooked a beautiful garden. That night we had dinner in the hotel that housed the restaurant of Gaultiero Marchesi, who greeted Mauro as an old friend. Gaultiero, who is also Mauro's patient, seems to respect the *Dottore* as much for his food and wine journalism as for his medical skills. Gaultiero's food was basically traditional cooking with some contemporary aspects. One memorable dish was a simple fried egg that formed a perfect circle in the center of a plate covered with truffle shavings.

The next day, we had lunch with Mauro and Floriana at their friend's restaurant, Miramonte L'Altro, in the village of Concesio, outside Brescia. We were greeted by the owner (whose name was also Mauro), his sister, and her French chef husband—all of them obviously close friends of the Febbraris.

We began our lunch there with herring and caviar in a small white dish covered with a purée of cauliflower. After this came seafood bisque with grilled white fish, then a martini glass with purée of *foie gras* on top of gelatin of *foie gras*. Bow-tie pasta with a meat sauce (Mauro's favorite) came next. The most amazing dish of all was Lamb Six Ways, presented

Top: A group photo after our first dining experience at Miramonte L'Altro. Above: An amazing display of fragrant truffles at da Vittorio.

The Zeidlers and Febbraris enjoy an evening together.

on a 12-inch-square platter. Then a cheese cart was rolled in with a 12-inch high wheel of Stilton and eight varieties of *mostarda*, the delicious relish made of mustard-infused fruits.

Desserts continued the over-the-top theme: a platter of sugar-frosted grapes with melon and a platter of chocolate petite fours. Just when we thought we were finally finished, a tall container of vanilla *gelato* was inverted into a bowl and served to us covered with strawberries and sauce. As we left I asked if the staff would come out so I could take a photo. I have found that everyone is delighted when I do this, and departing becomes easier.

The year after that, Mauro gave Floriana a surprise for her birthday. They took a trip to visit their sons, Ricardo and Nicolo, in Los Angeles. We joined the celebration, along with Mauro's friend Mauro, and his son.

We extended Floriana's birthday celebration the following evening by inviting everyone to our home for dinner, where we served a selection of California and Oregon Pinot Noirs. We began with *gougère* and a pizza topped with onions and anchovies, sat down to an espresso cup of beans and caviar followed by *panini* with celeriac slaw. To continue our Pinot Noir theme, we served salmon in a Pinot Noir Sauce, followed by chocolate chip ice cream and banana cake.

On their next visit to Los Angeles we picked up Floriana and Mauro at their son's apartment and took them to the London Hotel, where celebrity chef Gordon Ramsey has his restaurant. A highlight of that memorable lunch was his squash soup garnished with *ragout* of duck and a dollop of truffle foam.

Our delicious times with the Febbraris have been among the treasures of our life, and we look forward to many more visits with them, in Italy and Los Angeles.

**WHEN YOU GO,
YOU SHOULD KNOW:**

Ristorante Miramonti L'Altro
Via Crosette 34
25062 Costorio di Concesio (BS)
Italy
Tel: (030) 2751063
Fax: (030) 275-189
email: info@miramontilaltro.it
www.miramontilaltro.it

Hotel L'Albereta
Via Vittorio Emanuele II, N 23
25030 Erbusco (Brescia) – Italy
Tel: (030) 7760550
Fax: (030) 7760573
www.albereta.it

Da Vittorio
24060 Brusaporto (BG)
Via Cantalupa, 17
Italy
Tel: (035) 681024
Fax: (035) 680849
email: info@davittorio.com
www.davittorio.com

Floriana's Parmesan Toast
(Bruschetta alla Parmigiana)

One evening when Mauro and Floriana were visiting their sons in Los Angeles, they invited us to dinner. Floriana prepared *risotto* with dried porcini mushrooms followed by Chilean sea bass, which she explained is often served in Italy with a small salad on the same plate.

We began with this Parmesan Toast, which was delicious and simple to prepare: with only four ingredients, you have a perfect appetizer.

Makes 16 toasts

1 cup grated Parmesan cheese
1/2 cup dry white wine
   to moisten
1/4 cup olive oil
16 slices toasted bread

In a medium-size bowl, combine Parmesan cheese, wine and olive oil and mix well. Spread on toast and serve.

Mauro's Large Tubular Pasta with Pumpkin, Sage and Tuna Bottarga
(Paccheri con Zucca, Salvia e Bottarga di Tonno)

Ricardo explained that his father purchases all his pasta from a famous pasta maker in Abruzzo.

Serves 4

2 tablespoons olive oil
2 garlic cloves, minced
1-1/2 pounds pumpkin or other
   winter squash (butternut),
   peeled and diced
1-1/2 teaspoons dried sage
3/4 pound large tubular pasta
Olive oil for garnish
2 tablespoons grated
   tuna bottarga
1/2 cup grated Parmesan
   cheese (optional)*

In a skillet, heat olive oil and sauté garlic until golden, do not brown. Add pumpkin and sage and sauté until tender.

Boil pasta until *al dente*. Add pasta to pumpkin sauce and sauté, tossing to coat. Serve on shallow plate and top with olive oil and grated *bottarga*.

* If not using bottarga, serve Parmesan cheese on the side. Bottarga is dried tuna roe.

Mauro's Spaghetti with Garlic and Olive Oil
(Spaghetti all'Olio e Aglio)

Most of our friends who own restaurants in Italy serve fresh pasta to their customers, but often they cook dry pasta for a quick lunch or dinner or to serve the kitchen staff before the restaurant opens for patrons.

Ricardo Febbrari, Mauro's son, who is going to school In Los Angeles, helped me translate this recipe from his father's cookbook. He explained that he remembers his family eating this dish at least once a week, when he was a small boy. It was simple to make and the ingredients were always available. He also recalls that, although they served grated Parmesan on the side, it was rarely used.

In many versions of this spaghetti sauce, crushed garlic cloves are sautéed in olive oil until they are almost black. Then they are discarded and the spaghetti is seasoned with the flavored oil. In this recipe chopped garlic is sautéed lightly and left in the oil to be added to the spaghetti. The result is a fuller yet milder garlic taste with no trace of bitterness.

Serves 8

**1/2 cup olive oil plus
    2 additional tablespoons
5 garlic cloves, chopped
Salt
1 pound spaghetti or spaghettini
Freshly ground black pepper
    (6 to 8 twists of a pepper mill)
2 tablespoons chopped parsley
1/2 cup Parmesan Cheese**

The sauce can be prepared in the time it takes to bring the water for the spaghetti to a boil. When you have turned on the heat under the water, put 1/2 cup of the olive oil, the garlic and 2 teaspoons of salt into a large skillet. Sauté the garlic over very low heat, stirring frequently, until it turns a rich, golden color. Do not burn garlic.

Drop the spaghetti into boiling salted water and cook until *al dente*, tender but still firm to the bite. Drain immediately and transfer to the skillet with the olive oil and garlic sauce. Toss rapidly, coating all the strands of spaghetti, adding pepper and parsley. Mix an additional tablespoon or two of olive oil into the spaghetti and serve with Parmesan cheese.

Mauro's Roasted Sea Bass

(Il Branzino Arrosto)

Mauro has written two cookbooks, *Salute Grande Cucina* (*Healthy Grand Cuisine*) and *Salute e Buona Cucina* (*Health and Good Cooking*), and he shared this easy recipe with me. *Branzino* is equivalent to sea bass in the States.

A good alternative to the fried onion ring topping would be a simple tomato salsa.

Serves 8

**2-1/2 pounds sea bass fillets
2 tablespoons olive oil
1/2 cup unsalted butter
Salt and pepper to taste
2 large onions
1 cup flour
Oil for frying
1 lemon thinly sliced**

Preheat the oven to 375°F.

Wash and dry the sea bass fillets and remove skin. Brush an ovenproof baking dish with olive oil, arrange sea bass in it, and top with butter. Season with salt and pepper. Bake in preheated oven for 20 minutes or until cooked through, basting with butter that accumulates on the bottom of the baking dish.

While the fish is baking, slice onion and separate into rings. Dip onion rings in flour, shaking off excess, and fry in hot oil. Remove when golden and crunchy.

To serve, arrange sea bass on serving plates and top with onion rings and lemon slices.

Mauro's Hunter Stew with Chicken
(Pollo alla Cacciatora)

Mauro explained that in this recipe from Liguria, the onions, wine, and tomato pulp give the chicken a rich, luxurious quality.

Serves 4 to 6

1 (2-1/2 pound) chicken,
  cut in pieces
Salt and pepper, to taste
1/3 cup olive oil
2 tablespoons finely
  minced onions
1/4 cup dry white wine
1 cup chicken broth
1 cup chopped tomato pulp

Sprinkle chicken pieces with salt and pepper. In a large skillet heat oil and brown the chicken on all sides. Transfer the pieces to a platter lined with paper towels as they are done; the wings and breast may take less time than legs and thighs.

  In the same skillet, sauté onions until cooked through, stirring occasionally. Increase heat, pour in wine and stir until it evaporates. Add broth and tomato pulp, bring to a boil and simmer for 10 minutes. Add chicken, cover, and cook on low heat until tender.

Mauro's Veal Tongue in Hot Sauce
(Lingua di Vitello con Salsa Piccante)

Tongue has always been a favorite of mine, and I especially like this version from Mauro's collection of meat recipes.

Serves 6 to 8

1 large veal tongue
1 tsp salt
3 tablespoons olive oil
2 carrots, minced
2 celery ribs, minced
1 tablespoon breadcrumbs
1 tablespoon plus 1 teaspoon
  white wine vinegar
6 anchovy fillets, rinsed
  and minced
2 tablespoons capers, rinsed
2 tablespoons parsley
1 garlic clove, minced
1 tablespoon brown mustard
2 or 3 drops Worchestershire
  sauce
2 tablespoons tomato purée
1 tablespoon lemon juice

In a large roaster, add tongue, salt and enough water to cover. Bring to a boil over high heat, reduce heat and simmer for 2 hours or until tender. Drain and peel tongue while still warm. Cool and cut into slices, place them on a platter and cover with plastic wrap until ready to serve.

  In a pot, heat olive oil and sauté carrots and celery until soft. Cool. In a large bowl combine bread crumbs and 1 tablespoon vinegar. Squeeze dry. Add anchovies, capers, parsley, garlic, mustard, Worchestershire, tomato purée, lemon juice, carrot/celery mixture and remaining vinegar. Pour over sliced tongue and serve.

Cheese Puffs
(*Bombolini di Formaggio*)

I gave these classically french cheese puffs (*gougère*) an italian twist by simply changing the cheese from Gruyere to Asiago or any other semi-hard cow cheese. These make for an elegant appetizer or can be served with a salad, just before dessert.

Makes about 24

1 cup milk
4 tablespoons unsalted butter
1 teaspoon salt
1/8 teaspoon coarsely
   ground black pepper
1 teaspoon Dijon-style mustard
1/2 teaspoon dry mustard
1 cup flour
4 eggs
1 cup finely shredded Asiago
   or Fontina cheese

In a heavy saucepan, scald milk. In a medium size bowl, knead together butter, salt, pepper and mustards. Add to milk and blend with a wooden spoon. Bring to a rolling boil. Add flour all at once, stirring vigorously, until the mixture forms a ball and leaves the sides of the pan.

Transfer the mixture to the bowl of an electric mixer. Add eggs, one at a time, blending well after each addition. Blend until the dough is shiny and smooth. Add the cheese and blend well.

Spoon into a pastry bag with plain round tip. Place a Silpat onto a baking sheet and pipe cheese puffs in mounds 1/4 - 1/2 inch apart. Sprinkle with additional cheese and a few drops of milk. Cover with plastic wrap and refrigerate until ready to bake.

Preheat the oven to 400°F. Bake 40 to 45 minutes or until well puffed and golden brown. Serve immediately.

Suzanne Dunaway's Ricotta Tart
(*Torta di Ricotta*)

Everyone loves this *torta*, the perfect finish for an otherwise elaborate meal. It can be made a few hours before you need it. It will rise like a soufflé in the oven and then fall, becoming a thin, low calorie dessert for all occasions. Suzanne cuts designs out of paper before dusting with powdered sugar.

Serves 6

4 large eggs, separated
2/3 cup sugar
Pinch of salt
1 pound ricotta cheese
2 tablespoons flour
1 teaspoon baking powder
1/2 cup mascarpone or
   crème fraîche
1 tablespoon lemon zest
Pinch of cinnamon
Powdered sugar for dusting

Preheat oven to 375°F. Butter and flour an 8- or 10-inch non-stick springform pan. Mix the egg yolks, sugar and salt in a food processor. Add the ricotta, flour, baking powder, mascarpone, lemon zest, and cinnamon, and blend well. In the large bowl of an electric mixer, beat egg whites until stiff but not dry. Fold cheese mixture into egg whites. Bake in the prepared springform pan for 30-40 minutes or until center springs back. Let cool, slide the *torta* out onto a plate, dust with powdered sugar and serve.

LAGO DI ORTA (Coiromonte)
Erma Erbe
Le Tre Montagnette: Italian Hospitality

Some years ago we spontaneously made our first visit to Hotel San Rocco on Lake Orta just before returning to the United States. After settling into an enchanting room overlooking the lake, we asked the front desk attendant to recommend a place where we might enjoy a casual Northern Italian lunch. She described a restaurant several kilometers up the road into the mountains that sounded just right.

Following her directions, we arrived in the village of Coiromonte and drove along a rural road to the restaurant, Le Tre Montagnette. But the parking lot we pulled into was empty. Resisting this sign that the restaurant was closed, I persuaded Marvino that we should at least knock on the door.

A sweet-faced elderly woman in a flowered cotton dress answered the door and confirmed in Italian that the restaurant was indeed closed. Erma Erbe explained that her two sons, who usually worked in the kitchen, were away at cooking school. Our disappointment must have shown on our faces, because she surprised us by offering to cook for us herself.

Having long dreamed of a meal in Italy that was home cooked just for us, we immediately accepted her offer and settled down outside at a long wooden table overlooking the three mountains in the distance. Erma soon appeared with a crisp white tablecloth and napkins and laid a table nearby. She proposed a few dishes, but no sooner had she returned to the kitchen than Marvino mentioned how much he would like to begin with local *salumi* (salami). I entered the kitchen with this request just as Erma was about to drop homemade *gnocchi* into boiling water. She smiled and disappeared.

Later, we found that she had gone to the cellar where her family stored the dried meats and salami. She returned with two large platters laden with salami selections. When we exclaimed at the extravagance of the presentation, she said, "Eat what you want."

As we sat enjoying this selection of home-cured *charcuterie*, we caught sight of our host's husband in the vegetable garden just below us harvesting lettuce and vegetables by hand for our lunch.

Course by course, the meal of our dreams was served forth from the *signora's* kitchen: potato *gnocchi* in a light tomato sauce, roast veal with garden-fresh vegetables, a salad of fresh-picked greens and local cheese.

Above: Our gracious hosts pose for a memorable photo.
Right: Erma served the meal of my dreams.

For dessert, our hostess announced that she was making *crème caramel*. At this point, I invited myself into the kitchen to watch, explaining that I had never successfully made a smooth *crème caramel*. She was certain this had to do with the freshness of the eggs. Alas, our supermarket eggs in Los Angeles couldn't compare with hers, fresh from the hen's nest.

I always prefer crème caramel served in the cup it was baked in because when the cup is inverted the caramel sauce gets lost on the plate. If the custard is served in its baking cup, each spoon brings up a lovely bit of caramel sauce with the custard, making for a distinctly different taste sensation. I remember that the *crème caramel* at Le Tre Montagnette was perfectly smooth but not too creamy. Chef Erma told me that in order to get a creamy but firm custard the water in the *Bain Marie* should never be boiling hot.

After this memorable lunch we were about to say good-bye when our hostess presented us with two fresh eggs, wrapped in fabric. "If you use these eggs the next time you make *crème caramel*, the result will be perfect," she promised. Just as we were leaving, she climbed a ladder and picked for me a beautiful, fragrant rose that was growing on a trellis above the front gate: something to remember her by.

I'm afraid we were only minimally successful in conveying the details of our luncheon adventure to the hotel receptionist on our return. But, since it was impossible for us to return to the U.S. with our two fresh eggs, we did persuade her to hardboil them so we could eat them on our flight home.

When Marvino and I went back to Coiromonte recently we learned that Erma and her husband had retired and sold the restaurant but that their sons are continuing the family tradition as chefs elsewhere in the north of Italy.

It's surprises like Le Tre Montagnette that make our journeys through the Italian countryside a continual adventure. This simple yet perfect lunch became the country's going-away gift to us, and we still treasure the memory of it.

Pasta and Bean Soup
(*Zuppa di Pasta e Fagioli*)

Although the sun was shining as we sat in the garden above Lake Orta, there was a chill in the air. Erma's homey soup was a perfect way to warm up after the antipasti and before the *gnocchi*. Traditionally, the pasta used in this soup is *maltagliati* (which literally means "badly torn pasta"), but *tagliatelle* also works well.

Serves 6 to 8

1 cup dried white beans, soaked in water to cover overnight
2 tablespoons olive oil
1 small onion, minced
3 garlic cloves, minced

Drain the beans and and transfer to a large pot; add water to cover and boil until tender, about 1 hour, adding additional water as needed.

In a skillet, heat olive oil and sauté the onion. Add the garlic, then the tomatoes, tomato paste, salt, and pepper to taste.

Meanwhile, cook the tagliatelle in boiling salted water until *al dente* (still with a bite).

1 cup chopped tomatoes
1 tablespoon tomato paste
Salt
Freshly ground black pepper
4 ounces dried tagliatelle
1 tablespoon chopped
    fresh parsley

Before serving, add the *tagliatelle* and beans to the tomato mixture and cook everything together briefly. Sprinkle with chopped parsley and additional olive oil. Ladle into shallow bowls and serve immediately.

Erma's Caramel Custard
(*Crème Caramel*)

Erma served us the caramel custards right out of the ramekins in which they were baked. When we dipped our spoons into the custard, the caramel sauce at the bottom came with it, a great combination.

Makes 6 servings

Caramel (recipe follows)
2 cups whole milk
1/3 cup sugar
1 teaspoon vanilla extract
3 large (very fresh) eggs,
    at room temperature
1/2 teaspoon salt

Preheat the oven to 325°F. Adjust the rack to the center of the oven.

Prepare the caramel and quickly pour about 2 tablespoons into each of six 6-ounce ramekins. Carefully lift each ramekin and swirl the caramel to coat the bottom evenly. Place the coated ramekins in a large baking pan.

In a medium bowl, whisk together the milk, sugar, and vanilla. In another large bowl, whisk together the eggs and salt. Pour in the milk mixture. This is the custard base.

Fill each ramekin to the rim with custard. Fill the large baking pan with hot water *(bain marie)* until the water rises half way up the ramekins. Bake for 40 to 45 minutes. The custards are finished when they are set but have a uniform jiggle. They should not be brown, and should not have risen. Allow the custard to cool completely, then cover with plastic wrap and refrigerate in their ramekins until serving time. To serve, arrange the ramekins on (dessert) serving plates or run a knife along the outside of each creme, than turn over onto a dessert plate and allow the caramel to drizzle over the crème.

Caramel

1 cup water
1 cup sugar
3 tablespoons light corn syrup

In a medium saucepan, combine the water, sugar, and corn syrup. Stir them with a wooden spoon to make sure no lumps of dry sugar remain. Cover the saucepan and place it over medium heat for 4 minutes. After 4 minutes, remove the lid, increase the heat to high and bring to a boil. Do not stir from this point on. It will be very bubbly. If stray sugar crystals appear on the side of the pan, brush them down with a clean, wet pastry brush.

As the sugar cooks, the bubbles will get larger. Insert a candy thermometer, and when the temperature reaches 285°F to 300°F the mixture will be golden brown. Remove from the heat and quickly pour into ramekins.

BARBARESCO
Angelo Gaja – *Godfather of the Italian Wine Industry*

If you befriend a Piemontese, they are likely to be your friend for life. The best known of our treasured compatriots in this region is Angelo Gaja, whose impact on Italian wine production in the last thirty years is impossible to overestimate. He took over the family business in 1970 and is now owner and president of the Gaja Winery. Angelo and his wife, Lucia, live in Barbaresco with their son, Giovanni and two daughters: Gaia and Rossana. Lucia plays an active role in the daily management of the winery. Their daughter, Gaia is now the winery's sales representative..

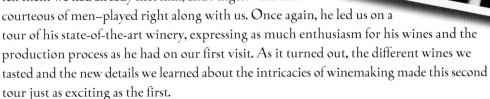

We were introduced to Angelo twice. First in 1986, by Antonio and Nadia Santini of Ristorante dal Pescatore, during our visit with them to the village of Barbaresco; then, on a later trip, when we were traveling with Carluccio and Itala Brovelli, owners of Il Sole on Lake Maggiore. The Brovellis, hoping to surprise us, didn't tell us where we were going. We had been driving for about an hour when we arrived again at the winery and home of Angelo Gaja. When the Brovellis proudly introduced us to him we didn't have the heart to tell them we had already met him, and Angelo–the most courteous of men–played right along with us. Once again, he led us on a tour of his state-of-the-art winery, expressing as much enthusiasm for his wines and the production process as he had on our first visit. As it turned out, the different wines we tasted and the new details we learned about the intricacies of winemaking made this second tour just as exciting as the first.

On yet another trip to Italy, while we were staying at a hotel in Rome, we got a phone call from Angelo. He said Antonio Santini had called to tell him that the Zeidlers were in Italy. Why, Angelo wanted to know, hadn't we called him? He invited us to visit him and said he would make a reservation for all of us at his favorite hotel/restaurant, Il Cascinalenuovo, outside of Asti. When we got to the hotel, he said we should ask for Walter or Roberto Ferretto. Walter is the chef, and his brother Roberto runs the front of the establishment. Before driving to the Piemonte area we had eaten lunch at our friends' restaurant, dal Pescatore. As always, lunch there involved twelve courses, and we stayed until 5:00 p.m.

On our way to Il Cascinalenuovo, Marvino and I agreed that there was no way we could eat dinner; we would just have to skip the meal. On our arrival, when Roberto asked what time we wanted to have dinner, we said that dinner was impossible for us because we had just finished lunch. We told him we would have only a light snack, and go to bed early.

The next morning when Angelo picked us up for a tour of the area and asked how we enjoyed our meal the previous evening, we admitted we had skipped dinner. Looking stricken, he told us he had planned a special truffle dinner for us with the chef–and that he had prepaid for everything. A truffle dinner is no small matter, and of course Marvino

Marvino and I share one of many memorable moments we've shared with Angelo Gaja.

and I felt terrible. But after a few tense moments, we were all able to joke about the extraordinary dining experience we had missed.

Angelo, Lucia and their daughters then spent the entire day with us. For lunch they took us to a local country restaurant just below the winery. One of the dishes he ordered, as a first course, was boiled agnolotti, filled with cheese and served without sauce in a straw basket lined with a napkin. We ate them with our fingers like French fries.

As we were preparing to leave Il Cascinalenuovo, we realized we couldn't go without purchasing several truffles to take home. Roberto weighed and packed them in rice for us to hand-carry aboard the plane. Walter explained how he uses a truffle slicer when he serves them on top of pasta, *risotto* or *polenta*.

Our last stop in Italy that trip was Sirmione, a village on Lake Garda, where we checked into the Villa Cortine Palace Hotel, leaving the truffles in the glove compartment of our car. The next morning, when we drove to the airport, the intense aroma of the truffles had permeated the interior of our car, even though we drove with the windows down. I have often wondered what the car rental company did about that indelible smell.

Agnolotti Boiled and Served in a Napkin
(Agnolotti Bolliti Serviti in un Tovagliolo)

Angelo's favorite pasta was served at the beginning of lunch. Cheese-filled Agnolotti are boiled and served without a sauce, in a basket lined with a napkin. They are eaten with fingers just like French fries.

Agnolotti (small tortellini) can be purchased dried, or in the freezer or cheese section of specialty markets. Just boil them in salted water, dry and serve immediately.

Baked Agnolotti with Marinara Sauce and Cheese
(Agnolotti al Forno con Salsa Marinare e Formaggio)

Since we are on the subject of agnolotti, I just had to include this recipe. The agnolotti are store bought, so it is simply a matter of boiling them, mixing them with sauce and cheese, baking and serving. I think even Angelo would love this dish.

Serves 6 to 8

2 tablespoons olive oil
2 cups marinara sauce*
  (recipe page 111)
1/4 cup minced fresh parsley
2 tablespoons fresh
  basil leaves, minced
1 pound cheese agnolotti
  or tortellini
6 to 8 thin slices of mozzarella
1/2 cup freshly grated Parmesan

Preheat the oven to 375°F. Brush an 8x8x2-inch baking dish with olive oil.

Prepare the marinara sauce, transfer it to a large bowl, add parsley and basil and mix well and set aside.

Cook the agnolotti in a large pot of boiling salted water until just tender, about 3 to 4 minutes. Drain and transfer to a large bowl. Add the sauce to the agnolotti and toss to coat. Transfer mixture to the prepared baking dish. Arrange mozzarella and Parmesan on top. Cover with aluminum foil and bake until the sauce bubbles and the cheeses melt, about 25 to 30 minutes. Serve immediately.

* Note: There are many acceptable store-bought marinara sauces available.

ALBARETTO DELLA TORRE
Cesare Giaccone – *The Spirit of Hospitality*

It was Angelo Gaja who introduced us to the shy, sweet and unassuming Chef Cesare Giaccone when we first visited his Ristorante dei Cacciatore di Cesare in Albaretto della Torre. In the fog and rain, we tailed Angelo up winding roads through a series of villages for about thirty minutes and arrived at the small house Cesare had converted to a country restaurant.

That evening, we sat at a long table in the center of Cesare's small dining room. Our mouths watered upon sighting leg of goat, rotating on a spit in a corner fireplace. This was a specialty of Cesare's, as was our first course: a peach and arugula salad dressed, with his own olive oil and wine vinegar.

Several years later, Cesare moved this restaurant a hundred yards down the road, to the home in which he was born. The restaurant's new site also had four rooms that he offered for overnight stays. During one of our stays there, Cesare greeted us and led us to our room, carrying a basket of fresh fruit and a bottle of water. About thirty minutes later, he returned with a bottle of Vin Santo and a plate of hot homemade hazelnut cookies, looking as though they were nuts on a branch from a real hazelnut tree! I'd never seen such an ingenious presentation for cookies. Marvino and I had been napping. Cesare pretended not to notice–even though Marvino answered the door wrapped with a towel, as I remained tucked in bed.

When it was time for dinner, we walked downstairs and through the kitchen. The wonderful aromas had us wondering what surprises Cesare woud be cooking up for us that night. We sat at our favorite table, in front of the fireplace. Cesare appeared after each course, to ensure our enjoyment. Between courses, I sneaked into the kitchen to photograph Cesare making *zabaglione* in a copper pot. The next morning, we joined him for a breakfast of fresh fruit, local cheeses, homemade bread and jam, and a chocolate and custard cake. We have returned to visit Cesare many times, and are always touched by his kind heart and hospitality that are his hallmarks.

Cesare recently closed his own restaurant and took over the kitchen at Villa Contessa Rosa Restaurant, located at the Fontanafredda Winery.

His vison has clearly inspired his two sons, Oscar and Filippo. Oscar, himself a fine chef, now operates his father's wine vinegar factory. Filippo worked with Cesare in the restaurant until 2004. He then worked in Germany with famous chef, Steinheuers Stefan and with Gino Angelini, at Angelini Osteria in Los Angeles, California. Soon, his heart grew heavy for home. In June 2010, he re-opened the doors to the restaurant once run by his father and great-grandfather, under the name, Filippo Oste in Albaretto.

WHEN YOU GO, YOU SHOULD KNOW:

Cesare Giaccone
Villa Contessa Rosa Restaurant
  at Fontanafredda Winery
Serralunga di Alba
12050 Italy
Tel: (017) 361-3161
www.cesaregiaccone.com
www.villacontessarosa.com

Filippo Giaccone
Filipo Oste in Albaretto
Umberto 12 street
12050 Albaretto Tower, Italy
Tel: (0173) 520141
www.filippogiaccone.com

Oscar Giaccone
Cesare's Fine Wine Vinegars
Tel: (0173) 520141
www.acetodibaorlo.it

Cesare's Peach and Avocado Salad with Balsamic-Olive Oil Dressing
(Insalata di Pesche e Avocado in Olio et Aceto)

Cesare's innovative peach salad inspired me to create my own version using the fresh ingredients that we have in California, which includes peaches, avocado, red peppers and corn kernels for color and texture, as well as flavor. When white truffles are in season, Cesare will often arrive from the kitchen to shave them on top of the salad.

Serves 6 to 8

1 avocado, peeled and diced
1 firm peach (preferably white), peeled and diced
1 cup corn kernels
1 red bell pepper, seeded and diced
4 cups arugula
1 tablespoon balsamic vinegar
1/4 cup olive oil
Salt
Freshly ground black pepper

In a large bowl, combine the avocado, peach, corn, red bell pepper and toss. Add arugula and toss.

Combine the balsamic vinegar and olive oil and mix well. Just before serving add the dressing to the salad mixture and toss to coat. Season with salt and freshly ground black pepper to taste. Arrange on salad plates and serve.

Oscar's Hazelnut Cookies
(Biscotti alla Nocciola)

Here is my adaptation of the hazelnut cookies that Cesare's son, Oscar, once made at Cesare's restaurant. Oscar replaces the hazelnuts in an actual tree branch with small rounds of cookie dough and bakes them, branch and all! This makes for a unique presentation. You can also be creative and use small branches from nut or fruit trees.

Makes about 7 dozen

1 cup hazelnuts
1/2 pound unsalted butter
1/2 cup powdered sugar
1 teaspoon vanilla extract
2-1/2 cups flour
1/2 teaspoon salt
Powdered sugar for coating, optional
Branches from hazelnut (or other nut or fruit trees), optional

Preheat the oven to 350°F.

Line a baking pan with aluminum foil or Silpat and toast hazelnuts in one layer in the middle of the oven for about 10 minutes or until they color lightly and their skins blister. Wrap hazelnuts in a kitchen towel and allow them to steam 1 minute. Rub nuts in towel to remove the loose skins (don't worry about any skins that fail to come off) and cool. Grind finely in a food processor.

In the large bowl of an electric mixer, blend the butter with the 1/2 cup of powdered sugar until fluffy. Mix in the vanilla. Add the flour and salt and blend thoroughly. Add hazelnuts and blend until completely incorporated. Work the dough with your hands into a smooth ball. Pinch off and roll the dough with your hands into 1/2 to 1-inch balls. Place them about 1 inch apart on ungreased baking sheets* and bake for 10 to 15 minutes, or until the bottoms are golden brown. Cool slightly, then roll in sifted powdered sugar. Let them cool and roll them in sugar again.

* If you are using branches to enhance the presentation of these cookies, at this point place each unbaked cookie in the leaf of a branch and bake the branches.

NEIVE D'ALBA
Romano Levi: *The Angelic Grappa Maker*

I will always remember Romano Levi's words to me:
"Do not cut trees. Do not destroy nature. Do not kill.
Do not take unless you give back." Giving was living for
Romano, widely known during his long lifetime as
"the angelic *grappa* maker."

The first time we met Romano was with Antonio and Nadia Santini, owners of dal Pescatore. The four of us had just finished lunch at Ristorante La Contea in Neive when Antonio began telling us about an odd character they knew who was the most famous *grappa* maker in Italy. Insisting that we must meet him, the Santinis drove us to a small farm in the countryside.

We arrived in the pouring rain in front of an old iron gate, behind which a small man with thick dark eyebrows appeared with a large black umbrella. He and Antonio exchanged a few words, the gate slowly opened, and we were invited in. We followed Romano Levi past a ramshackle house with a window, where we could see his office with simply a desk, an old table littered with papers, bottles of ink, paints, pens and brushes; stacks and stacks of books and periodicals—all illuminated by a single gooseneck lamp.

From there, we trooped on behind our gnomic host through a weedy, unkempt yard to his barn, where he produced an oversized key that opened a battered wooden door. Mice scurried as the door swung open, and Romano warned us not to disturb the thick webs housing spiders in the corners of the barn's opaque windows. He also asked us to watch where we put our feet, lest we step on any other living creatures.

In the center of the room stood two weathered wooden barrels where Romano aged the grappa he made exclusively from grape skins and seeds from Angelo Gaja's winery. A uniquely Italian drink, *grappa* is traditionally made from pomace, the residue that is a by-product of winemaking. For Romano Levi the distillation of grappa was his modest but essential contribution to the world. He worked alone, in this cramped barn, in his tiny Piemontese village, content to concoct the earthy distillates that the discerning came to his back yard to buy and which he sold only when the right mood was upon him.

On our first visit, Antonio asked Romano to give us a taste of his *grappa*, and we watched as Romano gently lowered a thimble-sized glass vessel on a silk thread into one of the barrels. We each took a sip of the precious liquid, which warmed us right down to our toes. We were hooked. Back in his office, we discovered that Romano himself drew and lettered individual labels for each bottle of his *grappa*—a longtime custom he insisted on honoring. When Antonio tried to persuade him to sell us a bottle to take back to California, he said he was sorry that he did not have time to design a personal label for us just then and suggested we come back another time.

It took one year and a return trip in the company of Angelo and Lucia Gaja (whose daughters are Romano's godchildren) for us to claim our first bottles of personalized

Romano Levi shows
pride as he shares
his liquid gold.

grappa. As before, Romano met us at the iron gate. As we walked through his garden, Angelo pointed out a rock garden designed by a local artist in the shape of the New York skyline. Before we left Romano gave us one of this artist's sculptures–a large rock

Above: A lesson in grappa-making, from the master himself.
Left: Our own personalized bottles of Romano's *grappa.*

with a leather rope laced through it so that it resembled a football. We left that day carrying not only our two personalized bottles of grappa but also a new sculpture for our art collection.

Romano, who died in 2008 at age 80, created many labels for his grappa depicting a "wild woman," often with flowers in her hair. I wonder if this might have been his affectionate depiction of Mother Nature, whose creatures he so fiercely protected and whose fruit residues he transformed into an extraordinary elixir.

Sour Cherries in Grappa
(Ciliegie Aspre in Grappa)

I developed this recipe in honor of Romano Levi and his extraordinary *grappa.* It's good to have these cherries on hand to serve chilled in stemmed glasses as a dessert. They are delicious spooned over vanilla ice cream to be eaten while sipping the infused *grappa* from a glass.

**2 cups fruity full-bodied
  red wine (Barbera d'Asti)**
1 cup water
1/3 cup sugar
**1 vanilla bean, split lengthwise,
  seeds scraped**
**2 cups unsulphered dried
  sour cherries (1/2 pound)**
1 cup *grappa*

Makes about 6 cups

In a medium nonreactive saucepan, combine the wine with water, sugar, vanilla bean and seeds and bring to a boil over high heat. Remove from heat and add dried cherries. Cover and let stand until plumped, about 5 minutes. Uncover and cool completely.

    Spoon cherries and their liquid into a clean jar. Add the vanilla bean. Pour the grappa on top. Cover and let stand at room temperature for at least 1 week to let the flavors deepen. These will keep for months in a tightly sealed jar.

BIELLA
Sesé Ferraro, My Italian Sister

Some people are nervous about traveling alone, but time on my own has often led to my most exciting discoveries. In 1978 Marvino and I arrived in the village of Biella in the mountains above Milan, where some of Italy's finest woolen fabric is woven and where Marvino often purchased fabrics for his men's fashion stores. We checked into the Hotel Astor, and the following morning Marvino headed off for a day at the mills after pointing me in the direction of the road that led to the main street of Biella.

In two days I discovered one of the original Il Fornaio bakeries, invited myself into the kitchen for a baking lesson, met Sese and joined in her son Marco's ninth birthday party, learned to make *Limoncello* with Sese and took a lesson in preparing *gnocchi* from Matilda, her cook.

The center of Biella is one long street lined with small shops and restaurants, and I was to be on my own all day. Delighted as I was about this new adventure, I had no idea how extraordinary it would turn out to be.

As I began my walk, I passed an interesting shop that sold paints, housewares, interior design materials, and gifts. I walked inside and, in my best broken Italian, asked a slim blond, blue-eyed woman if she spoke English. Her answer was, "Why yes, my oldest son, Paulo, was born in New York."

We talked for about fifteen minutes and when the store got busy I said goodbye, and walked up the street, where I found a bakery called Il Fornaio, The couple who owned it, their son and his wife, all worked in the store. After we had chatted for a while, I asked if I could watch them bake their breads and they said, "Of course." This is when I discovered the true meaning of *il fornaio*, which means "the baker." I took a lot of photos, especially of their granddaughter, and on my next visit I brought them the pictures. When I left, they filled my arms with breads, rolls and *biscotti*. I looked forward to visiting them every year, and each time I found them upgrading their kitchen with new ovens and machines to roll out their breads.

Later that morning, I went back into the shop where Sesé, the woman I had visited earlier, worked. Could she suggest a good restaurant for lunch, I asked, and would she like to join me? She said she would love to but that she was giving a birthday party for her 9-year-old son, Marco. Would I like to come along and have lunch with her friends? I hesitated only a moment before accepting her invitation. She said a friend would pick me up at 1:30, and I went back to the hotel to leave Marvino a note telling him where I would be.

Sesé's friend picked me up promptly, and we drove up into the hills, passed through a large wrought-iron gate, and approached a large two-story Mediterranean-style house.

Learning the art of *gnocchi*-making, from Matilda.

I found out later that Sesé didn't really work in the shop where we met, but was helping out a friend who owned it.

At the party many of Sesé's friends, smartly dressed young Italian women, spoke English. They were friendly and anxious to hear about my life and work in America. The delicious lunch featured several hand-made pastas. At the end of the meal Sese served homemade *Limoncello* and later gave me her recipe. The next day I was invited back for a cooking lesson with Sese's cook, Matilda, on how to make *gnocchi*. Thus began one of my most profound friendships. Twice a year, when Marvino and I went to Italy on business, I would call and visit Sesé. Usually Matilda would make a great lunch for us and I would leave with another recipe or cooking lesson. Spotting large looms in Sesé's bedroom upstairs on one visit, I discovered that she is a weaver of exquisite tapestries, using wool yarns manufactured by her husband.

The second year I visited Sesé she took me to a local coffee bar where, instead of espresso, we had a fresh-squeezed grapefruit drink. She explained that whenever she and her friends went shopping in Biella they would always meet at this famous bar for a fruit drink. On one visit the bar's owner took us downstairs to a huge basement, which contained a large banquet hall and a kitchen. Here I was introduced to an amazing machine that pressed dough into wafer-like cookies (*Canestrelli*) with a chocolate cream filling. On that day Sesé and I discovered that our birthdays are five days apart in the same year.

On many occasions I tried to persuade Sesé to visit us in Los Angeles. But, unfortunately, our Italian friends don't travel to California as readily as we travel to Italy. However, many years later, Sesé did come to Los Angeles, to visit her son Paulo's wife and children, who were vacationing in our hometown. We had a wonderful time reminiscing about our first meeting and telling each other how our families had grown.

Nowadays, when we stop in Biella many things are different—Dino Fortunio's Bar has given way to a sushi bar. But you can still find the local specialty, *Canestrelli*, in a number of the region's bars and shops.

At the Prinz Grill seasonal vegetables are still a specialty, and if you're lucky enough to visit in late March or early April, you'll find asparagus featured on local restaurant menus. One of my favorite dishes is *Asparagus Bismark*—steamed asparagus with a sunny-side-up fried egg on top. In the fall, when white truffles and wild porcini mushrooms are in season, these delicacies can be sliced and added to any dish on request.

Many travelers delight in the restaurant's trademark tableside salad service from a cart brimming with fresh seasonal vegetables: fennel, tomatoes, peppers, onions, mushrooms, carrots, and fresh marinated baby artichokes.

**WHEN YOU GO,
YOU SHOULD KNOW:**

Hotel Astor
Viale Roma 9
Biella Bl., 13900 Italy
Tel: (015) 402750
Fax: (015) 8491691

Prinz Grill Asparagus and Eggs
(Asparagi alla Bismack)

When we are in Italy during asparagus season, it is always a joy to see how many delightful ways they serve this vegetable. One of my favorites is the following recipe; the surprise is that instead of hollandaise sauce, the asparagus is topped with a golden fried egg over-easy. Informality is the key to enjoying this dish. Just pick up a spear with your fingers and dip it into the egg yolk.

Many years ago, I found a set of French asparagus plates in an antiques shop. They have elegant gold rims, and each plate has a deep well for sauce—or for holding a fried egg.

When I can find quail eggs, in a local market or Chinatown, I use two of them for each serving. The tiny fried eggs make a stunning presentation.

Serves 8

48 asparagus spears,
  trimmed and peeled
3 tablespoons unsalted butter
1 garlic clove, minced
8 eggs (or 16 quail eggs)
Salt
Freshly ground black pepper
Shaved Parmesan cheese

Tie the asparagus in a bundle with kitchen string and steam it standing up in a pot of simmering water or on a steam tray set above a large pot of boiling water. When it is tender-crisp, drain the asparagus, remove the string, and place 6 spears on each of 8 heated plates.

In a large skillet, melt half the butter with half of the garlic over moderate heat and fry four eggs sunny side up, with the yolks slightly runny. With a metal spatula, carefully transfer the eggs and place them on top of the asparagus. Repeat with the remaining eggs, and spoon the butter and garlic over all. Season with salt and pepper to taste, and cover with shavings of Parmesan cheese.

Pasta with Gorgonzola and Blood Oranges
(Pasta con Gorgonzola e Arancie Rosse)

One of our favorite restaurants in Biella was Black Cat (*Gatto Nero*). The owner was an Italian hippie and his food was original and delicious. One of his specialties that we will never forget is a pasta in a gorgonzola sauce garnished with cubes of blood oranges.

Serves 8 to 10

1 cup milk
1 cup cream
1/2 pound gorgonzola, diced
1 pound spaghettini
  or fettucini
3 to 4 blood oranges
  chopped into pieces

In a large frying pan, heat the milk and cream. Add the gorgonzola and as it softens mash with a fork until completely incorporated.

Boil the pasta according to directions until *al dente*. Heat gorgonzola sauce and transfer pasta to sauce. Toss until completely coated. Add 1/2 cup oranges and toss.

Spoon into heated serving plates and top with remaining orange pieces. Serve immediately.

Sese's Limoncello Spritzers
(Limoncello alla Menta)

This sparkling drink is especially refreshing on a summer day. Since making your own *Limoncello* is time consuming, it's good to know that you can purchase it in the liquor department of most supermarkets, as well as in liquor stores.

Ice cubes
1/2 cup fresh mint leaves
1 cup Limoncello
(recipe follows) or
bottled *Limoncello*
1 cup club soda or
enough to fill glass

Serves 4

Fill 4 tall glasses halfway with ice. Add mint leaves. Using the handle of a wooden spoon, coarsely crush mint leaves into ice. Pour *Limoncello* over, and stir to blend. Add club soda and serve.

Sese's Lemon Liqueur
(Limoncello)

My first taste of *Limoncello* was in Sese Ferraro's home. I was sitting in her spacious living room when she appeared in the doorway holding a frosty bottle filled with slices of lemon immersed in a bright yellow liquid. She carefully poured a little of this liquid into small glasses, and my first sip filled my mouth with a strong sweet lemony flavor with a sour/bitter undertone of lemon peel. As the lemon liqueur slid down my throat I became aware of its high alcohol content. *Limoncello* is traditionally served chilled as an after-dinner digestive.

8 lemons *
1 bottle (750ml or 4 cups)
100-proof vodka (or *grappa*)**
2 cups sugar
2-1/2 cups water

Serves 4

Wash the lemons with hot water and scrub lightly with a vegetable brush. Pat dry with paper towels.

Zest the lemons with a zester or potato peeler, avoiding the white pith.

Into a one-gallon glass jar pour one-half of the bottle of vodka. Add lemon zest. Cover the jar and let the mixture macerate at room temperature for at least 10 days and up to 30 days in a cool dark place. The vodka will take on the flavor and rich yellow color of the zest.

In a large saucepan, over medium heat, dissolve the sugar in the water; cook until thickened, about 5 minutes. Let the syrup cool before adding to the *limoncello* mixture.

Add the remaining vodka. Allow to rest for another 10 to 30 days.

After the rest period, strain into a bottle and close with corks or stoppers, discarding the lemon zest. Keep bottles of Limoncello in the freezer until ready to serve.

 * Choose thick-skinned lemons (easier to zest)

** Use 100-proof vodka, which has less flavor than a low proof one. Also the high alcohol level will ensure that the limoncello will not turn to ice in the freezer.

TORINO
The Zocchi Family
A Chance Meeting with Fellow Food Enthusiasts

It was Sunday and Marvino and I were in Torino—a city
we'd visited many times but never fully explored—and
we decided to follow the suggestion of our Italian friends
Antonio and Daniella Pironte, who live in both Los Angeles
and Torino, that we visit the Castello di Rivoli.

An imposing baroque building that is now a museum of contemporary art, Castello di
Rivoli's cutting-edge exhibitions are continually changing. Touring the museum, we
were captivated by the staircase that ascends to a sky-painted ceiling. When you reach
the top you feel as though you are in the clouds.

By the time we left Castello di Rivoli it was time for lunch.
We had read about a country restaurant close by, but it was
full; Sunday is family day, and most restaurants are booked
in advance. We tried our second choice, which luckily had a
table for two available. Sitting at the table next to ours was
a handsome young couple. We observed that the chef came
out periodically to personally serve them a special dish,
then returned to see how they liked it. Curiosity got the
better of us, and after exchanging smiles we struck up a conversation with them about food and wine.

That is how we came to meet Michele and Laura
Zocchi. Michele, a plastic surgeon, is passionate about
food and wine. President of a local gourmet group, he is knowledgeable
not only about food and wine but also about fine art. Laura, a stunning dark-haired
woman who was chicly but conservatively dressed, could not have been friendlier. We
exchanged cards, and Michele invited us to call them when we were next in Torino.

A year passed before we returned, and I wasn't aware that my husband had been corre-
sponding with Michele. After we had checked into the hotel Grand Mogal in Torino,
Marvino suggested we call the Zocchis, but I wasn't sure they would remember us.

When we called Michele at his office and told him where we were staying, he laughed
and said, "If you go outside the hotel and look up, you'll see me in my office window."
With all the hotels in Torino, it was amazing that we happened to check into the very
one where he had his office.

He asked what our plans were for dinner that evening and said he would pick us up
at 7:30. We drove to his home in the hills above the city, where Laura was waiting to greet
us with Lorenzo, the oldest of their three children. Six-year-old Lorenzo was dressed in a
jacket and tie, and the twins—a boy and girl—were asleep in their crib.

After Michele opened the champagne he allowed his son Lorenzo to serve us. Our

Top: Michele with his
wife, Claudia and their
combined families. Left:
A snapshot of our first
aquaintance with
Michele and Laura's
adorable children

memorable evening with the Zocchis began with caviar, followed by *foie gras* and moving on from there to Roast Spring Lamb with *Salsa Verde* and a wonderful cheese to go with his fine old bottle of Barolo. The whole dinner was delicious, and it was a special treat for us to dine in a private home in the suburbs of Torino.

When we visited the city the following year we were treated to another splendid dinner that included good friends of the Zocchi's whom Michele had invited to meet us.

Some years went by before we were able to visit Torino again. When we communicated by email, we learned that Michele and Laura had divorced and Michele had remarried. He invited us to dinner to meet his new family: his wife, Claudia, and their three children. We also renewed our acquaintances with his son Lorenzo, who had graduated from college and grown into a handsome young man, and the twins, who were now 16. On that occasion, not only did Lorenzo again serve the wine, he also opened the bottle.

We dined outside on the patio on that balmy evening. During dinner, Michele mentioned that Laura, his former wife, was out of the country but would like to speak to us. Obviously still on friendly terms with her, he called her on her cell phone, and we talked about our first visit and promised to see her the next time we were in Torino.

When we got back to Los Angeles, I was pleased to be able to send back to Michele photos of his new family, along with some I had taken of Laura and their children when we had our first dinner at their home.

Roast Spring Lamb with Green Sauce
(Agnello Arrosto con Salsa Verde)

Michele loves to cook, and he prepared this delectable roast lamb with peppers and potatoes for us at his home. Serve with Green Sauce, recipe page 38.

Serves 8 to 10

2 cups white vinegar

4 cups water

1 head garlic, peeled,
    4 whole cloves reserved,
    remaining cloves minced

6 to 8 pounds lamb shoulder,
    cut into 2-inch chunks

3 sprigs fresh rosemary leaves
    or 1 teaspoon dried rosemary

Salt

Freshly ground black pepper

1 red bell pepper, stemmed,
    seeded and thinly sliced

1 green bell pepper, stemmed,
    seeded and thinly sliced

2 potatoes, peeled and sliced
    lengthwise

1/2 cup olive oil

In a large bowl, combine the vinegar, water, mashed garlic and lamb. Marinate for 4 hours. Strain and discard the liquid.

Preheat the oven to 450°F.

Combine the rosemary and the reserved garlic cloves and chop coarsely. Add salt and pepper to taste. Toss with the lamb to coat evenly. Add the red and green peppers and potatoes and toss well. Place in a large roasting pan. Pour the oil over the meat mixture. Bake uncovered for 10 minutes. Reduce the heat to 350°F and bake covered for 1 to 1-1/2 hours, until tender.

LIGURIA

A private *focaccia*-making lesson with
a young chef at Ristorante Manuelina.
Recipe page 80.

RECCO
Ristorante Manuelina and Ristorante Vitturin 1860
Delectable Cheese Focaccia

Traveling on the Autostrada south of Genova, we rarely fail to exit at Recco to enjoy an order of Cheese *Focaccia* (*Focaccia col Formaggio*) at Ristorante Manuelina. This pizza-like dish, a specialty of the area, is usually served as a first course, but we often order it as our main dish. Manuelina also has an extensive menu specializing in seafood.

I had always wanted to know how their amazing cheese *focaccia* was made. After eating in the restaurant many times, and often standing at the kitchen entrance observing its preparation, one of the young chefs finally invited me in. Even though the kitchen was closed and the lights were off, he must have been touched by my longing look. He turned the lights back on, re-lit the oven and gave me a demonstration on the preparation of this pizza-like *focaccia*, along with the recipe.

On another visit, we left Manuelina and drove all the way to the south of France (over 4 hours), before realizing that the restaurant had neglected to return our credit card. When we called them, they apologized and offered to messenger it to us. We told them not to bother, knowing we could retrieve it on our return trip the following day. Of course, they sat us at a table and served us an order of *Focaccia col Formaggio* for our trouble. Nowadays when we visit they always remind us to make sure we have our credit card before we leave.

The establishment now includes Manuelina La Villa Hotel, for travelers who might crave *Focaccia col Formaggio* for breakfast as well as dinner.

On another visit we found Manuelina closed for a private wedding party. They suggested we try Ristorante Vitturin 1860, just up the road, and we were delighted to discover it, since Vitturin also produces a satisfying rendition of our favorite Ligurian specialty.

Vitturin's kitchen is downstairs, and they have an unusual arrangement for conveying food up to the dining room. An apparatus that functions like a windmill sits in the center of the restaurant and diners get to watch as it carries the dishes up from the kitchen.

**WHEN YOU GO,
YOU SHOULD KNOW:**

Ristorante Manuelina
(Manuelina La Villa Hotel)
Via Roma 278, Recco
(Genova) Italy
Tel: (0185) 74128-75464
email: manuelina@manuelina.it
www.manuelina.it

Ristorante Vitturin 1860
Via dei Giustiniani, 48
16036 Recco (Genova) Italy
Tel: (0185) 720225
Fax: (0185) 723686
vitturin@libero.it
www.vitturin.it

Hotel Cenobio dei Dogi
Via N. Cuneo 34, Camogli
(Genova) 16032 Italy
Tel: (0185) 7241
Fax: (1085) 772796
email: Cenobio@cenobio.it
www.cenobio.it

Recco's Cheese Focaccia
(Focaccia col Formaggio di Recco)

Cheese *Focaccia* is a Ligurian specialty, one of the glories of Italian cuisine. Driving north toward Genova on the Autostrada along the Italian Riviera, exit at Recco; if you make a left off the Autostrada you will have a choice of two restaurants that specialize in this cheese masterpiece: Ristorante Manuelina and Ristorante Vitturin 1860.

Serves 8 as an appetizer, 4 as a main course

1 cup flour
1-1/2 teaspoons salt
1/4 cup olive oil
2 tablespoons water (approx.)
1 pound Stracchino or
  Taleggio cheese,
  cut into cubes

In the bowl of a food processor, place flour and 1/2 teaspoon salt. With motor running, add 2 tablespoons of the olive oil and enough room-temperature water to create a soft dough that forms a ball around the blade (about 45 seconds). Turn dough out into a lightly oiled bowl, shape into a ball, cover, and let rest 30 minutes or longer.

Preheat the oven to 500°F. Generously oil a 14-inch pizza pan or heavy-duty cookie sheet.

Roll out half of the dough into a transparent circle about 16-inches in diameter, and line the pan with it. Top with dollops of the cheese. Roll out the second piece of dough in the same way and top the *focaccia* with it. With the aid of your rolling pin, trim excess dough to form a seal. Tear four small holes in the top to allow air to escape, brush with olive oil and sprinkle with the remaining 1 teaspoon salt. Bake for 8 to 10 minutes, or until lightly golden but not crisp. Serve hot, cut into wedges.

Chickpea Pancake
(Farinata)

Every Italian region has its comfort food, its local dish imbued with memories, tradition, and nostalgia. In Liguria, the region flanking Genova along Italy's northwest coast, that dish is *farinata*. A deceptively simple street food, *farinata* is somewhat like a large, thin chickpea *crepe* or pancake. It is traditionally baked in brick wood-burning ovens on pizza pans. Crisp and golden on the top and bottom, soft and moist on the inside *farinata* is a finger-lickin' food that nourishes the soul.

Like pizza, *farinata* can be topped with any vegetable, cheese, or sauce; or it can be eaten plain, right out of the oven. In some places minced onions or rosemary are sprinkled on top of the *farinata* before it is baked. My method calls for using a skillet on the stovetop, then moves the pancake to the broiler.

Makes 2

2/3 cup chickpea flour*
1/3 teaspoon salt
3/4 cup water
2 teaspoons finely chopped
  rosemary
6 tablespoons olive oil
1/2 cup chopped tomato
1/2 cup chopped onions

Sift the chickpea flour with the salt into a medium bowl. Slowly add 1/4 cup of the water, whisking constantly to form a paste. Beat with a wooden spoon until smooth. Whisk in remaining 1/2 cup of water and, if time permits, let the batter stand at room temperature for 30 minutes, then stir in the rosemary.

Preheat the broiler.

Heat 1-1/2 tablespoons of olive oil in a 12-inch non-stick ovenproof skillet. Stir the batter once, pour (about 3/4 cup of batter) into the skillet. Cook the pancake over moderately high heat until the bottom is golden

2 tablespoons capers, (optional)
1/3 cup freshly grated
   Parmesan cheese
1/2 teaspoon freshly ground
   black pepper

and crisp and the top is almost set, 2 to 3 minutes. Burst any large air bubbles with the tip of a knife.

Sprinkle half of the tomato, onion, capers (if using) Parmesan and pepper over the top, and drizzle the remaining 1-1/2 tablespoons of olive oil on top. Place the skillet under the broiler and cook until the pancake is golden and crisp, 3 to 4 minutes. Slide onto a wooden board; using a pizza cutter, cut into wedges and serve immediately. Repeat with the remaining batter.

* Chickpea flour is sold in Italian specialty shops and health food stores.

Onion-Anchovy Pizza
(*Pissaladiera*)

In restaurants on the Italian Riviera a dish called *pissaladiera* is often served as an *antipasto*. It consists of a thinly rolled pizza dough topped with a rich and savory mixture of slow-cooked onions and garlic, garnished with pungent anchovies and olives, and drizzled with olive oil. This is a great way to wake up your taste buds.

Makes 1 or 2 Pizzas Serves 12 or 24

Basic Pizza Dough
   (recipe follows)
5 tablespoons olive oil
2 pounds (3 large) onions,
   thinly sliced
2 garlic cloves, minced
Salt, to taste
Freshly ground black pepper,
   to taste
1 can (2-ounces) anchovy
   fillets, drained
1 cup chopped olives
   (optional)
Cornmeal for pizza pan

Prepare the pizza dough. Preheat the oven to 450° F.

In a large skillet, heat 4 tablespoons of the olive oil. Add the onions and garlic. Season to taste with salt and pepper. Cover and cook on low heat for 30 minutes. Stir occasionally to avoid sticking. Do not allow onions to brown.

Break off a golf-ball size piece of dough to make one 8-to10-inch pizza. Knead on a floured board to a round disc and roll out to a thin circle. Brush pizza baking pan with oil, dust with cornmeal and place the rolled out dough on top. Scatter enough onion mixture to cover pizza round generously. Garnish with 12 anchovies in a circular pattern and top with chopped olives (optional). Sprinkle with the remaining 1 tablespoon oil. Bake for 30 minutes on lower rack of oven, or until golden brown. Repeat with remaining dough if desired.

Basic Pizza Dough
(*Impasto per Pizza*)

Prepare this basic pizza dough, roll it out and select your own toppings: sliced mushrooms, anchovies, sliced onions, sliced zucchini, oven-baked tomatoes (see page 155), roasted peppers (see page 21) cut into strips. This recipe also serves as a base for Pizza *Margherita*.

Makes 3-4 pizzas

2 packages active dry yeast
Pinch of sugar
1-1/4 cups warm water
   (110-115°F)
1/4 cup olive oil

Dissolve the yeast with the sugar in 1/2 cup of the water and set aside until foamy.

In the bowl of an electric mixer, combine the remaining 1/4 cup water, the olive oil, and yeast mixture. Mix the flour and salt and stir in, 1 cup at a time, until the dough begins to come together into a rough ball. Spoon onto a floured board and knead until smooth and

3-1/2 cups flour
1 teaspoon salt
Cornmeal

elastic. Place the dough in an oiled bowl, oil its top, cover, and set in a warm place to rise for about 1 hour, until doubled in bulk.

Punch down the dough and break off golf ball sized pieces to make 8- to 10-inch or individual pizzas. Knead each piece of dough on a floured board for 1 minute, working in additional flour to make it smooth and no longer sticky. Roll it out into a thin circle. Brush a round pizza baking pan with olive oil, dust with cornmeal, and arrange the rolled out dough on top. Spread with assorted toppings.

Vegetarian Minestrone Ligurian Style
(*Minestrone di Verdure alla Ligure*)

Every region of Italy makes its own version of vegetable soup. This hearty minestrone, which we ate in a little restaurant outside of Genova, typifies the Ligurian style of cooking by its inclusion of potatoes and basil. Choose seasonal fresh vegetables and don't be too concerned with exact measurements. Substitute part chicken or beef stock for vegetable stock, if you wish. Be sure to allow time for soaking the beans overnight.

1 cup dried cannellini beans
   or Great Northern beans,
   soaked overnight
1/4 cup olive oil
2 medium onions, chopped
2 cloves garlic, minced
1 cup chopped carrots
1-1/2 cups chopped celery
1/4 cup minced fresh parsley
2 cups peeled and diced potatoes
2 cups unpeeled diced zucchini
2 cups chopped Swiss chard
1 can (28 ounces) peeled
   tomatoes with liquid
6 to 8 cups vegetable stock
1 tablespoon fresh basil, crumbled
1/2 teaspoon dried thyme, crumbled
1 bay leaf, crumbled
Salt
Freshly ground black pepper
4 to 8 ounces dried macaroni or
   penne pasta
1/2 head cabbage, cored
   and shredded
1 (12-ounce) can garbanzo beans,
   drained
Freshly grated Parmesan cheese

Serves 10 to 12

In a large heavy pot, heat olive oil over medium heat. Add onions, garlic, carrots, celery, parsley, potatoes, zucchini, chard, beans, and tomatoes. Sauté 5 minutes, stirring occasionally. Add stock, basil, thyme and bay leaf. Season with salt and pepper to taste. Cover, reduce heat to low, and simmer until beans are soft, about 2 hours.

Add pasta, cabbage, and garbanzo beans. Cook partially covered, for 30 minutes, stirring frequently. Serve in heated soup bowls and sprinkle with grated Parmesan cheese.

VARIGOTTI
Vincenzo and Emma Frumenta
Ristorante Muraglia Conchiglia d'Oro:
Best Fresh Seafood Restaurant in Italy

Vincenzo Frumenta's restaurant in Varigotti, a city north of Genoa, is our choice for the best grilled seafood in all of Italy. Relatively unknown among Americans, it first caught our attention when we read that the house specialty was fresh anchovy soup. Every coastal Italian province has its signature fish chowder, but this seemed especially distinctive..

Ristorante Muraglia Conchiglia d'Oro did not disappoint us, and each fresh seafood dish we chose from owner-chef Vincenzo's handwritten daily menu was more delicious than the previous one. Guests are invited to select their fish from two large ice-filled straw baskets displayed on a long counter that separates the dining room from the grill. After you make your choice, Vincenzo, a tall man with a magnificent beard, will suggest several ways your seafood might be prepared. (None of this conversation is in English, since the entire staff speaks only Italian). Chef Vincenzo, whose shuffling gait reminded me of Charlie Chaplin's, grills your selection over coals in an open fireplace.

We highly recommend the fresh anchovies, when they are available. During our last visit Vincenzo served the anchovies three ways: steamed, grilled and deep fried. Also on my "recommended" list is the raw seafood plate, accented with red peppercorns and thinly sliced fresh ginger.

Emma, the petite and beautiful wife of Vincenzo, oversees the formal kitchen in the rear, preparing appetizers, salads, pasta dishes and desserts. Like many restaurants in Italy, Muraglia is a family enterprise. The Frumentas' daughter, Ann, works by Emma's side as a chef, and their daughter Roberta as a server.

Throughout our dinner Marvino and I were eyeing the rolling dessert table prepared by Emma. Each dessert is a work of art, and you will want to try everything. The ones we saw included homemade candied ginger, at least three fruit tarts, seasonal berries, and fruit in syrup. There is always something new to choose from.

Here's a sample menu: To welcome us before we order, the wait staff always arrives with sparkling wine and hot *focaccini* (fried bread). I was surprised on our first visit to discover that Vincenzo shapes the same dough into a large pretzel to hold a rolled- up napkin, just as I have done for years. Following this we might eat seafood crudo (tuna, *trigilia*, *riccioli* pasta, fresh anchovies); barley-bean and vegetable soup with *riccoli*; fresh sardines, triglia, and/or grilled orata with cherry tomatoes, and for dessert a lemon cake covered with candied lemon peel; almond brittle and ginger candies.

Four guest rooms are now available behind the restaurant—the perfect place for an overnight stay and a walk on the oceanfront boardwalk after a leisurely lunch or dinner.

**WHEN YOU GO,
YOU SHOULD KNOW:**

**Ristorante Muraglia
Conchiglia d'Oro**
Via Aurelia, 133
17024 Finale Ligure Varigotti
(SV) Italy
Tel: (0185) 74128-75464
email: r.conchigliadoro@libero.it

Fried Bread
(Focaccine Fritte)

Before you place your order for lunch or dinner at Ristorante Muraglia Conchiglia d'Oro the wait staff welcomes you with complimentary sparkling wine and a platter of hot *focaccini*. There are many recipes for this fried bread, but I've found that using my pizza dough recipe results in the closest approximation to the delicious original.

Makes 8 to 10 dozen

Pizza Dough (see recipe page 81)
Olive oil for frying
Salt for dusting

In a deep pot, heat 4 inches of olive oil to 350°F. Divide dough into four parts and with a rolling pin roll out one part into a rectangle about 1/8-inch thick. With a pizza wheel, cut the dough into 1-inch squares. Repeat with the remaining dough. Fry the *Focaccini* a few at a time in the hot oil until puffed and golden brown on both sides. Transfer to paper towels to drain and sprinkle with salt. Serve warm.

Vincenzo's Fresh Anchovy Soup
(Zuppa di Acciughe)

Many dishes are prepared with canned anchovy filets because they add so much flavor to recipes. In sauces they combine especially well with garlic and parsley. For a change of pace, Chef Vincenzo uses fresh anchovies as the basis for this unusual and delicious soup.

Serves 6 to 8

1 pound fresh anchovies*
1/2 cup olive oil
2 garlic cloves, minced
1 onion, finely sliced
1 celery stalk, diced
1 large carrot, diced
2 tomatoes, diced
1 teaspoon dried oregano
1 tablespoon minced parsley
4 to 5 cups water
Salt to taste
Toasted bread slices

Remove heads and fillet the anchovies, wash them and dry on paper towels.

In a heavy pot, heat the olive oil and sauté the garlic and onions. Add celery and carrot and sauté a couple of minutes, then add tomatoes, oregano and parsley. Simmer for 5 minutes. Add water and bring to a boil.

Remove the pot from the fire. Add the anchovies and salt, and stir gently. Return to the fire, cover and let cook for 20 minutes. Shake the pot every 10 minutes, but do not stir as the anchovies may break. Ladle into heated soup bowls and serve toasted bread on the side.

* Anchovies can be found in the freezer section of specialty markets. Fresh sardines or smelts can replace the anchovies.

Vincenzo's Baked Sea Bass with Green Olives and Rosemary Sauce
(Branzino con Olive Verdi e Salsa al Rosmarino)

At restaurant Muraglia, Chef Vincenzo serves sautéed cherry tomatoes with many of his seafood dishes. The mixture of garlic, herbs and the tomatoes provides a savory complement to the mild sea bass.

Serves 6 to 8

4 cloves garlic, minced
1 cup green olives,
  pitted and chopped

Preheat the oven to 425°F.

In a medium-size bowl, combine garlic, olives, rosemary and parsley and mix well. Season with salt and pepper to taste and set aside.

2 tablespoons fresh
   minced rosemary
2 tablespoons minced parsley
Salt
Freshly ground black pepper
1/4 cup olive oil
2 pounds sea bass, cut into
   6 to 8 fillets
1/2 cup vegetable stock
Sautéed cherry tomatoes,
   for garnish (recipe below)

Heat olive oil in saucepan and sauté garlic mixture for 1-2 minutes. Transfer to a 9x13-inch glass baking dish and spread evenly. Arrange sea bass fillets on top of olive mixture. Sprinkle with salt and pepper. Spoon vegetable stock around sea bass. Bake for 15 minutes, or until cooked through, basting with juices. To serve, arrange fillets on heated serving plates with olive mixture and sautéed cherry tomatoes.

Sautéed Cherry Tomatoes

Serves 6 to 8

2 tablespoons olive oil
3 cups assorted cherry tomatoes
Salt
Freshly ground black pepper
1 to 2 teaspoons sugar

Heat the oil in a large non-stick skillet. Add tomatoes, salt and pepper and sauté until slightly tender. Add sugar and continue to cook for about 2 to 3 minutes. To serve, spoon over sea bass.

Chocolate Covered Candied Ginger
(*Cioccolat al Zenzero*)

Vincenzo's wife, Emma, makes fresh candied ginger at Ristorante Muraglia, and it is arranged on top of a lemon cake on the dessert cart. I was inspired to adapt it to chocolate covered ginger. When I am in a rush to bring chocolates to a friend I often use packaged candied ginger. These are a perfect after-dessert treat with espresso.

Makes about 1/4 pound

1/4 pound fresh ginger
1-1/2 cups water
1-1/2 cups sugar, plus 1/2 cup
   for tossing

Peel the ginger and slice very thin. Cut crosswise against the fibers, rather than lengthwise. Place slices in a heavy saucepan, cover with water and bring to a boil. Simmer for 3 to 4 minutes. Drain and repeat this step twice, for a total of three times.

Return ginger to the saucepan, add water and sugar. Simmer until the temperature on a candy thermometer reaches 222°F. Remove from the heat and let stand for one hour. Strain the ginger from the syrup through a strainer. Reserve the syrup for other uses.

Place remaining sugar in a shallow bowl or on a baking sheet and toss the ginger in it, separating the pieces with your fingers, to coat the ginger with sugar. Shake off excess sugar and store ginger in an airtight container in the refrigerator for up to two weeks.

To chocolate-coat candied ginger:

Serves 10

1 recipe candied ginger (above) or
   1 Package (8-oz.) candied ginger
1 cup melted
   semi-sweet chocolate

Line a baking sheet with wax paper. Using a teaspoon, dip each piece of candied ginger into melted chocolate, place on wax paper and refrigerate until firm.

TOSCANA

TOSCANA

TOSCANA

TOSCANA

TOSCANA

TOSCANA

PIETRASANTA
Life in an Italian Monastery

Pietrasanta is a small village in the foothills of the mountains above the Italian Riviera west of Lucca. It's a ten-minute drive from Forte dei Marmi, the Italian equivalent of Malibu, an area where many well-known artists have lived and worked. Fernando Botero, Henry Moore, Jacques Lipshitz, and Isamu Noguchi are among those who have created sculptures in the foundries and marble yards of this ancient walled city.

In the spring of 1982, we decided to rent a house for five months in Camaoire, a small village on the Mediterranean Sea close to Pietrasanta. After we visited Pietrasanta for the first time the previous year, we returned home knowing that, of all the places we had seen in Italy, Pietrasanta was the one where we'd like to spend more time, get to know the locals and live the way the Italians did. It had always been a dream of ours to spend more than just a few weeks or a month in one special locale, and the time was now right, since our children were older. We balanced our finances, made arrangements with friends and family to look after our house in Los Angeles, and decided to take the plunge.

The prior year, on our trip to Pietrasanta, we had seen a house we liked and made arrangements to rent it from owner, Andie Hoffman, an American artist. We also arranged to buy a BMW and drive it to Pietrasanta (BMW offers an economical program that allows you to purchase a BMW, pick it up in Germany, and drive it for your European travels. BMW will ship it to the United States). All of the pieces seemed to be in place. A few days before we were scheduled to travel, we received a call from Andie's husband. He told us there was a "small problem." It seemed that the previous year, Andie had rented her house to an American artist who was now refusing to leave. Because of the local housing laws, there was no way to force her to vacate.

The tenant had gone so far as to change the locks on the doors of the house. Andie actually had to break into her own home to get inside. The tenant called the police and reported her for trespassing–on her own property. The *polizia* arrived, arrested her, and threw her in jail.

With Andie in jail and the house unavailable, we had to quickly come up with an alternative. A friend, an American sculptor, who lived in Los Angeles, recommended we contact an Italian family who offered us the opportunity to rent a monastery in the hills above Pietrasanta, that had been in their family for over 300 years.

Attracted to the idea of staying in an old monastery, we jumped at the chance, especially after learning that the area was also a summer beach community.

Less than a week later, we took the exit off the *autostrada* at Pietrasanta and were met by Andrea, a tall sun-bronzed young man who might easily have been cast in an Italian movie. Andrea was the son of Laura and Giuseppi Raffo. Laura is a lawyer, and Giuseppi owns the local marble yard.

Lorianna and myself, enjoying our friendship.

Andrea explained that we would be staying in his grandparents' home until his parents returned from vacation and that they would need a little time to tidy up the monastery, since no one had actually lived there for a number of years. And so, several days passed before we finally got to see the place that would be our home for the next five months.

Nestled in the mountains above the center of the village, the monastery was a large three-story structure. Paula Raffo, Andrea's aunt, showed us around the building. She told us that it dated from the thirteenth century and had been used by the Medicis as their country house. We were to occupy the second level, which offered a stunning view of the sea and the surrounding area. Our living space consisted of a kitchen, a study, a bedroom, a bathroom and a living room that we could convert into a bedroom for guests.

On our introductory tour, Paula showed us a beautiful small chapel housed in the building. We could open an interior window in our hallway and look down into it. It had last been used for a family wedding, but since then had fallen into disrepair.

We were unpacking and exploring our new surroundings when we heard a knock at the door. A red-haired, middle-aged woman appeared with a big smile on her face. She introduced herself as Lorianna Conte and explained that she and her husband, another Andrea, were the caretakers of the monastery and lived on the top floor. They would help us if we needed anything. Neither of them spoke English, and at that time our Italian was less than fluent, but by using hand gestures and nods we managed to communicate fairly well.

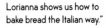

Lorianna asked which day we would like her to come and clean, and I was amazed at the vitality and enthusiasm she brought to her chores. Since it was not possible to drive our car up the dirt path, we always parked at the bottom, which meant that the only route to the monastery was on foot via a steep road. I once watched Lorianna carry a heavy crate of fresh peaches that she would soon use to make jam, striding up the hill with a big smile on her face.

We soon began to take Italian language lessons a couple of times a week. We felt badly that the young woman who was our teacher had to drive to our house on a dirt road, then had to walk about a mile uphill to get to where we were living.

A few weeks after our arrival, two workmen began to build a stone wall and a new road to the monastery. They started early in the morning, bringing their tools, a big lunch, and two jugs of red wine that they placed in a tub of water to keep cool. By the end of each day the wine jugs were empty; while progress on the job continued at a steady pace. It took three months to complete their task, and when it was done it was a work of art. We appreciated being able to drive up the new road to the monastery,

Lorianna shows us how to bake bread the Italian way."

though by that time we had become accustomed to our daily hikes up the hill.

There were a few things we needed to make our living conditions at the monastery more comfortable. To our surprise, it was not easy to communicate these to the village shopkeepers, or even to find out where to procure the necessary items. You would think it would be simple, for instance, to find large candles, in case the lights went out–which happened frequently in these parts. It took many gestures and much confusion before we finally succeeded in explaining what we wanted.

One of our priorities was to put screens on the bedroom windows so that bats and insects, especially mosquitoes, could not fly in and disturb us as we slept. At our local hardware store window screens were unheard of. We were told, "they would block the natural air...we might suffocate!" We finally prevailed and found acceptable substitutes–thumbtacks and plastic netting–to solve the problem.

Soon after our arrival, I asked Lorianna if we could take her and Andrea out for dinner. She immediately said yes, but when Andrea appeared and Lorianna told him about our invitation, he said it was impossible. They could not accept, he said, because of their position as custodians of the monastery. Lorianna looked crushed, but we finally persuaded Andrea, after assuring him that they could choose any restaurant in the area. That night they introduced us to their favorite local haunt, where we met many of their friends. During dinner Lorianna confessed that this was her birthday. We were amazed that I happened to pick that particular day to invite them to dinner, and it turned out to be a fun and festive evening.

Our days at the monastery quickly took on a comfortable routine. In the morning we would have a light breakfast of freshly squeezed orange juice, bread and a cappuccino made in an antique Italian coffee pot. The bread, which we bought fresh each morning, came from a bakery on one of the side streets near the main *piazza* in Pietrasanta. People would be waiting in line to pick up unusually shaped bread or pastries. The baker evidently made just enough for the locals and always seemed to run out by noon.

Eventually I summoned the courage to ask the baker's wife if he would allow me to watch him bake the bread. He agreed, on the condition that I arrive at 3:00 a.m., when he started. The bakery was about ten minutes walking distance from the monastery, so at 2:45 a.m. I awoke, dressed, grabbed my camera, and walked there through the dark streets.

To my surprise, he baked his breads, rolls and pastries in wood-burning ovens, and I was fascinated to see how he kept the ovens warm. With no electricity or gas available, he had to stop every 20 or 30 minutes to add wood to keep the fires going. There were three layers of ovens, so he had to stand on a ladder to put the loaves into the top ovens and take them out when they were done.

Continually snapping photographs, I watched him roll out the dough and shape it into breads and rolls. Then he put them on a flat board, climbed the ladder and slid them off into the oven. I have never forgotten this primitive way of baking–or how delicious these breads were. Or, for that matter, his unconventional baking attire, appropriate to

Lorianna and Marvino ham it up.

his inferno of a kitchen—a pair of shorts, a sleeveless t-shirt and sandals.

The next day, when I returned with the photos I had taken, the baker's wife was so pleased with them that she gave me bags full of bread to take home. From then on, whenever I arrived to pick up our daily bread, she always handed me an extra bag of *biscotti*.

We returned several years later to find the baker still using these same methods, but he confessed that it would soon be impossible because of the health laws and the new ways of baking. In many of the small villages in Italy, you can still see families baking bread the same way, but they are becoming more difficult to find.

On most days, after breakfast and shopping, we would head down to the ocean. Imitating the Italians, during the summer months we rented a space on the beach from the Ermione Hotel in Marina di Pietrasanta.

It was on this beach that we began a series of newsletters that we sent back to our family and friends. We would sit on the sand composing the letters, then return to the monastery, where we did our best to navigate the foreign keyboard on the typewriter we had bought. After typing up our letter, we would put it in the mail to our son Marc, who would copy it and send it on to the friends with whom we wanted to share our experiences. To this day, many of these people still use our newsletters as their guides to Italy.

We were living in Pietrasanta as if we were locals, and it was during that time we discovered the extraordinary festivals that take place during the summer months in the surrounding villages. We usually learned about these events from posters plastered on the sides of buildings that told us the name of the host village, the date of the festival, and the specialty dishes that would be served. The locals spend days and even weeks planning these festivals, which are annual fund-raising charity events in which everyone participates.

All the food is prepared by the women of the village, in quantities sufficient to feed hundreds. Tents are set up with long community tables and benches inside, and tickets are sold for the food that is picked up at central stations. The specialties, which vary depending on the location of the festival, have included *polenta*, *ravioli* and even frogs and snails; one festival was a celebration of the first-picked strawberries.

**WHEN YOU GO,
YOU SHOULD KNOW:**

Bistrot
Viale Franceschi, 14
Forte dei Marmi (LU)
Italy 55042
Tel: (0584) 89879
email: bistrot@bistrotforte.it
www.marcodavid.com

Hotel Ermione
Viale Roma, 183
Marina di Pietrasanta, Italy
Tel: (0584) 745852
Fax: (0584) 745906
email: hotelermione@virgilio.it
www.hotelermione.com

During another festival, we looked into the main room of a local city hall that was crowded with wooden tables covered with starched white linen cloths and laden with thousands of ricotta-filled *ravioli*. In still another village, the locals barbecued chicken on outdoor grills and topped each dish with a spicy sauce. One of my favorite festivals featured a hot *brioche* filled with homemade *gelato*.

On these occasions, there was always live music and a stage where the locals danced the tango. In Italy, tango dancing is an important art form and we would often see the same couples performing at different festivals. Even children participated, and it was common to see seven-year-old boys and girls dancing just as skillfully as the adults.

When attending these wonderful events we met many Italian families, and because we were so enthusiastic during the festivities, they often invited us to their homes for a *grappa* or *digestivo* to end the evening.

Italian Balloon Bread
(Focaccia Bomboloni)

Having dinner one night just north of Pietrasanta (near Forte dei Marmi) at a beachfront restaurant called Bistrot, we were served this *bomboloni* (balloon bread). Your guests will gasp when you place a platter of this perfectly-named bread on the table. The secret to making it is placing the rolled-out *focaccia* (or pizza) dough on the lowest rack in a very hot oven and baking it until it blows up like a balloon. An oven with a glass window is helpful here, since it allows you to take the *focaccia* out as soon as it has expanded and browned.

Makes about 6

**Basic Pizza Dough
  (see page 81)**
Olive oil
Cornmeal or polenta
Salt

Preheat the oven between 450°F to 500°F.

Prepare the pizza dough according to the recipe. Pull off a small piece of dough and knead it into a ball. Roll it out on a floured board, into a round as thin as possible (do not poke it with a fork).

Sprinkle a round baking pan or cookie sheet with olive oil and cornmeal or *polenta*. Place the round of dough on the prepared baking pan. Place the pan on the lowest rack in the oven and bake until the bread expands like a balloon.

Sprinkle generously with olive oil and salt and serve immediately.

Puccini Grilled Porcini Mushrooms
(Porcini Grigliati alla Puccini)

The first time I was served this simple dish was at a little restaurant in Torre del Lago where we had an early dinner before attending a Puccini opera. I realized these mushrooms would make a perfect light main course, since my experience was similar to that of eating a steak. A thick mushroom cap is brushed generously with olive oil, sprinkled with thinly sliced garlic and minced parsley, and grilled over hot coals. The stems, treated the same way, are also delicious.

The following recipe gives three options for preparing this dish: grilling, broiling or baking. When fresh Porcini mushrooms are not available, portobellos are the best substitute.

Serves 4

**4 porcini mushroom caps
  and stems (4 to 5 inches
  in diameter)**
1/2 cup olive oil
2 tablespoons minced garlic
Salt
Freshly ground black pepper
1/4 cup minced parsley

Gently clean mushrooms with a soft brush. Remove stems from mushroom caps and slice stems lengthwise.

To grill: Brush mushroom caps and stems with olive oil and sprinkle with garlic, parsley, salt and pepper. Place caps round side down on hot grill, with stems, and grill for 5-10 minutes. Using tongs, turn and grill until brown and tender, about 5-10 minutes.

To broil: Brush mushroom caps and stems with olive oil and sprinkle with garlic, parsley, salt and pepper. Place caps, round side down, with stems, on an oiled baking sheet. Broil 5 to 10 minutes (do not overcook). Using tongs, turn and broil until browned and tender but not mushy, about 5 to 10 minutes.

To bake: Preheat oven to 400°F. Brush a baking dish with olive oil. Place mushroom caps round side up, with stems on the baking dish. Brush mushrooms with olive oil. Sprinkle with garlic, parsley, salt, and pepper. Cover with aluminum foil and bake 20 minutes or until tender and juices run out.

Watermelon and Tomato Salad
(Insalata di Anguria e Pomodori)

Driving down a country road in Italy, we would often come across a stand selling watermelons. You could buy a slice and eat it on the spot or take a whole watermelon home.

When we were living in Pietrasanta, there was wild excitement over Italy winning the World Cup in soccer. I remember one young man in a red, white and green striped jersey (the colors of the Italian flag) riding his motorcycle while holding a big slice of watermelon (also red, white and green), rubbing it all over his face to express his joy.

Serves 6 to 8

3 cups (1/2-inch) diced tomatoes
3 cups (1/2-inch) diced
  watermelon
2 tablespoons minced fresh basil
3 teaspoons balsamic vinegar
1/4 cup olive oil
Salt and freshly ground black
  pepper, to taste
Pomegranate seeds

In a large bowl, gently toss the diced tomatoes, watermelon and basil. Just before serving toss with balsamic vinegar, olive oil and salt and pepper.

Spoon onto salad plates and sprinkle with pomegranate seeds.

Tuscan Baker's Country Bread
(Pane Toscano)

Traditional Tuscan bread is commonly made without salt and can accompany dishes eaten at any time of the day or night, for breakfast, lunch or dinner. Some say the reason Tuscan bread is made without salt is that in ancient times salt was very expensive. This salt-free bread may also be enjoyed with typical Tuscan salami, which are extremely salty, as well as with heavily sauced dishes, where the bread is dipped into the sauce.

Makes 1 small loaf

1 package active dry yeast
3-1/2 cups unbleached flour
Pinch salt
1-1/4 cups water

In a large bowl of an electric mixer, combine the yeast, 1/2 cup flour and 1/2 cup warm water (82°F to 84°F). Mix together to make a very soft dough.

Pour 2-1/2 cups flour over the mixture, cover with a towel and let the sponge rest in a cool spot for 30 to 45 minutes.

Using a dough hook and on low speed, slowly add 3/4 cup cold water and remaining 1/2 cup flour as necessary. Knead until dough clumps around the dough hook (comes together) and pulls cleanly from the sides of the bowl, Dough should be smooth and satiny.

Transfer to a large greased bowl, turning the dough to grease all sides. Cover with a damp towel and let rise in a warm place until doubled in bulk, about 1 hour.

Punch down, turn out onto a lightly floured board and knead for 2 minutes. Shape into a round or a long loaf. Sprinkle with flour and place on a baking sheet. Lightly cover with a cloth or plastic wrap and let rise again in a warm place until doubled in bulk, about 30 minutes.

Preheat the oven to 400°F. Bake for 35 to 40 minutes or until golden brown and bread sounds hollow when lightly tapped. Cool and serve. This recipe can be doubled, making 2 loaves or 1 large loaf.

Chicken under a Brick
(Pollo al Mattone)

Chicken Mattone can easily be prepared at home with fabulous results. Butterflied chicken halves are seared on the grill or in a cast-iron frying pan under a heavy stone to compress the meat. When I prepare it this way it is always moist and tender inside with a crisp skin and a barbecued flavor.

Serves 4

1 (3-pound) chicken
1/2 cup fresh lemon juice
1/4 cup olive oil
1 garlic clove, minced
A sprig of fresh rosemary or
  a pinch Italian seasoning
1 teaspoon chopped parsley
Salt
1 tablespoon whole
  peppercorns, crushed

To butterfly the chicken: turn the chicken breast side down on a cutting board to remove the backbone. Using poultry shears or a sharp knife, cut along one side of the backbone and then back down along the other. Remove the backbone (reserve for soup) and cut the chicken completely in half, pressing each half to lie flat.

In a shallow glass dish large enough to hold the chicken combine the lemon juice, olive oil, garlic, rosemary, parsley. Add salt and crushed peppercorns, to taste. Rub the chicken with this mixture before grilling.

In a heavy cast-iron skillet, preferably with raised ridges, sprinkle with salt and heat until smoking. Immediately place the chicken, breast side down, in the pre-heated skillet and place a heavy stone or brick on top of the chicken. Grill on the top of the stove for 10 to 15 minutes, until the skin is deep gold and crusty. Lift the stone off the chicken and turn the chicken over. Replace the stone and grill 5 to 10 minutes or until done. Pierce the thickest part of the thigh; if juices run clear, it is done. Remove the weight and serve.

Coffee Ice with Whipped Cream
(Granita al Caffe con Panna)

Coffee Ice takes only five minutes to make and is a perfect way to take advantage of leftover espresso. Make the Coffee Ice a day or two in advance, store in the freezer and serve topped with whipped cream.

Makes about 1 quart

Sugar Syrup (recipe follows)
2 cups espresso coffee
1-3/4 cups sugar syrup
1/2 cup whipped cream
  (optional)

Prepare the sugar syrup and cool.

In a large bowl, combine the coffee and sugar syrup. Blend well.

Freeze in an electric or hand-cranked freezer according to the manufacturer's directions. Or pour the mixture into flat-bottomed ice cube trays without their dividers or a freezer-proof glass bowl. Place in the freezer compartment of your refrigerator and stir with a fork every hour, scraping from the sides into the center. Continue stirring and freezing until the ice is set, 3 to 4 hours.

Spoon into small bowls and top with a dollop of whipped cream.

Sugar Syrup

Makes about 3 cups

1-1/2 cups sugar
1-1/2 cups water

Place the sugar and water in a large heavy pot over medium heat. Stir until sugar dissolves. Bring to slow rolling boil, reduce the heat, and simmer for 5 minutes. Pour into a glass bowl, cover with plastic wrap and chill.

Chocolate Covered Ice Cream Bites
(Dai Dai)

At the end of a meal there are many restaurants, especially in Tuscany, that serve as a complimentary sweet called *Dai-Dai*—frozen ice cream morsels covered in chocolate in a brown wrapper lined with aluminum foil. I often use ice cream sticks to make these irresistible bites easier to handle.

Makes 12 servings

1 pint Vanilla chocolate chip ice cream (see recipe page 99)
2 cups melted semi-sweet chocolate

Line a tray with wax paper and place it in the freezer. Remove the ice cream from the freezer to soften a little (about 5 minutes) if it is solid. Remove the chilled tray from the freezer. Using a small ice cream scoop, scoop out 12 bite-sized balls of ice cream and insert a toothpick in the center of each for easier handling. Place in the freezer for at least 1 hour.

Remove one ice cream ball at a time and, using a narrow spatula or knife, brush the entire surface with warm melted chocolate. Return the chocolate coated ice cream ball to the tray and continue with the remaining ice cream balls. I like to wrap them in wax paper and return to the freezer for at least one hour or until frozen solid.

PIETRASANTA
Janice and Ron Mehlman – *A Dusty Meeting in the Marble Yard*

Carrara, Italy's marble capital, is a village close to Pietrasanta. We heard about an outdoor sculpture event and decided to investigate. We found the main square roped off and about thirty artists from all over the world were working on large blocks of marble.

We strolled through clouds of marble dust, observing the intensive work on a variety of individual sculptures. In front of each artist was a sign with his name (all the sculptors were men) and country of origin.

Ron Mehlman, from New York, caught our eye because the sculpture he was creating was so different from the traditional carved marble figures many of the other artists were working on. His art, which featured layers of marble and glass in a geometric design, was strikingly contemporary. When Marvino asked Ron to tell us about his work, he spoke confidently and eventually invited us back to his studio for lunch, and to meet his wife, Janice. On our way there, Ron told us that the two of them generally spend summers in

Pietrasanta and were now on a year-long sabbatical working there full-time. We later learned that both are recognized artists who have shown their work in both American and European galleries.

Janice's heavy Brooklyn accent made us smile when she spoke Italian. She is an architectural photographer, and her great talent as a cook—evident at our first lunch—laid the basis for what has become an enduring friendship.

As for Ron, I don't know if it was his thick black beard and expressive eyes, or the fact that when he smiled—which was often—you couldn't help seeing the gap between his front teeth, but I immediately felt I had known him forever.

A few days later, we invited them to be our first dinner guests at our monastery home. At the end of a narrow hall in our quarters was a window with a spectacular view of the surrounding hills, and this is where we usually ate breakfast and lunch. We set a bowl of freshly picked wild-flowers in the center of the table, had a delightful dinner, and agreed that the four of us would do this again very soon. Our meal began with *bruschetta*, toasting slices of the bread from the local baker I had taken lessons from. The tomatoes were from the little vegetable stand in the *piazza*. A Caesar salad, *ravioli* purchased from the local fresh pasta shop and *gelato* from the local *gelateria* completed the menu.

Eventually, the Mehlmans bought a wonderful house from Arnaldo Pomodoro, a well-known Italian sculptor, to which they have now added a large work studio and a swimming pool. Their garden has many fruit trees, and we recently enjoyed some of Janice's homemade fig and walnut jam. They also make a pleasant wine from the small vineyard on their property. Both have been invited to show their work in the Pietrasanta Municipal Art Gallery exhibitions.

One evening we dined with Janice and Ron in a local restaurant, Emilio e Bona. The establishment was originally part of an old olive mill built along the river. Inside we saw olive presses dating back to 1700. We remarked on the delicious food, and I told Emilio, who ran the front of the house, that I would love to spend a day in Chef Bona Capelli's kitchen. When she came out to the dining room to greet us, I asked her if this was possible. She said in Italian, "Why not?" and Janice offered to take photos of our day with her.

We spent the whole next day with Bona learning to make some of her signature dishes. Her kitchen is unusually large, and the first thing I noticed was the huge pots filled with meat stocks boiling on top of the stove. She has a special space in a corner for making pasta, which is her specialty, and another devoted to desserts.

The time flew by as I took notes and Janice shot photo after photo. At noon, we were invited to have lunch and sample the dishes Bona had prepared.

It was at an event in Carrara, when we first met Ron Mehlman. We watched and admired his technique as he combined mediums of glass and marble. Bottom: Ron, and wife Janice. Daughter Elena, here perhaps 3-years-old, is today a grown woman!

**WHEN YOU GO,
YOU SHOULD KNOW:**

Ristorante Emilio and Bona
Via Lombrici, 22
Camaiore (LU), Italy 55041
Tel: (0584) 989289
email: info@ristoranteemilioebona.com
www.ristoranteemilioebona.com

These included Fried Sage Leaves with Anchovies (*salvia fritta*); two pasta dishes—one with spinach and ricotta and the other with cream, coriander, Parmesan cheese and pine nuts; and an assortment of desserts.

When Janice developed the photos and gave copies to Bona, she was so excited that she invited us back for another dinner as her guests. I suspect that our visit may have been one of the rare occasions when a guest took a personal interest in what this fine chef was doing.

Our friendship continued to grow, and the Mehlman's were blessed with a little girl, Elena, who today, is a grown woman. She lives in both New York and Italy and is fluent in English and Italian.

During one of the Mehlman's visits to Los Angeles, we introduced them to Bobby Greenfield, who has a gallery in Santa Monica. She now is their Los Angeles representative and houses a collection of their spectacular works.

Bona's Fried Sage Leaves with Anchovies
(Salvia Fritta con Acciughe)

The first time we were served these delicate, savory leaves was at the Maule wedding, the second at Emilio e Bona Ristorante. I later learned that sage is well known for its medicinal properties.

The leaves used in this recipe should be young and fresh. We always have eggs in the refrigerator and sage growing in our garden, so we can prepare and serve this appetizer on short notice with no shopping required.

Makes about 30 or 40

**Batter for sage leaves
   (recipe follows)
1 bunch of fresh sage leaves
2 (2-ounce) cans anchovy fillets
Olive oil for frying
Salt**

Prepare the batter, cover with plastic wrap and set aside.

Select the largest of the sage leaves and wash and dry them carefully. Sandwich two at a time together with an anchovy fillet in the middle. Press together and dip into the batter. Heat oil and fry sage sandwiches until lightly brown. Transfer to paper towels and sprinkle with salt. Serve immediately.

Batter for Sage Leaves

Makes about 3 cups

**2 egg yolks
3 tablespoons olive oil
1/4 cup vodka
1 cup ice cold water
1-3/4 cups flour
1/2 teaspoon salt
Pinch of sugar
2 egg whites**

In the bowl of an electric mixer, combine the egg yolks, olive oil, and vodka. Add ice water and flour with salt and sugar alternately and blend well. Beat egg whites until stiff and fold into the egg yolk mixture. Cover with plastic wrap and set aside until ready to use.

Bona's Spinach-Ricotta Tagliatelle
(Tagliatelle Spinaci e Ricotta)

Bona, the chef at Emilio e Bona, prepares a large quantity of the spinach and ricotta mixture in the morning. She shapes it into individual servings, and when a customer orders Spinach-Ricotta *Tagliatelle* it takes only a few minutes to cook the pasta in the sauce.

Serves 4 to 6

3 cups packed spinach or
   3 (5-ounce) bags baby spinach
3 tablespoons olive oil
6 green onions, thinly sliced
1 tablespoon minced sage
   (4 to 5 leaves)
2 tablespoons unsalted
   butter, melted
1 cup fresh ricotta cheese
1/2 pound *tagliatelle*
1/2 cup freshly grated
   Parmesan cheese, plus
   more for serving
Salt and freshly ground black
   pepper, to taste

Soak spinach leaves in cold water, drain and dry. Thinly slice the spinach leaves and set aside.

In a large deep skillet, heat olive oil, add green onions and sage, and cook over high-heat until lightly browned, 2 to 3 minutes. Lower the heat, add spinach and cook, stirring, until wilted. Add butter and ricotta and mix well. Cool.

In a large pot of boiling salted water, cook pasta until *al dente*. Drain thoroughly, reserving 1 cup of pasta cooking water.

Just before serving, heat the spinach mixture until blended, adding enough pasta water to make a sauce. Add the pasta and Parmesan and salt and pepper and toss to coat. Cook over medium low heat, tossing, until sauce is thick and creamy, adding more water as needed. Transfer to bowls and serve with grated Parmesan cheese.

Vanilla Chocolate Chip Ice Cream
(Gelato Stracciatella)

From our first trip to Italy, this recipe has become my signature *gelato*. It is always there in my freezer to be enjoyed—day and night.

The only ice cream we ever had in Los Angeles that compared was Wil Wright's, and it is no longer around, so we look forward to eating *Gelato Stracciatella* when vacationing in Italy.

The milk makes it light and the eggs help make it creamy. Serve with *biscotti* and top with chocolate sauce for serious chocolate lovers.

Although you can use vanilla extract, a plump, fragrant vanilla bean yields the best flavor. When buying the beans, make sure the exteriors are black and appear moist—signs of freshness.

Makes about 3 pints

2 cups milk
1 cup sugar
2 vanilla beans, split
   lengthwise, or 2 teaspoons
   vanilla extract
7 egg yolks
Ice water, for cooling custard
2 cups cream
8 ounces semisweet
   chocolate, melted

In a medium-size heavy saucepan, over medium heat, combine the milk with 1/2 cup of the sugar and bring to a boil, mixing until sugar is dissolved. Turn off heat, add vanilla beans, cover, and let steep 5 minutes. Remove vanilla bean and scrape seeds into milk mixture. Stir until seeds separate; then add pod (*if using extract, add it with cream as noted below*).

In a large bowl, using a wire whisk or an electric mixer, beat egg yolks and the remaining 1/2 cup sugar until light and fluffy. In a slow stream, pour 1/2 cup of the heated milk mixture into the egg mixture and blend well. Pour mixture back into the saucepan with the milk mixture, mixing to blend well. Cook over medium-low heat, stirring

constantly, to just below the boiling point (170°F to 180°F), about 5 minutes. Pour custard into a fine strainer suspended over a large bowl set over a larger bowl filled with ice water. Scrape up thickened cream that settles on bottom of pan. Add cream. *If using vanilla extract, add it now.* Mix until cooled. Cover with plastic wrap and refrigerate until cold.

Freeze in an ice cream maker according to manufacturer's instructions. When mixture is very cold and thick, and machine is still running, pour in warm melted chocolate in a thin stream. The chocolate will quickly harden and break up into small pieces. Continue to freeze ice cream. Spoon into plastic containers; cover and freeze until ready to serve.

Espresso with Ice Cream and Caramel-Nut Brittle
(Gelato alla Crema Affogato con Praline)

Almost every restaurant in Italy will serve you this special dessert, but you have to ask for it. The first time we discovered it was at Emilio e Bona. It has many names, depending on which city you are in, but for me it will always be known as *Affogato*. It is sometimes referred to as ice cream drowned in coffee. Often served in a deep saucer, sundae dish or wineglass, it is simply a scoop of *gelato* (Italian ice cream) with espresso poured over it and topped with Caramel-Nut Brittle.

Serves 8

1 cup Caramel-Nut Brittle (recipe follows)
8 large scoops of Vanilla Chocolate Chip Ice Cream (see recipe page 99)
2 cups freshly brewed espresso or very strong black coffee

Prepare the Caramel-Nut Brittle and set aside.

In 8 small bowls, place a scoop of *gelato* and pour 1/4 cup hot espresso over each. Sprinkle with caramel-nut brittle and serve at once.

Caramel-Nut Brittle

Makes about 3 cups

3/4 cup unpeeled whole or sliced almonds
1 cup sugar
1/2 cup water

Preheat the oven to 350°F.

Toast the almonds on a foil-lined baking sheet until lightly browned, 5 to 10 minutes. Cool.

In a small heavy saucepan, combine the sugar and water. Cook over medium heat, stirring until the sugar dissolves. Continue cooking, without stirring, until the syrup turns a light caramel color. Remove from the heat and stir in the almonds.

Pour the mixture onto a lightly oiled baking sheet or marble slab, spread it out with a metal spatula, and let it cool and harden. Break the brittle into small pieces; place them in a processor and process until coarsely chopped.

FLORENCE
Walter & Fiorella Mello – *An Italian Vegetarian Feast*

We met the Mello family at Citrus Restaurant in Los Angeles, where we were having dinner with our son, Paul, and his wife, Amber. The Mellos were sitting at an adjoining table, chatting away in Italian with a friend of ours, Silvio De Mori, who owned a nearby Italian restaurant. About halfway through dinner Silvio introduced them to us..

He told us that Walter and Fiorella Mello were in Los Angeles with their daughter Francesca for a short vacation. Walter, a tall dark-haired physician who specializes in gerontology, had just flown in from San Francisco, where he had attended a medical conference. Silvio explained that Walter and Fiorella were friends of his from Florence and they knew no one in Los Angeles.

Having become quite friendly with them during the evening, we invited them to our home the following afternoon for a glass of wine. After they arrived, we sat in the garden with them for a while, then took them for a walk in our neighborhood. Their comments on the local architecture, the trees and the flowers made us more aware of the beauty that surrounds us.

Earlier in the day, we had called our friends, Barbara and Sam Masket, who had invited us for dinner that evening, and asked if we could bring this Italian family with us. Not only did they immediately say yes, they also invited a friend's daughter to meet Francesca to help put her at ease.

The five of us drove together to the Maskets' two-story contemporary house in Santa Monica, which Barbara, an architect, had designed. Sam, a well-known eye surgeon, did all the cooking and we had a great time. Later that night, as we were saying goodbye, the Mellos insisted that the next time we were in Italy, we visit them in Florence and we promised we would.

Several months later, we arrived in Italy and were driving to Panzano. Sam and Barbara Masket were to join us in Tuscany in a few weeks, so we put off calling the Mellos until after the Maskets' arrival.

One morning as we were driving along the Arno River in Florence we heard some-one calling, "Marvino, Marvino!" We looked out the window and saw Walter and a friend riding by on their motorcycles, waving to us. Walter had recognized us and was surprised that we had arrived in the area without contacting him.

In our few minutes of conversation, we promised to phone, and they zoomed off down the busy street and disappeared around a corner. Later that day we called and made plans to get together for dinner at their home after the Maskets arrived.

On the night of the dinner, we bought a huge bouquet of flowers from a local florist and somehow managed to get it into our car. The four of us were to meet the Mellos on a corner near the train station and follow them to their home. When they drove up, however, we learned that we were not going to their home, but to a restaurant. We transferred our huge floral gift to their car and followed them to the restaurant.

We entered this local *trattoria*, just outside Florence, to find twenty of their friends, who were gathered to celebrate a birthday. Our original invitation had been for another night, and when we asked to change the date, the Mellos didn't have the heart to say that wasn't possible and arranged instead to include us in the birthday party.

Although the restaurant is usually open only for lunch, that night they prepared a special dinner for our friends. There was no menu, and the food just kept coming–course after course of wonderful salami, pasta with meat sauce, and a selection of roasted meats. This posed something of a problem, since the Maskets do not eat red meat. But Italian hospitality prevailed, and the chef made several meatless dishes especially for them.

When we left, Walter and Fiorella insisted that all of us come to their home for a vegetarian dinner the following evening, and we were delighted to accept.

When we arrived, the Mellos introduced us to their surprise guest, a lovely young woman who was going to play the harp for us. We were touched by their efforts to make this evening special for us.

Walter loves to cook, and the first course he prepared was spaghetti with fresh broccoli. The main course was traditional *bagna cauda*, which consists of a wide selection of raw and cooked vegetables to be dipped in individual ceramic bowls filled with anchovy sauce and set over a candle to keep the sauce warm.

Following the *bagna cauda*, Walter brought out a large package wrapped in a flowered cotton fabric tied with yarn. It contained *burrata*, a special cheese that is usually made only in the Puglia area. It is not found in Florence, but Walter, who comes from Puglia, enjoys it so much that he sought out a specialty food store in Florence that has it sent to them. This was our first experience with this wonderful soft cheese. Its name– *burrata*–refers to the distinctive buttery taste and texture of the cheese's center, which consists of fresh mozzarella combined with a high proportion of heavy cream. The outside of the cheese is wrapped in a skin made from stretched sheets of mozzarella that gives the exterior a springy quality that creates an appealing textural contrast with the luscious soft interior.

Then Walter brought out a bottle of 1988 Biondi-Santi Brunello and carried it to the table, carefully cradled in his arm. When he opened and poured it out, Marvino took a sip, realized it was oxidized, but said nothing. When Walter asked how we liked the wine, Sam took a sip and announced, "This wine has seen its day–it is definitely over the hill." Not understanding that Walter had kept this wine for a special occasion, Sam realized–too late–that honesty might not be the best policy at this particular moment.

The evening ended with more music and *grappa*, and we left promising to call before we returned to the States. In the Italian tradition, there was much hugging and kissing.

As we walked downstairs to our car, Sam said, "Marvino, do you think it would have been better not to say anything about that wine?" Marvino didn't really have to answer.

We still tease Sam about this, especially when we are with friends at dinner and he is asked to taste the wine.

Walter's Pasta with Broccoli
(Pasta e Broccoli)

Our Italian friends in Florence served us this pasta as a first course, followed by *Bagna Cauda*.

Serves 4

1 pound broccoli florets
1/2 cup olive oil
1 garlic clove
1 hot red pepper
2/3 cup chopped tomatoes
8 ounces rigatoni, crushed
1/2 cup cream
1 cup vegetable stock
1/4 to 1/2 cup grated Parmesan
Salt
Freshly ground black pepper

Steam or boil the broccoli until it is virtually mushy. In a skillet, heat oil and stew the garlic, red pepper and tomatoes until soft. Mix in the broccoli.

Cook the pasta in salted water until *al dente*. Drain pasta and add to the broccoli mixture. Blend in the cream and vegetable stock. Stir in Parmesan and salt and pepper to taste.

Walter's Warm Anchovy, Garlic and Olive Oil Sauce
(Bagna Cauda alla Piemontese)

Bagna Cauda is a delicious hot dipping sauce made with olive oil, garlic and anchovies. It is served whenever the Piemontese are hungry, usually with a glass of red wine. Raw or cooked vegetables—such as celery, peppers, and artichokes—are dipped into this "hot bath" for an explosion of flavors.

On one of our stays in Italy, the Mellos invited us to dinner and served this dish as a main course. We each had our own ceramic bowl with a candle at the bottom to heat the "bathing" liquid of fragrant anchovy sauce into which we dunked our vegetables.

Makes about 1 cup

1 whole head garlic, broken into cloves and peeled (about 1/4 cup)
1/2 cup water
12 anchovy fillets,
    finely minced
1/2 cup extra virgin olive oil
Salt
Freshly ground black pepper
Raw vegetables (fennel, carrots,
    celery, cucumbers, mushrooms,
    red radishes, Belgian endive,
    red bell peppers)
Steamed or grilled vegetables
    (artichokes, potatoes,
    asparagus, string beans)
1 large loaf country-style bread

In a small saucepan over high heat, cook the garlic and water, uncovered, for 10 minutes, or until garlic is tender. Drain. Mash the garlic and anchovies with a fork or in a food processor to blend thoroughly. Add the olive oil in a thin stream. Season with salt and pepper, to taste. (The mixture may resemble separated mayonnaise.)

Transfer the anchovy sauce to a medium saucepan and simmer over low heat until hot, about 5 minutes.

To serve, keep warm in an ovenproof casserole or terra-cotta *bagna cauda* set. Dip raw and cooked vegetables into the anchovy sauce, scooping up some of the sauce. Hold a piece of bread under the dipped vegetable so you don't dribble the sauce on the table. Eat the vegetable and then the bread.

Burrata Salad with Arugula
(Insalata con Burrata e Rucola)

Inspired by the *burrata* we were served at the home of Walter Mello in Florence, this colorful salad can be served as a first course or after the main course and before dessert. It is important to toss the arugula with the olive oil just before serving.

6 cups arugula, thinly sliced
3 to 4 tablespoons olive oil
Salt and freshly ground
   black pepper, to taste
1 pound fresh *burrata*,
   cut into 8 wedges
4 tablespoons balsamic vinegar
1/2 cup pomegranate seeds

Serves 8

Place the arugula in a large bowl and toss with olive oil and salt and pepper.

Arrange arugula on serving plates with wedges of *burrata*. Drizzle balsamic vinegar around the arugula and sprinkle pomegranate seeds on top. Serve immediately.

GREVE
The Grape Harvest Festival

While in Florence one September on business, we read about a Grape Harvest Festival taking place in the village of Greve, in the center of the Chianti area. Since we had a rented car, we decided to drive to Greve without having a clear idea of where it was.

Attempting to follow a map, we got completely lost. We would stop at almost every intersection and ask, *"Dove Greve?"* ("Where is Greve?") But the hand signals and directions in Italian were more confusing than helpful. We were almost ready to give up when we stopped to ask one more person, in our limited Italian, where Greve was. He asked if we spoke English–and we finally found this amazing village.

We parked the car and walked to a narrow street that was lined with long tables. Some were crowded with wine bottles and glasses, others displayed magnificent platters of roasted meats. Some were piled with loaves of a flat sweet bread covered with grapes, which we later learned was called *Schiacciata con L'Uva.*

The name refers to the somewhat squashed appearance of the pastry. Flavored with olive oil and fresh rosemary, this delicacy is studded with ripe Sangiovese grapes. I have made it with concord or seedless grapes, and though this version is not quite as authentic, it is just as delicious. It is available in almost every coffee bar and mini market during the grape harvest, and no two ways of preparing it are exactly the same.

Not until our five-month stay in Tuscany, did we discover where to buy our favorite version. It was at Bar Marconi, just 30 minutes outside of Florence, about 10 minutes from Greve. Every day during the grape harvest a large sign appears in the window: *"Oggi, Schiacciata con L'Uva"* (Grape Bread Today). Their *Schiacciata*, which is sold by the slice or whole, resembles a giant chocolate chip cookie and is delectable.

**WHEN YOU GO,
YOU SHOULD KNOW:**

Bar Marconi
Via Chiantigiana per Ferrone 52
(FI), Italy 50023
Tel: (055) 207031

Bar Marconi's Sweet Grape Bread
(*Schiacciata con L'Uva*)

In Falciani, just 30 minutes outside of Florence, is the extremely popular Bar Marconi. Almost every day, from August through October during the grape harvest, a large sign appears in the Bar's window: *"Oggi, Schiacciata con L'Uva"* (Grape Bread Today).

Their *Schiacciata*, a flat, round cake that resembles a giant chocolate chip cookie, contains grapes, anise and rosemary. It is baked in a wood-burning oven until crisp and sugary around the edges. They sell it by the slice or whole.

Makes 2 pastries

1 package active dry yeast
1 cup warm water
3/4 cup sugar
1/3 cup olive oil
2 eggs
3-1/2 cups flour
1 teaspoon salt
1/4 cup minced fresh rosemary
3 cups concord or red grapes

In a measuring cup, stir yeast into 1/2 cup of the warm water with a pinch of sugar and let stand 5 minutes until frothy. In the large bowl of an electric mixer, blend the remaining water, olive oil, eggs, and 1/2 cup of the sugar and mix well. Add yeast mixture, 3 cups of flour, salt and rosemary and blend until smooth and dough begins to come together. Dough will be a little sticky.

Transfer to a floured board and knead in remaining flour. Add grapes and gently knead into the dough. Add additional flour if dough is too sticky. Place dough in an oiled bowl, cover with a towel, and let rise in a warm place until doubled, about 1-1/2 hours. Turn dough out onto a lightly floured board and divide in half. Stretch each half into a (9 or 10-inch) round and arrange on 2 lightly oiled baking pans. Cover pastry with a towel and let rise until doubled, about 1 hour. Sprinkle with remaining 1/4 cup sugar.

Bake at 400°F for 15 minutes; reduce heat to 375°F and continue baking for 15 minutes or until golden brown.

THE FLAVORS OF TOSCANA

IMPRUNETTA
Tuscan Hospitality

Count Ugo Bonacossi and Contessa Lisa Bonacossi

Our friendship with the Bonacossi family began through friend, Faith Willinger. She invited us to a lunch at the Capezzana Villa and Winery, also home of Count and Contessa Ugo and Lisa Bonacossi. This was an event we almost didn't attend because we were to drive that morning from Todi to the Rome airport, to pick up friends—a 2-hour drive. But, we trusted that we would somehow get to Capezzana (which is just outside Florence) in time for the lunch. Despite our friends' flight being late, we did manage to arrive at the winery close to the 1p.m. appointed hour, with our jet-lagged friends in tow.

By the time we had arrived, graciously greeted by Count Ugo, the entire family was seated at a long table, starting their *antipasti*. Those in attendance were helping themselves from large platters filled with sliced salami, sausages and roasted peppers. Our friends, who had left Los Angeles just 24 hours earlier, felt transported to a magical place, and so did we.

Since then we have returned to Capezzana several times for special dinners featuring their wines. They have also invited us to teach cooking classes there for students from America as well as Italy.

At one of their banquets, the dinner was presented in an unusual manner. It started with the usual selection of *antipasti*. Then, for the second course, the buffet table's offerings were changed to a variety of soups. After these were cleared away, a selection of pasta dishes appeared on the table—at least three varieties, including *tagliatelle* and *ravioli*, for guests to choose from. When that course was finished, they returned to the buffet, which was now laden with main courses; followed by desserts, in the same manner.

Count Ugo is a man who, even in the most informal situation, never fails to embody the perfect image of a gentleman. One morning when we had stayed overnight at the villa, he appeared, dressed in vest, tie and jacket, to invite Marvino to join him for a walk. Four hours later, having wandered up and down rolling hills on a dirt path, they returned just in time for lunch.

Beatrice and André Benaim

Flash forward two years later. Marvino and I were looking into renting a villa in Italy for several months. We asked the advice of an Italian friend and restaurant owner, Jean Louis De Mori, who lived in Los Angeles. He suggested a house in Tuscany that he and his wife were renovating, in Imprunetta, a village about 30 minutes south of Florence. He said it

Above, right: A group photo of a cooking class Marvino and I once held at Capezzana.

would be ready in May and that we would be able to stay for an extended period, until they were ready to move in with their family.

We agreed to rent it and made our arrangements. One month before we were to leave for Italy, Jean Louis called and said he had bad news, but also good news. The bad news was that his house would not be ready in May because of normal construction delays in Italy. The good news was that we could rent the adjacent house from his friends and neighbors, André and Beatrice Benaim. They were going on vacation and would stay with Beatrice's parents–Count Ugo Bonacossi and Countess Lisa Bonacossi. We were delighted and accepted.

We arranged to meet Beatrice at the Certosa exit of the *Autostrada*, outside Florence, and follow her to the house. It was dusk, and on an unfamiliar road we seemed to be driving a considerable distance, but we were excited at the thought of living in the Tuscan countryside for five months.

At the time, we didn't realize that we had met Beatrice a few years earlier at Capezzana Villa and Winery, owned by her parents, the Bonacossi. Since then, Beatrice (Bea) had married André Benaim, an architect from Florence. They were now expecting their first baby.

When we arrived at the Benaims' house it was beginning to get dark. André, worried that we would not have anything to eat the next day and took us to the local market in Imprunetta, where we bought vegetables, olive oil, eggs, milk and supplies.

When we returned from our marketing, Bea had prepared dinner for us, including a salad of tomatoes along with sautéed green peppers, a mild and meaty local variety. This was followed by a simple pasta dish with tomatoes and basil from their garden, and roasted chicken with potatoes. Bea served Capezzana wine with every course and for dessert an ice cream cake from the *gelateria* in the *piazza* of Imprunetta. This would be our new hangout for cappuccino in the morning and *gelato* in the evening. Later that summer we were surprised to discover that the *gelateria* was closed for vacation from July 15 to August 15. I think that says a lot for the Italians.

After dinner we gave them a few gifts we had brought from the States. One was a copy of my newly published cookbook, *The Gourmet Jewish Cook*. Bea remarked that she was especially delighted to have it because André is Jewish and they celebrate all of the Jewish holidays.

They left at about 9:30 for Bea's parents' house. Alone now in this unfamilar house with strange noises, we tucked ourselves into bed and slept until morning.

And what a beautiful morning it was. We took a walk and discovered that the house was surrounded by an extensive garden filled with artichokes, zucchini, tomatoes, eggplant, lettuce, fruit trees and grapevines. For the rest of the summer we dined from that garden, including its vegetables in almost all of our salads, soups and pastas. Fruit trees on the property gave us fresh peaches, plums, apples and pears for breakfast and desserts after dinner. When we had a craving for ice cream we drove to the center of Imprunetta for *gelato*.

We had several guests visiting from Los Angeles during our stay. We enjoyed preparing lunches in the garden for them. Sitting out there one day, Marvino saw a wild

A toast to our hosts, Bea and André.

**WHEN YOU GO,
YOU SHOULD KNOW:**

Tenuta di Capezzana
Via Capezzana, 100
50042 Carmignano, (PO)
Firenze, Italy
Tel: (055) 8706005
Fax: (055) 8706673
email: capezzana@capezzana.it
website: www.capezzana.it

Osteria da Ganino
Piazza dei Cimatori, 4/r
Firenze, Italy
Tel: 39 (055) 214-125

boar emerge from the vineyard. I quickly ran into the house to get my camera, but by the time I returned the beast was waddling back into the vineyard.

At least once a week we would drive into Florence for the day and have lunch in one of the many small restaurants. One of our favorites is Osteria da Ganino, in a little *piazza* where, to our surprise, there was always a truck near the restaurant selling tripe sandwiches (*panini di lampordotto*).

A few years later, when Bea was expecting another baby, they offered us their house again. After arriving, we realized that she and André had moved into the renovated barn with their son, Oscar, so that we could stay again in the area we had so much enjoyed. We were overwhelmed to be the beneficiaries of their extraordinary hospitality.

Bea's Sautéed Small Sweet Green Peppers
(*Pepperoni Verde Dolci*)

Two of our Italian friends, Beatrice Benaim and Sammie Daniels, served us these delicious small green peppers, called *frigitelle*. They resemble jalapeños, but with a twisted wrinkled shape and without the heat. Sautéed in olive oil until charred and crisp on the outside and garnished with lemon, they make a delicious appetizer.

Serves 6

1/4 cup olive oil
1 pound small mild green peppers
Salt
Freshly ground black pepper
Juice of 1 lemon

In a skillet, heat the olive oil and sauté the peppers turning to brown them evenly. Season with salt and pepper to taste. Sprinkle with lemon juice and serve hot.

Marinated Artichokes
(*Carciofi Marinati*)

Using the small artichokes that were abundant in the garden of the house we rented from Bea and André, we prepared this appetizer. It originally came from Piermario and Paola Meletti Cavallari, a couple who produce a wine called Grattomacco in Tuscany. Paola often prepares lunch for us when we visit them. When artichokes are in season, she makes a huge batch and puts them in jars to serve as antipasti. While the wine and vinegar are coming to a boil, trim the artichokes.

Serves 4 to 6

12 small artichokes
Juice of 2 lemons
6 sprigs flat leaf parsley
1 cup water
1/2 cup white wine vinegar
2 cups dry white wine

Trim the stems of the artichokes, leaving about 2-inches. Using a heavy, sharp knife, cut about 1-inch off the tops. Pull off several layers of the outer leaves close to the base until you reach the tender pale yellow leaves, and trim the bottoms smoothly and evenly with a small sharp knife. As you work, generously rub each artichoke with lemon to prevent the flesh from darkening, and place in a bowl of cold

1 bay leaf
2 teaspoons salt
1 teaspoon whole
black peppercorns
1 cup olive oil

water to cover with lemon juice and parsley sprigs.

In a large saucepan, bring the water, vinegar and wine to a boil. Add bay leaf, salt, peppercorns, and trimmed, drained artichokes. Boil for 10 minutes, or until tender, depending on the size. Cool. Drain and transfer to a glass bowl and pour over enough olive oil to cover artichokes. Cover with plastic wrap and refrigerate.

Cold Tomato Soup with Mozzarella Cheese
(*Crema di Pomodoro Freddo con Mozzarella*)

I developed this recipe while we were renting Bea and André Benaim's house, where we often picked tomatoes from their garden. This soup, based on the famous Italian *Caprese* salad, is fresh, colorful and easy to prepare, especially if you have a tomato press.

This handy little Italian-made gadget separates the seeds and skins from the pulp, leaving a fresh tomato purée. The device is made of heavy red acrylic, with a stainless steel strainer and a strong suction cup on the bottom that attaches to any work surface. In America you can find it at most cookware stores for about $30.

For another version of this recipe, you could purée yellow tomatoes and spoon them over diced cucumbers and cubed squash; sprinkle julienned fresh arugula over the top as a garnish.

Makes 6 servings

6 medium tomatoes, peeled,
seeded and *puréed*
(about 3 cups)
2 tablespoons sugar or to taste
2 teaspoons balsamic vinegar
1 teaspoon salt or more to taste
Freshly ground black pepper
2 tablespoons minced fresh
basil leaves
6 ounces soft mozzarella cheese,
cut into 1-inch cubes
2 cup diced cucumbers, peeled
(2 small cucumbers)
2 cups fresh corn kernels
Extra-virgin olive oil, for garnish

Strain the puréed tomatoes into a glass bowl. Add the sugar, balsamic vinegar, and salt and pepper to taste. Add the basil and mix well.

Spoon an equal amount of mozzarella, cucumbers, and corn kernels into the center of 6 shallow bowls and ladle some tomato mixture over each. Drizzle with olive oil, and serve.

Stewed Baby Artichokes (in the French Style)
(*Carciofi alla Francese*)

With baby artichokes growing in the garden in the Imprunetta home we rented from Bea and André Benaim, I was inspired by a dish that Roger Verge prepared for us when he was in Los Angeles and appeared as guest chef on my television show and at Citrus Restaurant. The stewed artichokes are tossed with a garlic-orange *gremolata*, which I developed for the dish.

Makes 6 servings

***Gremolata* (recipe follows)**
12 very small artichokes

Prepare *gremolata* and set aside.

Trim the stems of the artichokes, leaving about 1-inch. Using a

1 lemon, cut in half
Juice of 1 lemon
3 tablespoons olive oil
1 large onion, thinly sliced
2 carrots, thinly sliced
2 sprigs fresh thyme
    or 1/2 teaspoon dried thyme
1 bay leaf
3 garlic cloves, finely chopped
Kosher salt and freshly ground
    white pepper, to taste
1 cup dry white wine

sharp knife, cut about 1-inch off the tops. Tear away several layers of outside leaves close to the base, and trim the bottoms smoothly and evenly with a small sharp knife. As you work, rub each artichoke with the lemon half to prevent the flesh from darkening, and place in a bowl of cold water and lemon juice.

Heat the olive oil in a pot large enough to hold artichokes side by side. Sauté the onion and carrots for 10 minutes, or until soft but not brown. Add thyme, bay leaf and garlic.

Arrange artichokes on top of the vegetables and sprinkle with salt and pepper. Pour in the wine and enough water to barely cover the artichokes. Cover and simmer for 20 minutes, adding more water as needed. Uncover, raise the heat to high, and reduce the broth until syrup-like, about 15 minutes, or until artichokes are tender when pierced with a fork (turn artichokes periodically during this time).

Just before serving, sprinkle the artichokes with salt and pepper and carefully stir in the *gremolata*. To serve, spoon the artichokes into shallow soup bowls with the vegetables and juices.

Gremolata

Serves 6

3 large garlic cloves
1/2 cup packed fresh parsley
1/4 cup basil leaves
2 to 3 tablespoons grated orange
    or lemon zest
Salt and freshly ground
    black pepper

In a mini food processor pulse the garlic to coarsely chop (or chop by hand). Add parsley, basil and zest and pulse a few more times to finely chop. Be careful not to turn into a paste. Add salt and pepper to taste.

Fried Cheese with Classic Tomato Sauce
(*Mozzarella Marinara*)

This is another of those dishes that is so impressive in Italian restaurants and easy to prepare at home. The mozzarella cheese cubes should be soft and melted inside, so it's important to fry them just moments before serving. Have the sauce prepared and ready to spoon onto the individual serving plates, place the fried cheese on top, and serve at once.

Serves 8-10

Classic Tomato Sauce
    (recipe follows)
1 pound mozzarella cheese,
    finely diced
6 eggs
1-1/4 cups dried bread crumbs
1 teaspoon dried oregano
2 garlic cloves, minced
1/2 teaspoon salt
2 tablespoons dry vermouth
    or brandy

Prepare the Classic Tomato Sauce.

In a double boiler, soften the mozzarella over hot water. Transfer the softened cheese to the large bowl of an electric mixer and beat in 2 of the eggs at medium-speed. Add 1/4 cup of the bread crumbs, the oregano, half the garlic, and the salt; mix well. Press the cheese mixture into a lightly oiled 5x7-inch glass dish. Cover and chill at least 1 hour, or until firm.

In shallow bowl, lightly beat the remaining 4 eggs. Blend in the vermouth. Set aside.

In a food processor or blender, blend the remaining 1 cup bread crumbs, Parmesan cheese, parsley, basil, and remaining garlic. Transfer to a small bowl.

2 tablespoons grated
  Parmesan cheese
2 parsley sprigs, stems
  removed
4 fresh basil leaves
1 cup flour
Vegetable oil for frying

Cut the cheese mixture into 1-1/2 to 2-inch cubes (about 15 cubes). Dip each into the flour, then the egg mixture, and finally into the bread crumb mixture to coat evenly. Place on paper towels and chill 30 minutes in the refrigerator.

In a heavy skillet or deep fryer, heat 3 inches of oil until it registers 375°F on a deep-frying thermometer. Fry the cheese cubes, a few at a time, until evenly golden brown on both sides. Drain on paper towels. Serve at once with heated Classic Tomato Sauce.

Classic Tomato Sauce
(*Marinara Salsa*)

Makes about 4 cups

3 tablespoons olive oil
3 garlic cloves, minced
2 onions, finely chopped
1 red bell pepper, chopped
2 carrots, finely chopped
2 celery stalks, finely chopped
1 can (28-ounces) whole
  peeled tomatoes
1 cup dry red wine
1 tablespoon fresh oregano,
  or 1 teaspoon dried
1 tablespoon fresh basil,
  or 1 teaspoon dried
2 tablespoons minced parsley
1/2 teaspoon sugar
Salt
Freshly ground black pepper

In a heavy skillet, heat the oil. Add the garlic, onions, red pepper, carrots, and celery and sauté until the onions are transparent. Add the tomatoes with their liquid, red wine, oregano, basil, parsley, and sugar. Bring to a boil and simmer on medium heat, stirring occasionally, until thick, about 30 minutes. Season to taste with salt and pepper. Transfer to a bowl, cover with plastic wrap, and set aside.

PANZANO
Setting up Housekeeping
Another Five-Month Adventure

In 1986, an introduction to an American innkeeper in Tuscany became our key to an Italian home of our own for future sojourns—and the beginning of yet another important friendship. Sammie Daniels, who lives in Northern California, has adopted Italy as her home, but this is a lady who seems at home anywhere.

At the entrance to Panzano, just south of Florence, Sammie had transformed a small Tuscan home into an inn, where she welcomed Americans and entertained and employed her considerable cooking talents to cater private parties. Since then, Sammie has moved to another location in Panzano, where she performs the same miracles. Over time, she has also become the leasing agent in Northern Italy for all sorts of homes available for short- or long-term rental. Anyone planning an extended stay in Italy would be wise to call her.

Sammie welcomed us on our first evening at her bed and breakfast by throwing a dinner party to introduce us to some of the locals. A couple of the characters around the dining table that night looked straight out of central casting. One we especially enjoyed was Manuccio, owner of the *trattoria* up the way, who instantly dubbed us Marvino and Marvina. Past middle age, he wore an army coat stretched over his great potbelly and a wide smile that revealed no more than one or two teeth. Another was Count Giorgio, with his glossy black hair slicked back, puffing on his pipe and looking immensely sophisticated in his simple sweater, shirt and tie.

Not long after our visit, Sammie began working with the Manetti Family, owners of Fontodi Winery as well as the Manetti Terracotta Factory, to remodel several barns on their vineyard property and make them available for rent. On the basis of our first meeting with Sammie, we rented one of these cottages from her for five months the following year, sight unseen—a decision we've never regretted.

The place we rented was part of a group of living spaces called *La Rota*, located in the middle of the vineyard. *Casa La Rota* is a grand old farm house in the famous Conca d'Oro region of Chianti Classico, about 2.5 kilometers from the center of Panzano-in-Chianti as one travels along State Road 222, the famous "Wine Road," toward Siena. *La Rota* has views toward Panzano and the Castello di Rampolla winery.

The main house has been divided into two elegant living quarters: "*Il Gelso*" (*Casa No. 1*) and "*Il Ciliegio*" (*Casa No. 2*)–each with all modern facilities including central heating, telephone, TV and electric household appliances. There is also a small apartment where Sammie Daniels lives six months of the year. The large garden surrounding the

Top: Peaceful and serene *La Rota.* Above, right: Wine and Travel consultant, Sammie Daniels,

house has a swimming pool and barbecue. The house has views of Panzano Castle and the parish church.

Adjoining the house is the old barn that has been converted into a particularly attractive apartment, "*La Capanna*" (The Old Milk Barn), where we usually stay. Because of its spacious and private garden terrace, it is especially well suited to the outdoor meals we always enjoy.

The rooms are furnished with handcrafted Tuscan country-style furniture. With its peaceful and refined atmosphere, *Casa La Rota* is ideal for those who appreciate the quiet of the countryside and the beauty of Tuscan landscapes.

Before our arrival, Sammie arranged to have a vegetable garden planted for us, so that every morning we were able to pick zucchini, tomatoes, artichokes and basil for our lunch or dinner.

We discovered that the local open farmers' markets arrived in the surrounding villages on particular days of the week, and we managed to visit them all. We learned that if we slept late we missed out, because all of the interesting products sold out early.

Of special mention, is the small market in the *piazza*, held every Sunday. To us, the highlight is the *rosticceria*–roasted chickens on a spit. I once took a photo of the owner holding up the chicken. The next time I saw her, I gave her the photo and I was an instant friend. Now when we meet, her eyes light up and she slips in "surprise sides" along with our chicken order...like her wonderful fried potatoes or polenta.

Maria and Dino Manetti

I became friends with Maria Manetti, the owner of Fontodi Winery, the first day we arrived. When she dropped in to welcome us, I was just taking a tray of *biscotti* out of the oven. She left with a plate filled with my cookies, and that was the beginning of our friendship.

During our five months in this beautiful setting, we became close to Maria and Dino and have often recommended their rental offerings to friends asking where they should rent in Italy. For three hundred years this family has been renowned for the manufacture of terracotta, and it was not until 1968 that they decided to move into winemaking with the purchase of the Fontodi Winery.

The Manettis have three grown children: Giovanni (who now runs the winery, since his father's death in 2007), Marco (who runs the family's terracotta factory) and Giovanna (who helps Sammie Daniels with their villa rentals).

We have eaten many excellent meals at the Manettis' home. Their cook's *bistecca fiorentina*, cooked in an open fireplace in their kitchen, is melt-in-your-mouth delicious. She also takes justifiable pride in her apple cake, and always gives us a couple of slices to take home.

Above: Maria and Dino Manetti. Left: Son, Giovanni Manetti pours the family wines for a tasting.

Our first year at La Rota we decided to have a July 4th party in our small private garden. Sammie helped by borrowing from other *La Rota* apartments the wine glasses, cutlery and plates we needed. Our guests included not only local Italians we had met but also people from all over the world, including a couple from Switzerland and several friends from Los Angeles. Bea and Andre Benaim came from Imprunetta, and even our artist friends from Pietrasanta, Janice and Ron Mehlman, showed up. Guests from a variety of places who were renting the apartments at *La Rota* also joined us.

We decided that the food should be potluck and asked everyone to bring something. Our own contribution was potato salad and pizza. Many guests brought wine. The Manettis brought Fontodi wine and their cook's apple cake, and Teo Loeffler brought his delicious herring salad. Our butcher friend Dario Cecchini contributed his famous roasted meats and a jug of wine. For dessert we had *gelati* with sugar cones.

Since the 4th of July is not an Italian holiday, we had little hope of finding fireworks, but on asking around we learned of a stationary/gift store in San Casciano (the next village) that might stock some. Amazingly, they had just what we wanted–hidden under the toy counter, and not sold to everyone.

Our little garden bordered on the vineyards, and as the fireworks were going off some sparks must have blown in that direction. But, knowing how much celebrating our Independence Day meant to us, no one said a word–not even the Manettis–except for the barking dogs at a farm close by.

Grazia the Cheese Lady

We had begun by purchasing Grazia's ricotta from the local market, but soon learned that we could visit her small home dairy and buy this magnificent cheese directly from her. On our first visit we drove down a dirt road to her place, marked by a battered wooden sign that pointed us up a hill onto another dirt road. The fierce barking of a large white Maremma dog failed to discourage us from our quest, and we entered a small barn where Grazia stood swirling a soft mass of white curds in an enormous copper bowl with a long wooden paddle.

Top: Maria Manetti and myself. Middle: *Signora* Grazia showing us the tricks of her trade. Right: Duilio sharing wine secrets with Chef Bruce Marder.

After a decisive final stir, she scooped the curds on top of the mixture into small plastic baskets dotted with holes. The curds were still warm and very soft as she held out a spoon for me to "take a taste." I breathed in the sweet, creamy scent, and the moment that smooth velvet substance hit my tongue, I knew I had, at long last, discovered real ricotta.

We took home the precious container of warm ricotta we bought that morning and ate it topped with chestnut honey. This is the best way I know to start the day. Since then, we've also eaten it often for lunch or dinner with olive oil and freshly ground pepper.

Needless to say, it soon became a ritual for us every morning to walk the mile or so to the "cheese lady's farm" to pick up a container of this freshly made warm ricotta, a piece of Pecorino cheese and chestnut honey.

We have of course eaten ricotta before, but it was the type available in supermarkets, with a texture somewhere between cottage cheese and yogurt; but we had never before experienced this warm, soft, sweet substance that made us close our eyes and savor the moment. Which, come to think of it, is the heart of what our Panzano adventure was all about.

Enoteca del Chianti Classico

We bought our wine from Duilio's wine shop located on the main street of Panzano. A charming man with a ready smile and a passion for wine. Duilio not only sells wine, but offers a running commentary, in Italian, about any bottle you consider purchasing.

When we first discovered his wine shop, it was much smaller and in a less central location than his present one. He himself had designed and built the dark brown wooden shelves that held the wine bottles. There was a section for each winery, with each of their varietals in a separate bin. In front of each bin a small shelf jutted out holding one bottle, so the customer could see at a glance which wine and vintage was in each bin.

A few years after we met Duilio, he bought a larger space on the main street of Panzano. In the space on one side were his distinctive wooden wine shelves, and on the other side, tables for wine tasting and a bar where he kept salami and cheeses to go with the wines.

If a customer selected a high-priced wine and Duilio knew of a less expensive one that was just as good, he would always offer the alternate selection. He followed this same pattern with his olive oils and balsamic vinegars. Never would this kindly wine seller take advantage of a customer.

WHEN YOU GO, YOU SHOULD KNOW:

Sammie Daniels
c/o Tenuta Fontodi
Panzano-in-Chianti 50020
P.O. Box 769
Larkspur, California 94977-0769
Tel: (415) 322-5841
Fax: (415) 925-0322
Italy Tel: (055) 85 2817
email: sammie@stayitalia.com
website: www.stayitalia.com

Fontodi Winery
50022 Panzano in Chianti
Florence, Italy
Tel: (055) 852005
Fax: (055) 852537
website: www.fontodi.com

Duilio's Wine Shop
Enoteca del Chianti Classico
Tel: 39 (055) 852495
Via Chiantigiana, 15-29
50020 Panzano
Chianti, Fl.

Nittardi Winery
Peter Femfert
53011 Castellina in Chianti
(Siena), Italy
Tel: (05) 77740269
Fax: (05) 77741080
email: info@nittardi.com
website: www.nittardi.com

Ristorante La Mora
Via Ludovica 1748
Fraz. Sesto di Moriano, Ponte a Moriano
(Lucca), Italy
Tel: 58 340 6402
Fax: 58 340 6135
email: info@ristorantelamora.it
website: www.ristorantelamora.com

Badia a Coltibuono
53013 Gaiole in Chianti (SI) Italy
Tel: 0577 74481
Fax: 0577 744839
email: info@coltibuono.com
website: www.coltibuono.com

Osteria del Cinghiale Bianco
Borgo S. Jacopo, 43 r.
50125 Firenze, Italy
Tel/Fax: (055) 215706
email: info@cinghialebianco.it
website: www.cinghialebianco.it

Fresh Fava Beans and Pecorino
(Fave Fresche con Pecorino)

While we were living in Panzano, a neighbor invited us over one day to see her vegetable garden. Standing in the midst of rows and rows of fava bean plants that were five or six feet high almost took our breath away. We picked as many beans as we could carry, took them home, cooked them, and served them with a young Pecorino cheese and a glass of Tuscan red wine. Marvino brought the seeds home to Los Angeles and planted them. Every year around April, our plants are ready for harvest.

Our Panzano experience inspired me to create this recipe using freshly shelled fava beans, Pecorino cheese and olive oil. I often serve this dish in cappuccino or espresso cups and top it with a spoonful of salmon caviar.

**4 pounds fresh young
fava beans***
**1 cup Pecorino cheese,
diced in 1/8-inch cubes**
1/2 cup olive oil
Salt
Freshly ground black pepper
Salmon caviar, optional

Serves 8 to 10

Shell fava beans and discard the pods. If fava beans are tiny, there is no need to boil them, serve them raw. Parboil the beans in boiling water until they puff up, about 5 minutes. Cool and pop them out of their skins.

Just before serving, spoon the fava beans and Pecorino into a bowl. Drizzle with extra virgin olive oil and add salt and pepper to taste. Spoon into small bowls or cups.

* If you have fava bean plants growing in your garden, be sure to use the leaves for salads.

Stuffed Squash Blossoms
(Fiori di Zucca Ripieni)

When we are cooking in Italy we can never resist buying zucchini blossoms at the open market. We serve them stuffed with a choice of two sauces: puréed roasted peppers or Classic Tomato Sauce. This light vegetable dish makes a perfect small course for a dinner that consists entirely of *primi piatti* (first plates).

**20 to 24 squash blossoms
with tiny zucchini attached**
1 pound fresh ricotta cheese
1 cup grated Parmesan cheese
2 egg yolks or whole eggs
1/2 teaspoon salt
Freshly ground black pepper
**1/4 pound Gorgonzola cheese,
cut in small dice**
1/2 cup olive oil
**Puréed Roasted Peppers or
Classic Tomato Sauce
(recipe page 111)**

Serves 10

Preheat the oven to 375°F.

Carefully open blossoms wide; remove the pistils* from inside the zucchini blossom and discard. Set blossoms aside.

To prepare the stuffing: In a large bowl, beat the ricotta, Parmesan, egg, salt and pepper until smooth. Taste for seasoning; the mixture should be highly seasoned. Cover with plastic wrap and refrigerate.

To fill the blossoms: The easiest way is to spoon the filling into a large pastry bag, but a small spoon will also work. Fill the clean blossoms about three quarters full. Push a piece of Gorgonzola into the center of the filling and gently twist the petals together on the top of the filling.

Brush two (8x10-inch) baking dishes with olive oil and arrange the stuffed zucchini flowers in the dishes. Sprinkle the blossoms with salt, pepper and olive oil. Cover with foil and bake 20 minutes or until the cheese is puffy and the juice from the blossoms begins to bubble.

To serve, ladle desired sauce into each serving plate and arrange two stuffed blossoms on top.

* The pistil is the fuzzy yellow floret found in the center of the squash blossom.

Judy's Fresh Ricotta

If you can't travel to Panzano to have Signora Grazia's ricotta here is my simple and quick recipe that creates a smooth and velvety ricotta. It is delicious with honey or Nadia Santini's *Mostarda* (recipe page 36) and enjoyed for breakfast, lunch or dinner.

Makes about 1/2 pound

1 quart whole milk
1/2 cup cream
1 teaspoon salt
3 tablespoons lemon juice
Honey, for garnish

Heat the milk, cream and salt over low heat until it is about to boil. Add the lemon juice, stir a few times and when mixture begins to curdle, remove from the heat. Let curds rest for a minute or two. Using a slotted spoon, skim the ricotta curds from the whey and place them in a colander or wire sieve lined with cheesecloth. Drain for 15 minutes. Serve warm or at room temperature, with a drizzle of honey.

Bruschetta with Spinach and White Beans
(*Bruschetta con Spinaci e Fagioli Bianchi Cannellini*)

When we are living in Panzano and drive into Florence for the day we often eat at Massimo Masselli's Ristorante Cinghiali Bianco, where he serves this hearty Tuscan appetizer, consisting of thick slices of country toast rubbed with a clove of garlic and olive oil, then topped with cooked spinach on one half and cannellini beans on the other.

Makes 4 servings

4 tablespoons extra-virgin
   olive oil
1 small onion, peeled and
   finely chopped
6 garlic cloves, minced
   (about 2 tablespoons)
2 teaspoons dried thyme
2 teaspoons dried sage
1 teaspoon crushed red
   pepper flakes
One (15-ounce) can
   cannellini beans with liquid
Salt
Freshly ground black pepper
1 pound fresh spinach,
   washed, blanched, drained
   and finely chopped*
6 to 8 (1/2 to 1-inch) thick
   slices French or Italian bread

Heat 2 tablespoons of the olive oil in a medium saucepan over medium heat for 30 seconds. Sauté the onion until golden, about 3 minutes, add the garlic and cook 1 minute more. Add thyme, sage and pepper flakes. Stir a moment, then add the beans and their liquid. Simmer for 10 minutes, or until thick. Season with salt and pepper to taste.

In a 10-inch nonstick skillet, heat 1 tablespoon of olive oil, add spinach, salt and pepper, and sauté until heated through, about 5 minutes. Transfer to bowl.

In a medium non-stick skillet, heat the remaining tablespoon of olive oil and lightly brown the bread on both sides; or toast it briefly on a baking sheet in the oven.

To serve, arrange the toasted bread on small plates. Mound the beans on half of each slice of toast and the spinach on the other half. Serve with a knife & fork.

* Note: To blanch the spinach, wash and stem the leaves. Place the spinach leaves with the water that clings to them in a heavy saucepan and steam over medium-high heat until wilted. Squeeze the water out and finely chop the leaves.

Panzano Bread Salad
(*Panzanella*)

Known as *Panzanella*, this is a traditional Italian peasant salad and an excellent way of using up old bread. There are many variations; some are mixtures of marinated vegetables placed on crusty bread, others are layers of bread and vegetables. This one reminds me of the Middle Eastern Tabbouleh Salad, substituting bread for cracked wheat and adding a colorful array of diced green and red vegetables.

Serves 6 to 8

6 slices day-old country-style
   bread, without crust
1 small red onion, sliced or
   diced (about 1 cup)
2 cloves garlic, minced
1 yellow bell pepper, seeded
   and diced
2 medium-size ripe, firm
   tomatoes, diced (2 cups)
1 cucumber, peeled and diced
1 cup fresh basil leaves, torn
   into small pieces
1 tablespoon capers, rinsed
   and dried
2 anchovy fillets, drained and minced
1/4 cup olive oil
2 tablespoons red wine vinegar
Salt
Freshly ground black pepper

In a bowl, soak bread in water to cover for a few minutes. Squeeze dry and drain well. Crumble into a large bowl.

Add onion, garlic, bell pepper, tomatoes, and cucumber; toss with bread. Add basil, capers, and anchovy fillets and mix well. Add enough olive oil to moisten. Then add vinegar, salt, and pepper to taste and toss.

La Mora's Spelt Salad
(*Insalata di Farro*)

While in Panzano we enjoyed many side trips, including one to Lucca, which is famous for its walled city. Just outside the city walls is the restaurant La Mora. The owners, Sauro and Angela Brunicardi, were always at the restaurant—she in the kitchen and he in the dining room, a charming host. It is a perfect lunch or dinner stop. One of their specialties is cooking with *farro*.

Farro, or spelt, is a form of wheat berry imported from Italy that makes a good basis for a salad (or soup) because it holds up well after cooking. Combined with tomatoes, arugula, olive oil and balsamic vinegar, the salad makes a fine main course for lunch. *Farro* is available from retailers of gourmet Italian foods. We are fortunate to have arugula growing wild in our garden.

Serves 6 to 8 as a main course, 10 to 12 as a side dish

2 cups spelt (*farro*)
2 quarts water
Salt
2 tablespoons lemon juice

In a saucepan, combine the spelt, water and salt. Bring to a boil, cover the pan and boil the spelt until it is tender (just starting to split open), about 30 minutes. Drain well and cool.

In a bowl, whisk in the lemon juice and a large pinch of salt, the shallot, then the balsamic vinegar and olive oil. Set aside.

1 shallot, finely chopped
2 tablespoons balsamic vinegar
1/2 cup olive oil
2 cups trimmed arugula
5 Roma or plum tomatoes, diced
1/4 cup chopped parsley

Rinse the arugula and cut any large leaves in half. Place in a large bowl. Add the drained spelt, tomatoes and parsley. Toss well with dressing. Add additional olive oil if desired.

Tuscan Bean and Tuna Salad
(Fagioli Toscani e Tonno in Insalata)

During our five-month vacation in Chianti, much of my time was spent creating new recipes from Tuscany's fabulous array of farm-fresh produce in local markets. I grew addicted to this combination of arugula, tuna, and cannellini beans for leisurely lunches in the garden overlooking the grapevines and the pool.

Serves 8

2 (15-ounce) cans cannellini beans, drained or 1 cup dried cannellini beans or Great Northern beans
About 1 cup olive oil
1 cup diced fennel
2 (6-1/8 ounce) cans tuna in oil, drained and flaked
Salt and freshly ground black pepper, to taste
4 cups thinly sliced arugula or radicchio leaves
1/8 to 1/4 cup balsamic vinegar
1 small red onion, thinly sliced, (optional)

If using dried cannellini beans, soak them overnight in water to cover. Drain beans and place in a pot with enough cold water to cover by 2 inches. Bring to a boil and simmer until tender, about 1 hour, adding additional water to cover beans, as needed. Drain well and cool.

In a large bowl, toss beans with 4 tablespoons of the olive oil, fennel and tuna. Season with salt and pepper to taste.

In another large bowl, toss arugula with olive oil; season with salt and pepper to taste. Arrange arugula in the center of each serving plate and spoon the bean mixture on top. Sprinkle each serving with additional olive oil, balsamic vinegar and garnish with sliced onion.

Spelt Soup
(Zuppa di Farro)

Farro (spelt), a traditional grain grown in Lucca and Umbria, makes a good basis for a soup as well as a salad. This is another specialty of Ristorante La Mora, where owners Sauro and Angela take great pride in what they do.

Serves 6 to 8

1-1/2 cups spelt (or wheat berries or barley)
1/4 cup olive oil
1 onion, thinly sliced
1 leek, white and light green part only, thinly sliced
2 garlic cloves, minced
2 stalks celery, thinly sliced

Soak spelt in cold water, to cover, for 2 hours or overnight.

In a large Dutch oven or stockpot, heat the olive oil and sauté the onion, leek, garlic, celery and carrots, stirring occasionally, until soft and lightly browned, about 5 minutes. Add the spelt, borlotti beans, puréed beans, and tomato paste, stirring so that the tomato paste is well blended. Add water to completely cover the mixture. Bring to a boil, then lower the heat and simmer gently for 1 hour. Add additional water and continue cooking until the spelt is tender.

2 large carrots, thinly sliced
1 (15-ounce) can borlotti
   beans, drained and rinsed
1 cup borlotti beans, puréed
2 tablespoons tomato paste
Water
Salt, to taste
Freshly ground black pepper,
   to taste
3 tablespoons fresh basil leaves,
   cut into thin slices
Freshly grated Parmesan cheese

To serve, ladle into heated soup bowls and garnish with basil and Parmesan cheese.

Chef Klaus' Green Tomato Marmalade
(Marmellata di Pomodori Verdi)

While living in Panzano we were invited to a cooking class at Nittardi Winery in Tuscany, taught by Chef Klaus Trebes, chef/owner of Gargantua Restaurant in Frankfurt, Germany. One of the recipes he shared was this Green Tomato Marmalade. It is so versatile that I always keep a jar in the refrigerator. Not only is it delicious on toast or a *frittata* for breakfast, it's also a perfect accompaniment to a *burrata* salad or a meat or chicken course.

Green tomatoes are simply under-ripe red tomatoes. If you don't have tomato plants, look for green tomatoes at your farmers' market.

Makes about 3 to 4 cups

2 cups sugar
1/2 cup water
8 cups (2 pounds) green
   tomatoes, diced (about
   4 large tomatoes)
1 cup fresh squeezed
   orange juice, heated
Grated zest of 1 orange and
   1 lemon
10 - 15 mint leaves, sliced
   (optional)

In a large heavy skillet, combine the sugar and water and bring to a boil, stirring constantly until the sugar dissolves. Reduce the heat and simmer until the sugar begins to turn golden. Add the tomatoes, orange juice, and zest, and bring to a boil. Reduce heat and simmer until the tomatoes are soft and the liquid has reduced to a thick syrup, about 20 to 30 minutes. Mix in the mint leaves, if using. Cool.

Lorenza's Lemon Risotto
(Risotto al Limone)

Lorenza de Medici has a cooking school in an old Abby in Tuscany and often invites us to join her for dinner with her class. The family also has a small restaurant close by on the property. Lemon *Risotto*, the specialty of the restaurant, is a popular dish there. The zesty flavor of the fresh lemon makes this a simple and unusual way to enjoy the pleasure of *risotto*.

Serves 8

6-8 cups vegetable broth
2 tablespoons unsalted butter
1 tablespoon olive oil

In a saucepan, bring broth to a steady simmer.

In a heavy pot, heat butter and olive oil over moderate heat. Add onion and sauté for 1 minute, until it begins to soften, being careful

1/2 cup minced onion
1-1/2 cups arborio rice
1/2 cup freshly squeezed
  lemon juice, about 2 lemons
1/4 cup brandy, optional
1/4 cup cream
1/2 cup grated
  Parmesan cheese

not to brown.

Add rice to the onions; using a wooden spoon, stir for 1 minute, making sure all the grains are well coated.

Add the lemon juice and brandy and stir until they are completely absorbed. Begin adding simmering broth, 1/2 cup at a time, stirring frequently. Wait until each addition is almost completely absorbed before adding the next 1/2 cup, reserving about 1/4 cup to add at the end. Stir frequently to prevent sticking.

After about 18 minutes, when the rice is tender but still firm, add the reserved broth, cream, and cheese. Stir vigorously to combine with the rice. Serve immediately.

Panzano Garlic-Rosemary Roasted Chicken
(*Pollo Arrosto all'Aglio e Rosmarino*)

On Sunday, at the open market in Panzano, we always buy a fresh barbecued chicken from the truck. If we are in the mood for chicken during the week, we buy a fresh chicken from Dario Cecchini, our local butcher, and roast it with garlic and rosemary.

Serves 8

1 (4-pound) or 2 (2-pound)
  whole chickens
1 onion, sliced and diced
2 garlic cloves, minced
4 carrots, peeled and
  thinly sliced
1 parsnip, peeled and
  thinly sliced
2 tablespoons minced parsley
Salt and freshly ground
  black pepper, to taste
1 head garlic, unpeeled cloves,
  separated

Marinade:

1/3 cup olive oil
2 tablespoons fresh rosemary
6 cloves garlic, thinly sliced

Split the chicken along the entire length of the back, removing backbone from tail to neck. Open it out, skin side up. With a mallet, (for big chickens) or the heel of your hand, flatten with a firm whack, fracturing the breastbone and rib cage. If you wish to serve this boneless, you can then turn the chicken over and remove the rib cage and cartilage. Use a very sharp boning knife, taking care not to break the skin.

Line a large roasting pan with heavy-duty foil. Add onion, garlic cloves, carrots, parsnip and parsley, salt and pepper and whole garlic cloves. Place the chicken on top, skin-side up.

Preheat the oven to 400°F.

For the marinade: in a small bowl, combine the olive oil, rosemary and garlic and mix well. Working with your finger-tips, separate the skin from the meat of the chicken, beginning at the neck end, being careful not to tear the skin. Place the olive oil mixture under the skin. Rub the top of the chicken with olive oil, salt and pepper.

Pour white wine around the chicken and bake for 10 minutes; reduce the oven temperature to 375°, and bake for 45 minutes to 1 hour or longer, depending on the size of the chicken. Baste every 20 minutes. If chicken browns too quickly, cover it loosely with foil. If the wine cooks away too quickly, add more. Remove the foil during the last 10 minutes, allowing the chicken to brown.

Twice Baked Almond Cookies
(Biscotti alle Mandorle)

These are the cookies I was making when Maria Manetti knocked on my door to introduce herself. Known as Cantucci in parts of Italy, these almond cookies are baked twice, resulting in a crisp, flavorful biscuit. This recipe is versatile. You can substitute some whole wheat flour for the white. Possible additions include chocolate chips, poppy seeds or dried fruit.

Makes about 6 dozen

2 cups flour
1/2 teaspoon baking powder
1/2 teaspoon baking soda
1/4 teaspoon salt
1 teaspoon fennel seeds
3/4 cup toasted, ground
   unpeeled almonds
1/2 cup toasted, whole
   unpeeled almonds
2 eggs
1/2 teaspoon anise or
   almond extract
1/4 teaspoon vanilla extract
1 cup sugar
1 egg white

Preheat the oven to 350°F.

Place the flour, baking powder, baking soda, salt, and fennel seeds in a mound on a floured board. Surround the outside of the mound with the ground and whole almonds. Make a well in the center. Place the eggs, anise and vanilla in the well. Beat the sugar into the eggs, blending well. Quickly beat the egg mixture with a fork, gradually incorporating the flour and almonds to make a smooth dough.

Divide the dough into 3 to 4 portions. With lightly oiled hands shape each portion into an oval loaf shape. Place the loaves 2 inches apart on lightly greased non-stick baking sheets. Brush with the egg white and bake for 15 to 20 minutes or until lightly browned.

Remove the loaves from the oven, use a spatula to transfer to cutting board and cut into 1/2-inch thick slices. Place the slices cut side down on the same baking sheet and return them to the oven. Leave the *biscotti* in the oven for 5 to 10 minutes per side or until golden brown. Transfer to racks and cool. Store in plastic containers.

Individual Ricotta Soufflés
(Piccoli Soufflés di Ricotta)

This soufflé-like cheesecake dessert makes a wonderful finale for a special dinner. When we are living in Panzano, I prepare it with Grazia's fresh ricotta cheese, which makes it especially delicious. I mix the cheese, egg yolks and lemon zest several hours before the guests arrive. Then after dinner I fold the meringue into the egg yolk mixture, fill the soufflé molds, and bake. No one minds the wait, especially after they taste these warm, light and flavorful soufflés.

Makes 8

2 tablespoons unsalted butter
   for molds
14 ounces fresh, unsalted
   ricotta cheese
6 large eggs, separated
2 tablespoons grated
   lemon zest
1 tablespoon Sambuca or
   other anise-flavored liqueur
3/4 cup granulated sugar
Pinch of salt
2 tablespoons confectioners'
   sugar

Preheat the oven to 350°F. Brush 8 (6-ounce) soufflé molds with butter and place in the refrigerator.

In a large bowl, strain the ricotta (for a creamy consistency) by pressing it through a fine sieve or strainer. Add the egg yolks, one at a time, until well blended. Mix in the lemon zest and Sambuca. (At this point you can cover the mixture with plastic wrap and refrigerate up to 4 hours before folding in the meringue.) In the large bowl of an electric mixer, beat the egg whites until foamy. Add 1/2 cup of the sugar and salt and beat until stiff peaks form. Gently fold into the ricotta mixture.

Dust the prepared molds evenly with the remaining 1/4 cup sugar. Line an ovenproof pan that is large enough to hold the cups with a cloth. Place the prepared molds in the pan and carefully spoon the ricotta mixture into the molds. Fill one third of the pan with hot water and bake for 20 minutes, or until soufflés are puffy and golden brown. Dust with confectioners' sugar and serve immediately.

MORE FRIENDS IN PANZANO
Carlo and Valeria Fabbri: *Italian Soul Mates*

On one of our first visits to Panzano, Sammie Daniels invited us to a small restaurant for dinner to meet her friends, Carlo Fabbri and his wife, Valeria. The Fabbris make their home in Bologna. Years ago, he inherited his aunt's winery, Sauvinola Paolina,, located in Greve (which bears her name—). Since then, Greve has become their second home. We became instant friends during our first evening together. We were delighted when Carlo invited us to their annual BBQ dinner.

These dinners are always a lot of fun. Everyone brings a course, and Carlo grills sausages and lamb in an open fireplace in the dining room. Valeria provides the pasta and desserts.

Valeria, an excellent and dedicated cook, always seems to be up to her elbows in the kitchen preparing her special peppers stuffed with anchovies or baking a cake.

One of the highlights of our time with her was a fascinating lesson she gave us on making *Nocino*, a walnut liqueur. The tradition is that the walnuts are picked green (when the outer shell is still soft) on the night of June 23, the feast of San Giovanni Battista. Carlo and Valeria often bring the nuts from their home in Bologna to Panzano, where they prepare this high alcohol-content liqueur.

When the four of us met in their kitchen for our *Nocino* lesson, we began by filling a large jar with whole green walnuts that had been washed. The nuts steep in alcohol and a sugar syrup for several months, but the bottle with its contents must be shaken and turned every day. When the Fabbris were away from the winery we became the babysitters for their *Nocino*.

One year we brought Carlo a shirt, "bowling shirt-style," with his name embroidered on the front and "BBQ and *Nocino* Bar" on the back. We named him *Presidente* of this enterprise. When we meet, he reminds us that he is the *Presidente* and Marvino the *Vice Presidente*.

The menu at Carlo's third annual BBQ and *Nocino* Bar event included *Bruschetta di Funghi Cavolo Nero* (toasted bread topped with mushrooms and kale), *Torta di Theo*, *Pomodoro Capuccio*, *Taglialini con Fagioli* (pasta–handmade by Valeria–with beans), Carlo's Barbecue *Misti* (a variety of meats grilled on the barbecue), *verdure alla bracci* (vegetables grilled on the barbecue), *pomodori verdi con L'Uva Sangiovese* (green tomatoes with grapes), *purée di melanze con formaggio* (puréed eggplant with cheese) and *gelato e biscotti* (ice cream with cookies).

The 150-year-old winery has a *cantina* on the ground floor and Carlo and Valeria's living space on the second floor. On the third floor is a spacious apartment where we often stay while vacationing in Tuscany; it is unbeatable for its lovely views and its walking distance from the Greve Saturday market (where parking is all but impossible).

Their daughter, Ludovica, is the winemaker at Sauvignola Paolina Winery. She also lives on the estate with her husband, Antonio, and their two children. The winery is tiny by American standards, with only 20,000 bottles of Chianti Classico, Chianti Classico *Riserva* and a Super Tuscan produced annually. They also produce extra virgin olive oil and

Carlo and Marvino have become close friends.

Valeria and myself, stuffing peppers with anchovies.

a small amount of *grappa*. About half of their wine and olive oil are sold in the U.S., but unfortunately Los Angeles, our home town, isn't one of their prime markets.

The Sauvignola Paolina estate is hidden away but convenient to get to, set in the midst of rolling hills. Its beauty is enhanced by flowering plants among the grapevines. A visit to this boutique winery for a personal tasting with Carlo is a special treat, and you will also find jars of Valeria's famous preserves available for sale. You might even be lucky enough to find the charming apartment above the Fabbris' home available for a weekly or monthly rental.

**WHEN YOU GO,
YOU SHOULD KNOW:**

Savignola Paolina Estate Winery
Via Petrolo, 58
50022 Greve in Chianti (FI), Italy
Tel/Fax: (055) 854 6036
email: info@savignolapaolina.it
website: www.savignolapaolina.it

Carlo and Valeria's Walnut Liqueur
(*Nocino*)

I often serve chocolate chip ice cream (*straciatelle gelato*) with *Nocino* drizzled over the top.

Makes 1 liter

30 (green, unripe) walnuts
4 cups of 100 proof vodka
1 large strip lemon zest
Juice of half a lemon
2 cinnamon sticks
5 cloves
2-1/2 cups sugar

Clean the walnuts with a damp towel and cut in quarters. (Be careful; they will stain your hands!) Place in a large jar, add the vodka, lemon zest, lemon, cinnamon sticks, cloves and sugar. Cover with a lid. Shake the jar once a day for a month. Filter and save the liqueur. Serve in tiny glasses at the end of a meal.

Valeria's Fresh Fruit of the Season Salad
(*Macedonia di Frutta*)

Most family-style restaurants in Italy, especially in the Northern Regions, serve fresh fruit known as Macedonia for dessert. To my taste, Valeria's version is the best.

Traditionally, a large bowl or jar of macerated fresh fruit is placed on a table with small bowls or tall glasses, and spoons. The basic fruits used are apples, pears and bananas, with orange and lemon juice. It may vary depending on which fruits are in season. Often sweet wine is added. This is a perfect light dessert after a big dinner, and it's especially tempting served with a scoop of *gelato* on top and *biscotti*.

Serves 6

1 pound cherries
2 quarts fresh strawberries
1 pound seedless grapes
4 medium peaches
2 pears
6 tablespoons lemon juice
1/2 to 1 cup Kirschwasser*
   (to taste)
2 tablespoons sugar

Wash and clean cherries. Cut 2 slices from the sides of each cherry and discard center section with its stone. Place slices in a large serving bowl. Wash, hull and quarter strawberries. Add to bowl. Wash grapes and cut them in half (optional). Add to the same bowl. Peel peaches, pit them, cut them into small wedges and immediately immerse in lemon juice in a separate bowl. Peel and seed pears. Add to lemon juice with peaches.

Stir Kirschwasser and sugar into fruit mixture and toss. Drain peaches and pears. Add to fruit mixture and toss. Chill, toss before serving.

* Kirschwasser is cherry brandy

PANZANO
Dario Cecchini: Butcher of Panzano, and Our Italian Son
Antica Macelleria Cecchini, Solo Ciccia,
Officina della Bistecca and MacDario's

The first time we heard the name Dario Cecchini was at dinner in Florence in the kitchen of our American friend, Faith Willinger, an American journalist, who has been living in Italy for over 20 years. She explained that every week she received a delivery from a butcher in Panzano, a village about 45 minutes outside of Florence, whose meat was the best in Italy. We should meet him, she said, when we were in Panzano.

The day we arrived at our rental house in Panzano we found Dario's butcher shop in the village. We walked in and introduced ourselves to this tall, handsome man with a knock-out smile. Although Dario does not speak English, his charm and high spirits made an immediate connection with us as he brought out glasses, poured red wine and sliced meats he had roasted the night before, for us to sample.

Later we learned that he prepares his classic roasted meats every night before he goes home, returning in a few hours to take them out of the oven, ready to serve the next day.

It soon became a ritual for us, stopping by every morning on our walk from our rented villa to say good morning to Dario. He was always on the phone, but would give us a big hug, often inviting us to the bar around the corner for an espresso.

Dario's butcher shop has been in his family for 250 years. He had originally intended to become a veterinarian. But after his mother died when he was 15 and his father passed away just three years later, Dario decided to devote himself to the family's butcher shop. He has made it far more than a simple butcher shop. His creations with meats, local herbs and spices quickly set his establishment apart from traditional shops. He spends months researching recipes that were used in Italy during the 17th and 18th centuries.

One day we discovered that Dario's birthday was the following week. To celebrate we suggested a kite-flying picnic to which he could invite all his friends. Since Dario loves dramatic celebrations, he immediately embraced our idea.

We found a perfect hill for flying kites and invited a lot of people–Italians, Germans and Americans. Dario also invited some friends who specialize in kite making. One of them made a kite so big that it had to be tied to the back of a small Volkswagen and driven up and down the hills of Tuscany to generate enough wind to get it into the air. We made a kite using the wrapping paper of Dario's store, and he still has our creation hanging on display.

On the hill a long table was set up laden with typical Tuscan breads baked in a wood fireplace, salami, cheeses, roasted meats and *pâtés*. Another table held wine glasses and bottles of red wine. Everyone had a great time feasting and flying kites, and the party lasted until dark.

Dario sports an apron from one of many memorable trips has taken to Israel.

Top to bottom: We have enjoyed many meals together at Dario's restaurant, Solo Ciccia; a Mac Dario burger; Dario shows off his olive oil cake; jars of red pepper jelly, as displayed in his butcher shop.

It was this moment in time, when we felt that we'd built a special relationship with Dario. He was so touched that we had organized such a wonderful party for him. He explained to us how meaningful our relationship was to him. It was then that he dubbed us his honorary parents and began calling us "Mama," and "Papa."

Dario has a powerful, operatic voice and is renowned for his spontaneous recitations of Dante's *Inferno* to customers in his butcher shop. One day we stopped by and told him we had friends coming to visit and that one of the women was an opera singer. Dario immediately announced, "We will have a *festa* and she will sing."

We all invited friends and arrived at Dario's at 6:00 p.m. to find that he had created, in the room next to his shop, a small café with a buffet loaded with food and wine.

In the rear of the room, up a small stairway, is a huge antique marble meat counter. At one point during the evening our opera singer friend, Gail Gordon Drabkin, quietly walked up the stairs, stood behind the marble bar and began singing an *aria* from Carmen. All conversation and motion in the room stopped as she descended the steps and strolled around the room singing to each guest in turn. Dario wore an expression of sheer joy and there were tears in his eyes.

When Gail finished singing he stood behind the bar and began reciting Dante. I think it was his way of thanking her. This Chianti butcher, who can recite Dante's *Divine Comedy* from memory, is now courted by TV stations and is in demand to perform at charity events throughout Italy–especially those involving children, for whom he has a special concern.

On one of our recent visits to Italy, to celebrate Marvino's birthday, our favorite butcher invited us to his house for a dinner that featured some of Marvino's favorite dishes, including *Bistecca Fiorentina*, which Dario prepared in a cast iron frying pan. Marvino had always admired Dario's outrageous color-coordinated outfits–for example, one that combined bright green pants, purple socks and a red shirt topped with a green sweater. Dario's birthday present for him consisted of a selection of Dario's own multi-colored striped socks.

Dario's gregarious personality seems to require continual expansion into new spaces. In the old building where he was born, across the street from his shop, he recently opened a restaurant called *Solo Ciccia* (which means "Only Meat"). This establishment features a striking contemporary-style interior that includes several large rooms connected by glass staircases that resemble bridges. On the floor below is a brick-walled room that looks like a wine cellar, where patrons dine at a large family-style table.

Dario has also transformed a large space above the butcher shop into a dining room where he offers cooking classes and provides banquet facilities. The décor in this room is a lively combination of colors, with red walls that slide open to reveal dishes and tableware. Adjacent to this area is a small kitchen where he prepares his delicious roasted meats.

Yet another addition to Dario's growing enterprise is an outdoor porch behind the butcher shop where he serves hamburgers. True to his spirit of fun, he has christened it "Mac Dario."

When Dario was in Los Angeles recently he visited a local meat supplier to restaurants, to choose cuts of beef to prepare in various dishes. Russ Parsons, who accompanied him on this shopping expedition, wrote an article for the *Los Angeles Times* describing both the cuts of meat Dario chose and how he prepared them at the home of Chef Bruce Marder, owner of Capo restaurant in Santa Monica, California. The steaks were custom-cut for Dario about three fingers thick, from aged beef, and he insisted on their being allowed to rest at room temperature for at least five hours before cooking (though twelve, he said, would have been ideal). "You have to get the cold out of the meat for the fibers to relax," he said. He cooked the steaks to medium-rare on a grill and seasoned them afterward with coarse salt and good olive oil.

For other meat dishes he often uses a combination of seasonings he calls *profumi di Chianti*, which include garlic, rosemary, thyme, lemons, and fennel.

WHEN YOU GO, YOU SHOULD KNOW:

Dario Cecchini
Antica Macelleria Cecchini
Via XX Luglio, 11 Panzano in Chianti
50020 Firenze, Italy
Tel: (055) 852020
Fax: (055) 852700
email: macelleriacecchini@tin.it
website: www.dariocecchini.com

Dario Meets Pastrami

On another note, Dario loves pastrami. He stayed with us on his first visit to Los Angeles, and we took him for lunch to The Broadway Deli in Santa Monica, where he ordered a pastrami sandwich. It was a "new discovery," as he called it, and he became obsessed. He called it "the worlds' greatest meat gift."

The next year when Dario and his *fiancé*, Kim, came to Los Angeles, we decided to have a Pastrami Festival at the Broadway Deli in his honor. We invited many of the people who had visited him in Panzano, or those who had read of his success in Italy.

It was a huge event, with over 250 people attending, and Dario had a great time. Pastrami pizza, mini pastrami sandwiches and Dario's famous olive oil cake that he makes for his Ristorante Solo Ciccia, were all on the menu.

He was so touched by this special event that before the evening was over he stood up on one of the tables and recited Dante's *Inferno*.

Everyone cheered as he ended with tears of emotion. He added a few words in English "thank you Mama Judy and thank you Papa Marvino. We were overwhelmed.

Dario and Kim Get Married in Panzano

When we arrived in Panzano, two days before the marriage of Dario and Kim, Dario took us aside and asked if we would take the place of his *mama* & *babbo* at the ceremony. With their early passing, he felt that we were the closest to parents he had. We were flattered by his request, and of course agreed.

The wedding was to take place in a park-like meadow. If it rained, it would instead be at the butcher shop.

Dario and Kim would furnish the wines and bread. Guests were asked to bring a potluck dish. One friend had an oversized pan on the fire with a lovely *paella*. At the last minute, we made an American potato salad.

With almost everyone assembled in the park at noon, and a tarp covering the food, it began to rain. Soon the guests crowded under umbrellas as it poured.

We all waited for the rain to stop. When that didn't happen, Dario phoned Kim, who was still in Panzano, dictated a change of plans and everyone happily hightailed it back to the butcher shop.

Dario was proudly dressed in red and white and Kim was glowing in a satin wedding gown. Her mother, father, Marvino and myself all walked up the stairs into a room above the butcher shop and stepped out on to a Romeo-and-Juliet-style balcony. Crowds of applauding guests gathered below to watch.

Marvino welcomed everyone in both English and Italian, and spoke to Dario and Kim. We had a wine glass wrapped in a red napkin. Marvino explained to the crowd that Dario was about to partake in the Jewish wedding tradition of breaking a glass. He spoke of how each piece of broken glass would bring a year of health, happiness and symbolize

Dario and Kim during a playful moment at the pastrami festival at the Broadway Deli in Santa Monica, California.

Top left, clockwise: The wedding ceremony; Dario and Kim's unique 3-tiered wedding cake consisted of custard-filled crepes; Igor's Klezmatic Florentine Group entertained guests. Below: Chef and caterer, Jeff Thickman, baked a special wedding cake just for the bride and groom!

long life. He asked Dario if he was ready—and with one big stomp, the glass was broken into small chards! Dario sprinkled the glass chards below the balcony and onto the street below. He wished a long life to everyone. The guests shouted "*Mazel Tov*," and applauded with joy!!!

To add to the festivities Marvino introduced the music group, Klezmatica Fiorentina that we invited from Florence to help celebrate Dario and Kim's wedding.

When we walked to the butcher shop the next morning, we excitedly read about the event and were delighted to read and view the photos that we discovered in the 3 local newspapers that had given this "celebrity" wedding a large amount of coverage.

Dario's Meat Loaf Rounds with Red Pepper Jelly
(Polpettone con Mostarda)

Dario's butcher shop in Panzano is like no other shop in the world. Larger-than-life meatballs fill an extra-large baking sheet garnished with parsley.

Polpettone is delicious eaten cold as a lunchmeat. In Italy, it is often served with what they call *mostarda*, which translates literally as "mustard" but is not mustard as most of the world understands it. A good substitute for Italian *mostarda* is a red pepper jelly.

2 pounds ground beef
1 small red onion, finely chopped
1 egg
2 garlic cloves, finely minced
1 teaspoon thyme leaves (or dried thyme)
Salt and freshly ground black pepper, to taste
6 ounces fresh bread, ground up into crumbs (or store-bought)
Red Pepper Jelly (recipe follows)

Serves 6 to 8

The best cut of beef is from the shin, also known as the shank. The meat is very lean, with an intense flavor.

In a large bowl, mix the beef, onion, egg, garlic, thyme, salt and pepper. Shape into one very large meatball, then roll in bread crumbs.

Cook in a deep roasting pan at 425°F for 15 minutes. Then lower the heat to 375°F and cook for one hour. Serve hot or cold.

Dario's Red Pepper Jelly
(Mostarda)

Enter Dario's butcher shop and you are immediately offered a glass of wine, a slice of roasted meat (which Dario prepares fresh every night), and a plate filled with Pecorino cheese and his famous Red Pepper Jelly. The jelly also makes an interesting accent for cold meats, poultry, cream cheese or goat cheese.

1-1/2 pounds sweet red peppers (about 4 large)
1 cup apple cider vinegar
1 teaspoon salt
1 teaspoon chili powder or 1 small red chili
Pinch crushed chili
5 cups sugar
1/3 cup fresh lemon juice
6 ounces liquid pectin

Makes about 6 to 8 (8-ounce) jars

Wash and cut up peppers, discarding seeds and stems. Place pieces, a few at a time, in food processor and chop fine. In a large pot, combine chopped peppers, vinegar, salt, chili powder or chili and crushed chili. Bring to a boil, reduce heat and simmer for 10 minutes. Add sugar and lemon juice, mixing until sugar dissolves. Bring to a boil. Stir in pectin and bring to a boil, stirring constantly, for exactly 1 minute. Remove from heat and skim off foam with metal spoon.

Ladle into hot, sterilized jars and seal immediately.

Dario's Carpaccio and Arugula Salad
(Carpaccio con Rucola)

In this salad from the master butcher of Panzano, slices of rare steak are fanned out in a circle on the plate and drizzled with olive oil. The arugula and radicchio are tossed with vinaigrette and mounded in the center, topped with shavings of imported Parmesan. A simple, attractive, and satisfying dish.

Serves 2

4 ounces rare cooked rib steak, thinly sliced

4 ounces arugula and radicchio, mixed

1 tablespoon olive oil

1 teaspoon balsamic vinegar

Arrange the steak slices in a circle around the outside of the plate. Drizzle olive oil on top. Toss arugula and radicchio with olive oil and vinegar and mound in the center.

Dario's Tuna of Chianti
(Tonno del Chianti)

After Dario's visit to our home in Los Angeles, he was invited to the 30th anniversary party of Chez Panisse, in Berkley, California, where he recited Danté and served his famous *Tonno del Chianti* – which in its final presentation, resembles a tuna fish, although it has no actual relation to seafood! This is also a refreshing dish for summer if served cold.

Serves 8

2-1/4 pounds lean boneless veal shoulder, trimmed of fat

2 teaspoons coarse salt (kosher)

1 tablespoon black peppercorns, crushed

2 bay leaves, crushed to a powder

1/2 teaspoons crushed fennel seeds

2 sprigs thyme

2 cups olive oil

1 small head garlic, cut in half

1 small red onion, thinly sliced

2 tablespoons red wine vinegar

Toasted sliced baguette (bread)

Cut meat into 2-inch chunks. In a small bowl, stir together salt, peppercorns, bay leaves, fennel and thyme. In a large, plastic sealable bag place meat and salt mixture. Squeeze out all the air, seal tightly and refrigerate for 6 hours or overnight.

Do not drain meat; place pieces into a medium ceramic or enameled cast-iron casserole in a single layer. Pour on olive oil to cover completely. Cover with a sheet of crumpled parchment and a lid, and set over very low heat and cook until the oil comes to a boil, 30 to 40 minutes.

Preheat the oven to 250°F.

Add garlic, transfer the pan to the oven and cook for 2-1/2 hours. The oil should bubble gently; the meat should not brown. To test, remove one piece and tap it lightly, it should break (almost fall apart) into smaller chunks and be a soft pink color. Remove from the oven and let stand until completely cool. Refrigerate up to 5 days, being sure the veal is completely covered in oil; add additional oil if necessary.

Before serving, reheat the veal slowly. Soak onion slices in 1 tablespoon vinegar for 30 minutes. Drain veal in a colander set over a bowl to catch the juices; discard garlic and thyme. Set bowl of juices aside to settle and break up the veal cubes roughly with a fork. When juices have settled, reserve 1/2 cup and use the remaining olive oil for cooking.

Stir the meat juices into the meat along with enough of the reserved olive oil to make the shreds shiny and slightly sticky. Taste and add seasoning to taste. Spoon meat mixture onto the warm toasted bread and top with a little pickled onion.

Dario's Rosemary Scented Veal Roast
(Vitello Profumato al Rosmarino)

This succulent roast is an adaptation of a recipe from our "Italian son," Dario Cecchini, the famous butcher of Panzano. Dario uses veal or beef, I find that veal is more convenient for the home cook.

Serves 6 to 8

1 cup olive oil, divided
1 (3 to 4) pound boneless veal
shoulder roast (or beef)
1 tablespoon coarse
    kosher salt
1 tablespoon dried rosemary
1/2 teaspoon ground
    black pepper
2 pounds shallots, thinly sliced
1-1/2 cups thinly sliced fresh
    fennel (from 3 large bulbs)
1 (500-ml) bottle Vin Santo

Preheat the oven to 375°F.

Rub 2 tablespoons olive oil over roast. In a small bowl, mix salt, rosemary and pepper, and rub over the roast. In a large, heavy pot, heat 2 tablespoons olive oil, add veal and cook until golden brown on all sides, about 5 minutes. Transfer veal to a plate.

Add remaining olive oil, shallots and fennel to same pot. Sauté until vegetables are golden brown, stirring frequently and scraping up browned bits, about 10 minutes. Add Vin Santo, boil 3 minutes. Return veal to pot, on top of vegetables, and top with some of the vegetables. Cover and roast until instant-read thermometer inserted into center of veal registers 165°F, about 1-1/2 hours.

Transfer meat to a platter. Season cooking liquid with salt and pepper to taste. Spoon vegetables and cooking liquid around roast. Slice and serve.

Dario's Marrow-Braised Beef
(Brasato)

Here is another recipe from the master butcher of Panzano, Dario Cecchini. Have your butcher remove the bone from the beef, cut the bone in half lengthwise, trim excess fat and remove blood vessels and ligaments from the meat. It's helpful also to have the butcher flatten the meat slightly with a mallet to make it easier to roll. From the split bone, you can easily scoop out the marrow from each side with a small metal spatula.

Serves 8

5 pounds beef shank (about
    5 pounds including bone)
Marrow from shank
Sea salt and freshly ground
    black pepper
1 teaspoon chopped
    fresh rosemary
2 tablespoons olive oil
2 pounds shallots, peeled
1 cup beef or vegetable stock
1/2 cup Vin Santo

Preheat the oven to 350°F. Season both sides of beef with 2 teaspoons salt and 1/2 teaspoon pepper. On cutting board, lay open the boned meat with the fat side down. Place marrow in the center of the opened meat, along the same direction as the grain. Sprinkle one-quarter teaspoon salt, and pepper and rosemary over the marrow. Roll meat tightly, enclosing marrow, and tie meat with butcher string.

In large ovenproof casserole, heat 2 tablespoons oil over medium high heat until nearly smoking. Sear tied beef on all sides until well-browned, about 12 minutes.

Remove beef from pan and set aside. Add peeled shallots to pan and cook over medium heat until they begin to turn gold brown, about 5 minutes. Increase heat to high and stir in beef stock to deglaze pan, scraping up any brown bits at the bottom of the pan.

Return the beef to the pan, cover and cook for 1-1/2 hours. Add Vin Santo and cook for another 1-1/2 hours. Baste meat a few times during cooking. Remove beef and allow to rest for 10 minutes. Cut strings, slice across grain and spoon the shallots and sauce over it.

Dario's Florentine Roast Beef
(*Arrosto Fiorentino*)

The herbal infusion used by Dario Cecchini, the great Panzano butcher, adds luscious depth of flavor to a simple roast beef.

Serves 4 to 6

2 pounds beef for roasting

Allow the meat to come to room temperature.
   Preheat the oven to 450°F.
   Prepare the herb infusion (recipe below).
   Place the beef in a shallow roasting pan and roast uncovered for 35 minutes. Remove from the oven and pour the herb infusion over the beef, cover with foil and let sit until ready to serve. Serve thin slices with the herb-infused oil.

Herb Infusion

1/2 cup fresh rosemary, finely chopped
1 cup fresh sage leaves, finely chopped
Pinch of fresh chili pepper
Salt, to taste
Freshly ground black pepper, to taste
1/2 cup olive oil

In a medium bowl, combine the rosemary, sage, chili, salt and pepper. Add olive oil to cover and whisk to blend.

Dario's Florentine Steak
(Bistecca Fiorentina)

The first time we discovered this delicious grilled beefsteak was in Florence, at a restaurant near the *Ponte Vecchio*. When a diner ordered the steak, the chef shuffled hot coals under a grate, cut the meat and began to cook it. Traditionally the meat comes from the Maremmana or Chianinia oxen. Though it is usually prepared on an open grill or barbecue, this indoor method works well for those who don't have year-round access to one of these. The cooked steak is often topped with olive oil. Serve with roasted potatoes.

Serves 3 to 4

1 (2-1/2 to 3 pound) rib steak
3 tablespoons olive oil
1-1/2 tablespoons kosher salt
2 teaspoons coarsely ground
   black pepper
2 to 3 large onions, cut into
   1-inch chunks

Brush steak with olive oil, sprinkle well with salt and pepper, and let rest, uncovered, at room temperature for 30 minutes. Position one oven rack in the top third of the oven, a second rack in the bottom of the oven and heat to 500°F (not on broil)

Fill a 13x9-inch baking dish with enough onions to completely cover the bottom. Place the baking dish on the lower rack. Place the steak directly on the top rack, positioned above the dish of onions. Use tongs to turn the steak after 15 minutes, and check occasionally to make sure it is not burning. For medium rare, roast until the internal temperature registers 125°F, about 35 to 40 minutes.

Place steak on a cutting board to rest for 5 minutes before serving. To serve, brush steak with olive oil, place on a bed of arugula and serve onions on the side.

Dario's Olive Oil Cake at Solo Ciccia
(Solo Ciccia Torta All'Olio)

Solo Ciccia (Only Meat) is the name of Dario's *Ristorante*, and when he opened it this was the dessert that he served. I have a photo of him holding up a 30-inch round cake still in the pan. Everyone went for seconds. Simonetta works with Dario and makes this cake every day. In sharing this recipe she said the last ingredient is "love for what you are doing." I have adapted this recipe to make a large round cake, but not the size of Dario's.

Makes 1 large round cake

1/4 cup ground almonds
5 eggs
2 cups sugar
2 oranges, finely chopped
   (pulp and peel)
1/2 cup olive oil,
   plus 2 tablespoons for top
4 cups flour
2 teaspoons baking powder
1/2 cup raisins, plumped in
   Vin Santo to cover (and
   slightly drained)
Sugar for garnish
1/2 cup toasted pine nuts

Preheat the oven to 375°F.

Brush a 10- or 12-inch springform pan with olive oil and dust with ground almonds.

In the bowl of an electric mixer, beat the eggs with the sugar. Add orange peel and pulp and mix well. Slowly add the olive oil alternating with the flour and baking powder and mix until smooth.

Let rest for 10 minutes, stirring from time to time. The oil is light, but tends to separate from the batter; mix well.

Stir in raisins, spoon batter into the prepared pan. Dust with sugar, drizzle with olive oil and pine nuts. Bake for 35 to 40 minutes or until a toothpick inserted in the center comes out clean.

PANZANO
Teo Loeffler and Brigette Brodbec
Tuscany by Way of Germany

From their home in Stuttgart, Germany, Teo Loeffler and Brigette Brodbec used to make annual pilgrimages to Panzano to dine in their favorite restaurant, where they would linger over lunch on the patio enjoying a view of the rolling hills below. One year they arrived to find the place closed and learned from the owner that he planned to sell the business. Devastated at the thought of losing their cherished eating place, they bought it on the spot. Since they owned a kitchen supply store in Stuttgart, they were in no position to maintain the restaurant as a business, so they made it their holiday home, and many years later it became their permanent home.

Teo, a robust man with a broad, mustachioed face, installed a modern kitchen, stainless steel from ceiling to floor, that would rival that of a first-class restaurant. A passionate cook, he began preparing meals for friends that were as creative and delicious as those of a three-star chef. His kitchen, he told us, cost him as much as a Ferrari, due to the expense of transporting all the equipment from Germany. But the pleasure he takes in cooking there clearly makes his outlay worthwhile.

We met Teo and Brigette at Dario Cecchini's butcher shop, and our friendship with them has developed through many visits and even more dinners. One of these dinners celebrated Teo's 65th birthday. Teo insisted on catering his own party, that was attended by at least 100 guests from all over Europe and America.

Dinners with Teo are often surprising and occasionally problematic. I remember one large potluck dinner we arranged in our rented home at *La Rota*. For the occasion, we rounded up plates, glassware and silver from all the neighboring apartments and borrowed the villa next door for the meal, since it offered a larger dining space.

Teo brought a salad of fresh fava beans and fish that had taken hours to prepare. The dining room was at the bottom of a flight of stairs, and just as he reached the bottom step he tripped, spilling the entire salad on the floor. Devastated as he was, he taught us a great lesson about recovery, picking up all of the chunks of fish, washing, seasoning and serving them up with aplomb. During the rest of the evening Teo and Brigitte kept reenacting the disaster, which amused us all and provided me with the perfect title for the recipe: "Fish Salad Tossed Down the Stairs."

I made notes on all the dinners Teo prepared for us, and I have especially fond memories of a *paella* he prepared one night for 20 friends, placing in the middle of the table a steaming three-foot-wide pan that emitted tantalizing smells of saffron, rice, sausages and chicken. At another dinner he served a memorable chopped herring salad made from ingredients he had brought with him on his drive from Germany; the meal's *antipasti* included a homemade liver *pâté* and *foccacia* topped with tomatoes, mozzarella and basil.

Dinners with Teo often involved bizarre situations. Brigitte, who ran the kitchen supply business, needed to spend considerable time in Stuttgart, so Teo was often alone in Panzano. One evening, while she was in Germany, we invited Sammie Daniels and Teo to our Panzano rental, for dinner. As the dinner hour approached it began to rain. We looked out the window and saw Teo walking through our garden in a downpour, carrying an over-sized black umbrella.

Some minutes later, when he finally knocked on our door, he was holding a bag in one hand and a large box under his arm. The bag contained a bottle of his homemade unfiltered olive oil, which he claimed is the best in Italy, and several rounds of fresh local goat cheese. In the box was a shivering, water-soaked wild rabbit. Teo had spotted it in the swimming pool, scooped it out of the water with his umbrella, and put it into the box to dry.

I suggested we use a hair dryer to dry the creature, and I held the dryer while Teo cradled the terrified animal. We were successful in saving its life, and we lined the box with a large towel on which the rabbit rested in our living room as we ate dinner.

Marvino suggested several times during the evening that we might cook the rabbit for dinner, at which Teo became furious—until he realized that Marvino was joking.

After dinner, as Teo was preparing to head home, he suggested we leave the rabbit inside our house overnight. We thought better of that idea and placed the box outside the door.

The next morning, the rabbit was gone. For the rest of our stay in Panzano, we were certain that every wild hare we saw near our house was the one Teo had rescued.

Top and Center: Enjoying an evening together with friends. On this particular evening, Dario Cecchini joined us.
Above: Teo loved to spend time in Dario's butcher shop, Antica Macelleria Cecchini, in Panzano.

Teo's Porcini Pâté on Toast
(*Crostini di Porcini*)

Teo combines dried porcini and fresh mushrooms with garlic, a touch of tomato paste and white wine to produce a fragrant spread that is the essence of mushrooms' musky meatiness. Satisfying as a first course or as an accompaniment for a simple vegetable soup or green salad.

Serves 8 to 10

1/3 cup dried porcini (soaked in warm water to cover)
2 tablespoons olive oil
1 pound fresh porcini mushrooms, thinly sliced*
2 garlic cloves, minced
2 teaspoons tomato paste
1/4 cup dry white wine
Parsley leaves, minced
Salt
Freshly ground black pepper
8 thick slices Tuscan bread, cut into thirds and toasted

Drain the dried porcini and chop, reserving the liquid.

In a large skillet, heat olive oil. Add mushrooms and garlic and sauté over moderately high heat until soft, about 10 to 15 minutes. Meanwhile, in a small bowl, dilute tomato paste with wine and the reserved porcini liquid and stir in 1/4 cup water. Stir wine mixture into mushrooms and cook until absorbed, about 3 minutes. Add parsley, salt and pepper to taste. To serve, spoon mushrooms onto toast and serve.

* If fresh porcini are not available, use Portobello, Cremini or white button mushrooms instead.

Teo's Chicken Liver Pâté
(*Crostini di Fegatini di Pollo*)

Teo always serves this chicken liver *pâté* to us while still warm. He uses fresh chicken livers that are sautéed, finely chopped, and served on toasted bread.

Serves 8 to 10

3 tablespoons olive oil
1 small onion, finely chopped
1 pound chicken livers
Salt
Freshly ground black pepper
2 garlic cloves, minced
Zest of 1 lemon
2 teaspoons minced fresh sage leaves
1 tablespoon capers, drained
1 teaspoon fresh lemon juice
8 thin slices of crusty white or brown bread, toasted
3 tablespoons minced parsley

(Serve with red pepper jelly, see recipe page 130)

In a large heavy skillet, heat olive oil and sauté the onion until soft, about 5 minutes. Sprinkle the chicken livers with salt and pepper and add to the onion. Add the garlic and sauté, browning the livers on both sides.

In a wooden chopping bowl or on a board, chop the lemon zest and sage together. Spoon the warm chicken liver mixture and the capers on top of the sage and lemon mixture and continue to chop until well blended. Mix in the lemon juice and season with salt and pepper, to taste. Transfer to a bowl or a crock, serve immediately, or cover with plastic wrap, and refrigerate until ready to serve. To serve, spoon on toast and sprinkle with parsley. Or line a small bowl with plastic wrap, spoon in the *pâté*, cover and unmold when ready to serve.

Teo's Chopped Herring, German Style
(Aringa Tagliata)

The secret ingredient in Teo Loeffler's treat for herring lovers is the green apple, which modulates the intense taste of the herring. The traditional chopped egg makes an attractive garnish.

Serves 8 to 10

1 pound jar pickled herring
    fillets in wine sauce
2 slices white bread
1 medium onion, cut
    into quarters
1 green apple, peeled, cored,
    and sliced
2 hard-boiled eggs
4 teaspoons vinegar
2 or 3 tablespoons safflower
    or vegetable oil
1/2 loaf thinly sliced
    corn rye bread

Soak the herring in cold water overnight. Drain well. If necessary, debone and skin the herring. Cut into pieces. Soak the bread in cold water for a few minutes and squeeze out the water.

Place the herring, bread, onion, and apple in a food grinder and grind. Chop the hard-boiled egg whites and combine with 3 teaspoons of the vinegar. Mix the whites into the herring mixture. Spread the chopped herring on a platter. Mash the egg yolks with the remaining 1 teaspoon vinegar and spread over the top of the chopped herring. Cover with plastic wrap and chill. Just before serving, pour 2 or 3 tablespoons of the oil over the top. Serve with thinly sliced corn rye bread.

Tuscan Porcini Soup
(Crema di Porcini alla Toscana)

For another special dinner Teo, delighted with the fresh porcini mushrooms he had found in the market, was inspired to create this delicious soup. Although porcini mushrooms work best, other varieties of fresh mushrooms work well, especially with the addition of dried porcini.

Serves 6 to 8

1/2 cup olive oil
1 small onion, minced
1 medium stalk celery, diced
1/4 cup minced parsley
12 ounces porcini mushrooms
    (or other mushrooms such
    as portobello or shiitake)
    cleaned and thinly sliced
4 ounces dried porcini
    mushrooms, soaked in warm
    water to cover and drained*
1 cup dry white wine
4 small ripe tomatoes, peeled,
    seeded and sliced
1-1/2 quarts chicken or
    vegetable broth
Salt
Freshly ground black pepper
6-8 thick slices crusty bread

In a skillet, heat 1/4 cup olive oil. Add onion, celery and parsley and sauté until onion is lightly browned. Add the fresh mushrooms and the drained dried porcini, and sauté for 3 to 4 minutes, stirring often with a wooden spoon. Add the wine and allow it to evaporate completely.

Add the tomatoes, the hot broth and the liquid from the dried mushrooms; add salt and pepper to taste. Cook over medium heat, covered, for 20 minutes.

Place bread in separate serving bowls, add the soup and drizzle with remaining 1/4 cup olive oil. Serve hot.

* Carefully drain the dried mushrooms; reserve the liquid, but discard the dirt particles that accumulate at the bottom.

GAIOLE IN CHIANTI
Lorenza Sebasti
Castello di Ama Winery

The first time we met Lorenza Sebasti she was very young and had just taken over management of the winery Castello di Ama in the province of Siena. A dynamic dark-haired woman, she was obviously destined to go far in whatever business she chose. Her knowledge of the wine industry was incredible for such a young person, and her outgoing personality and mastery of the English language were also important assets.

Castella di Ama is a small *borgo* (hamlet) containing a group of farmers' cottages and the original villa and chapel that were built on the property. Walking through the *borgo* is like walking in a small village, surrounded by vineyards and olive groves.

A few years after we met Lorenza she married the winemaker, Marco Pallante, and they now have three children.

For many years Lorenza and Marco have been collecting significant contemporary works by artists from all over the world. They own pieces by Kendell Geers, Giulio Paolini, and Anish Kapoor, one of the most influential sculptors working today. What a treat it is to take a tour of their collection, which is displayed all over their extensive grounds.

As you walk down the stairs to their wine cellar you become aware of yet another extraordinary art work, this one by Michelangelo Pistoletto: the trunk of a tree that appears to have been sliced in half, with a metallic piece that incorporates shards of mirror inserted between the two segments. The drama continues at the bottom of the stairway, where there are aging barrels in rows, with a five-foot neon sign by artist Kendell Geers behind them that reads "Revolution"(in reverse)–which, in this context, is a good description of their wines.

We were fortunate to be included in many of Lorenza's fabulous wine tasting parties. One occasion was a birthday celebration for a well-known winemaker friend of hers. Another was an invitation to Castello di Ama for a 10-year vertical tasting of Lorenza and Marco's Chianti wines. I also remember with special pleasure a garden party they gave for 100 people to celebrate the installation of a stunning new contemporary sculpture.

During one of the garden parties on this art-rich estate we met Lorenza's godmother, whom she considers part of her family. As usual, the garden was filled with guests, and we were drinking champagne as appetizers were being passed. All of a sudden, Lorenza

Top: A visit to Lorenza and Marco's with Nadia and Antonio Santini, of dal Pescatore. Left: No...it's not backwards! It's the way artist Kendall Geers intended this fabulous work of art for Castello di Ama.

beckoned the two of us to follow her down the road past the winery, where we stopped in front of a small house. She gently knocked on the door, which was opened by a sweet looking woman who ushered us into the kitchen where she was preparing a frittata for her husband's lunch. To our amazement, she insisted on our sharing the delicate and tasty frittata. Of course I asked for the recipe, which she gladly gave me. As we returned to the party with Lorenza we considered ourselves fortunate to have experienced yet another instance of Italy's extraordinary hospitality. And no one seemed the wiser about our little detour.

At another of Lorenza's parties at the winery, Chef Claude Sadler of Milan catered a lunch at which the first course was a delicious tuna *tartare* topped with minced fresh vegetables—as pleasing to the eye as to the palate. Raw fish is becoming deservedly popular in restaurants in Italy. Not only is it nutritious, it also has a distinctive flavor and texture. But it must be prepared fresh on the day of serving.

**WHEN YOU GO,
YOU SHOULD KNOW:**

Castello di Ama
Lorenza Sebasti
Località Ama
53013 Gaiole in Chianti
(SI) - Italy
Telephone: 0039 0577 746031
Fax: 0039 0577 746117
Email: info@castellodiama.com
website: www.castellodiama.com

Godmother's Paper-Thin Omelette
(*Frittata Sottilissima*)

During a party at Lorenza Sebasti's Castello di Ama winery, she spirited us away and escorted us down the road to the home of her godmother, whom we caught preparing an afternoon snack of frittata for her husband. She insisted we partake of the frittata and shared her recipe with me.

Because we always have eggs in the refrigerator and sage growing in our garden, this recipe is a perfect last-minute appetizer or supper to share with friends who stop by unexpectedly. My red onion marmalade makes a nice accompaniment.

2 eggs, lightly beaten
1/4 cup minced fresh sage
  (or 2 teaspoons dried)
Salt
Freshly ground black pepper
2 tablespoons unsalted butter
Red onion marmalade
  (see recipe page 52)

Serves 4

In a medium bowl, beat the eggs and 2 tablespoons of the sage, salt, and pepper, to taste. Blend well. In a 10 or 12-inch non-stick skillet heat the butter over low heat. Pour the egg mixture into the skillet distributing it evenly. Cook, uncovered, at medium-high heat, until firm, about 3 minutes, lifting the outer edge with a spatula to loosen as it cooks. Carefully transfer the frittata to a large platter and cut into pie-shaped wedges. Sprinkle with the remaining sage and serve immediately. Serve with Red Onion Marmalade.

Above: Lorenza and her godmother
shared a frittata during one of our visits.

CERBAIA
Old-Fashioned Elegance
La Tenda Rossa Ristorante

La Tenda Rossa is on the edge of a small *piazza* in the village of Cerbaia. You must ring a bell to enter the restaurant, as in the old speakeasies. A member of the family is there to welcome you and asks if you have a reservation. Italians are formal people, and if you haven't reserved a table, even when the restaurant is not fully booked, they may not seat you. We often joke about the possibility of using a nearby phone booth or a cell phone to call for a reservation if they turn us away.

For the past 30 years, this two-star Michelin restaurant has been owned and operated by two families that came together when Silvano Santandrea met and fell in love with Maria Salcuni. All family members work in the restaurant—either in the kitchen or in the front of the house. The early-60s decor is too formal for this little village, but we love the restaurant, the family, the food and the personal service.

On our first visit, we met Michele Salcuni, Maria's soft-spoken bespectacled brother. He is in charge of the wine and also runs the front of the restaurant when Maria's husband, Silvano, is away. Before we selected our lunch from the menu, we looked at the wine list and discussed our selection with Michele, who told us about his experience making homemade wine. We had a wonderful meal. The atmosphere here is formal, the food creative and fresh. We dined on *ravioloni* covered with squash blossoms and sliced pigeon and livers with a wonderful sauce. For dessert we ate a chocolate cupcake soufflé and a meringue with chocolate *mousse*. Before we left, he presented us with a bottle of his own wine to take home. Later we discovered he had left the restaurant between serving our main course and our dessert to go home and get it for us. On our next visit, we met Silvano, who is usually in charge. An elegant, gray-haired gentleman in a perfectly cut gray suit and semi-tinted rimless glasses, he managed to convey to us—without speaking a word of English—that the three women chefs in the kitchen were his wife, Maria, and her sisters: Fernanda and Paola Freschi. He explained that Paola and Toni Salcuni take care of the vegetable garden; while their daughters, Barbara, Cristiana and Natascia, are servers—as professional as those in the most demanding of establishments.

We like La Tenda Rossa so much, that for special occasions it is our first choice. When we arrive, we always peek into the kitchen and are greeted by members of the families. We return as often as we can, each time bringing locals or friends who may be visiting from the States.

Our most memorable evening there was with friends from Los Angeles. I doubt

Top: A memorable evening at La Tenda Rossa. Left: Silvano pours champagne for a toast.

**WHEN YOU GO,
YOU SHOULD KNOW:**

La Tenda Rossa Ristorante
Piazza del Monumento
Cerbaia in Val di Pesa (FI), Italy
Tel: (055) 826132
Fax: (055) 825210
email: ristorante@latendarossa.it
website: www.latendarossa.it

if anything like it has happened in the restaurant before or will ever happen again.

We were welcomed by Silvano, who escorted us to our table. We ordered wine and water, and he made some suggestions. Each of us chose a different first course. All of the beginning dishes were delicious.

Then the main courses arrived. I was surprised to find the meat not to my personal taste. I decided not to eat this course since I had already enjoyed so much wonderful food.

As she was clearing our main course dishes, our server, Barbara, remarked that I had not eaten my steaks. When she asked about it, I reluctantly explained it was because of personal preference. But, I added that everything else had been perfect, and I told her not to worry. A lovely selection of desserts followed.

During coffee, Silvano pulled a chair up to our table and announced that the kitchen was sorry that not everything was perfect. We repeated that everything was fine and urged him not to be concerned. When we asked for the check, he said there would not be one. Marvino was shocked and said it was not possible. He told Silvano that we would not leave until he presented us with a check. Silvano's smiling response was to offer to set up beds in the restaurant for us. We argued to no avail; he simply would not allow us to pay. He then requested that before leaving we stop for a moment in the reception area.

As we were departing, to our amazement, all the chefs in the kitchen were assembled, each holding a champagne glass. Then Silvano came into the room carrying a magnum of champagne. The entire family toasted us and again apologized. Their pride and genuine concern were unmistakable. Never had we experienced such a concerned staff at any restaurant. We all toasted each other, drank the champagne, hugged and kissed. When we left we were still in shock–loving this Italian family more than ever.

Cold Pepper Soup
(*Zuppa Fredda di Peperoni*)

This delicious cold soup, perfect for warm weather, was inspired by one of the many creative dishes we've eaten at La Tenda Rossa.

Serves 6

3 tablespoons olive oil
3 tablespoons unsalted butter
5 large red bell peppers, chopped
1 onion, minced
3 stalks of celery, chopped
1-1/2 quarts vegetable broth
Salt to taste
Cayenne pepper to taste
3 tablespoons fresh lemon juice
Italian parsley sprigs for garnish

In a saucepan heat oil and butter over low heat. Add peppers, onion and celery, and cook, stirring occasionally, until onion is soft but not browned. Add broth and season with salt and cayenne. Bring to a boil, cover, reduce heat and simmer for 20 minutes.

Strain broth into a bowl. Place the vegetables in a food processor or blender with a little broth and purée. Return to the remaining broth. Add additional salt and pepper to taste. Chill until ready to serve, then stir in lemon juice and garnish with parsley.

VAL DI ARNO
Bettina and Wolf Rogosky
Two Passionate People Achieve Their Lives' Dreams

The first time we met Wolf Rogosky was at Ristorante Cibreo in Florence. An American friend, Faith Willinger, called to tell us about the results of a wine tasting she had just attended. Sassicaia and Ornalaia—at that time the best and most expensive wines in Italy—had come in second and third after a wine called Caberlot, made by someone she insisted we meet.

When we arrived for lunch at Cibreo, our friend was sitting at a corner table near the window with a bespectacled man who sported a carefully trimmed salt-and-pepper beard and a friendly smile. This was Wolf Rogosky, who was there with his son Philip. When he stood up to greet us his handshake was so strong it almost hurt.

During lunch he poured his wine, Caberlot, and we later learned that he makes only 100 cases of it a year and bottles it only in magnums. The Caberlot was full bodied, with lots of fruit. Wolf seemed to relish our enthusiasm for his wine, and every time my glass was empty–which was often–he refilled it.

He explained that it was a clone of two varietals, Cabernet Sauvignon and Merlot, from which the name Caberlot derived, and that he was responsible for developing the clone used to make this unique wine. Before we finished lunch he invited us to pick

grapes at his vineyard the following week and help with the crush. After the *vendemia*, he said, we would all go to a local restaurant for lunch.

Originally from Germany, Wolf and Bettina also lived in Paris, worked in New York and came to own the Podere il Carnasciale Winery in Chianti. Wolf was a graphic designer whose dream was to own a vineyard in Italy and make the best wine possible.

We arrived at noon at Wolf's house, which is in the village of Mercatile, and he introduced us to his wife, Bettina, who explained that she had decided, at 4:00 that morning, that she would personally prepare lunch for all of us at their home. She had gotten up very early to call her purveyors and order everything she needed for her menu. It was evident during that first lunch, that her culinary talents were extraordinary.

But before sitting down to Bettina's feast, we had work to do. The clusters of grapes we picked were hand-forced through wooden slats into a large open barrel. When Wolf asked who wanted to get into the barrel and crush the grapes barefoot, I shyly accepted the invitation. Three of us, two young Englishwomen and I, took off our shoes and socks and rolled up our jeans. After Wolf made sure we had all washed our feet, we climbed into the barrel and proceeded to stomp in circles. It was great fun. Later on, Wolf always

remembered that this was the wine I had helped crush, and whenever we visited he gave me a bottle of it to take home. Any time we were in the area, Wolf and Bettina would always invite us for a country meal, which we often ate in the garden, tasting the current vintage and enjoying the Tuscan landscape.

On one visit we made plans to meet at Ristorante Vicolo del Contento, near their home. Wolf and Bettina were friends of the owners, and our party–which included Wolf and Bettina's son, Phillip, and his *fiancée*, Sara–sat in the center of the room near the bar. The chef prepared a special lunch for us, and Wolf brought a magnum of 1993 Caberlot, the wine I had stomped. The menu was exceptional: we began with fried seafood in a picante broth. Wolf ordered salmon, which was very moist, served with green mayonnaise and a green salad. Next came a hard-wheat pasta called *Strozzapreti* (Priest-Stranglers) with fried seafood. A second pasta course was *tagliatelli* with tomatoes and seafood, and a third was *tortelli* with vegetables served with fried onions. For dessert Bettina had brought along chocolate champagne truffles from France, and gave us a box to take home.

On one occasion when we were invited to lunch, Bettina and Wolf had also invited Burton Anderson, a well-known food and wine critic. We sat in the garden, and Bettina prepared each course and carefully carried the food over the rocky walkway from the house.

Wolf helped her, and proudly served a *focaccia* that he had made topped with whole sliced tomatoes, onions and rosemary. It wasn't hard to tell that this bread was prepared by a graphic designer, because the topping formed a perfect geometric design. Of course I asked for the recipe, and we often serve it to friends.

Our last visit with Bettina and Wolf was lunch at La Rendola, a restaurant near their house, where Chef Francesco prepared a delicious meal for us. Marvino and I were due to leave in a few days for Los Angeles, where I was to have shoulder surgery. Wolf gave me a big hug and said they would be at Lorenzo's restaurant in Forte di Marmi on the day of my operation and he would raise a glass of sparkling wine and think of me.

A week after my surgery, we received a call from Bettina telling us that Wolf had passed away. We were in shock at the loss of our wonderful friend, whom we miss terribly. Bettina continues to make Caberlot in the same manner and style as Wolf, and the wine has received recognition as one of the top wines of Italy. After her winery received 20 out of 20 points from Guida L'Espresso (and she was the only woman ever to have received this top rating), the local press in Tuscany dubbed her *La regina del vino* (queen of Italian wine).

We still visit Bettina often and reminisce about our times with her and Wolf while enjoying her delicious food. Now a grandmother, she is as gracious and charming as ever.

During one of our visits, Bettina served champagne and *focaccia*, and we all sat in the kitchen at a big round table. Behind us was a stunning sculpture of 12 hanging chickens made of canvas, each painted in a distinctive way. I loved this clever sculpture, and hope

Lunch with Bettina is always memorable. She often serves on the patio, overlooking the Chianti hills. Just below, she poses with Marvino.

one day to meet the Swiss artist who created it and commission a similar piece for our home.

As we watched, Bettina prepared a *risotto* with chopped fresh rosemary, explaining that she had begun the dish a little in advance so it would not take the usual 20 minutes. *Bistecca Fiorentina* was grilled on the open fire and served with fresh *fagioli* and fried potatoes. For dessert Bettina had prepared a chocolate *mousse*, one of the most delicious I have eaten. I coaxed her into sharing her recipe, and I love making it because it reminds me of our special friend. I also use it as one of the fillings for my homemade chocolates.

We had a great time and, as we were leaving, I took a photo of Bettina standing in the doorway of her house, with her lovely smile and easy, graceful stance. It captured her as the elegant European lady she is.

As always, we promised to write often and visit again as soon as possible. We are still trying—as of yet unsuccessfully—to persuade Bettina to visit us in Los Angeles. We continue to look forward to the day she may.

WHEN YOU GO, YOU SHOULD KNOW:

Podere Il Carnaschiale (Il Caberlot - Bettina Rogosky)
Mercatale Valdarno 52020 (AR)
Tel: (055) 9911142
Fax: (055) 992957
email: bettina.rogosky@caberlot.eu

Cibreo Ristorante, Trattoria Cibreo & Caffe Cibreo
Teatro del Sale
Via dei Macci 118/R
50122 Firenze, Italy
Tel: (055) 2341100
email: cibreo.fi@tin.it
edizioniteatrodelsalecibreofirenze.it

Bettina's Beet and Parmesan Salad
(Insalata di Barbabietola e Parmigiano)

Cooked or roasted beets are now available in many markets in the States, as well as in Italy, ready to include in a salad, add to a soup, use as a filling for *ravioli* or prepare as part of a sauce.

Makes 4 servings

2 bunches (12 small) boiled
  or roasted beets, peeled
  and thinly sliced
1/2 small red onion, peeled
  and thinly sliced
1/4 cup extra-virgin olive oil
Juice of 1 lemon
Kosher salt and freshly
  ground black pepper to taste
Whole coriander, crushed or ground
Shaved Parmesan cheese

Arrange the sliced beets on a large platter in a single layer. Top with onion slices. Sprinkle with olive oil, lemon juice, salt, pepper, and coriander. Just before serving arrange shaved Parmesan cheese over the beets.

Note: The best way to shave Parmesan cheese is with a potato peeler.

Bettina's Rosemary Cracker Bread
(Focaccia al Rosmarino)

Fresh rosemary gives this thin cracker-like *focaccia* added color and flavor. I like to serve it along with the *antipasti* or at the beginning of the meal.

Makes about 6

Basic Pizza Dough (see page 81)
1/2 cup fresh minced rosemary
Olive oil
Cornmeal
Salt, to taste

Preheat oven to 400°F.
  Prepare the pizza dough according to the recipe. Spoon onto a floured board and knead in the rosemary.
  Pull off a small piece of dough and knead it into a ball. Roll it out on a floured board, into a round as thin as possible.
  Sprinkle a round baking pan or cookie sheet with olive oil and cornmeal or polenta. Place the flat round on the prepared baking pan and sprinkle with salt. Pierce the dough all over the surface using the tines of a fork. Place on the lowest rack in the oven and bake until golden brown. Remove from the oven and transfer to a serving plate. Repeat with the remaining dough.

Wolf's Tomato, Onion and Rosemary Focaccia
(Focaccia Pomodoro, Cipolla e Rosmarino)

Wolf's *focaccia* is faster to make than ordering pizza from takeout, and it tastes so much better. Use my basic dough, and you can make this fragrant *focaccia* in no time at all.

Makes 4 *focaccia*, or 32 pieces / about 16 servings

1 recipe Basic Pizza Dough
  (see recipe, page 81)
1/2 cup extra virgin olive oil
1/2 cup cornmeal

Preheat the oven to 450°F.
  Prepare the Basic Pizza Dough. Divide into 4 parts. Brush four 12x14-inch baking sheets with oil and sprinkle with cornmeal. Roll out each piece of dough to 8x10-inches; place in the prepared baking

8 medium tomatoes, thinly sliced
4 medium yellow onions,
   peeled and thinly sliced
1/2 cup fresh rosemary, stemmed
Salt, to taste
Freshly ground black pepper,
   to taste

sheet and gently push dough with finger tips reaching as close to the edges of the baking sheets as possible without tearing the dough.

Arrange the tomato slices in a single layer on top of the rolled out dough; top with the onion slices, and sprinkle with rosemary. Drizzle with olive oil, and then sprinkle with salt and pepper. Bake on the lowest rack of the oven for 20 minutes, or until golden brown. Cut into 3x4-inch pieces and serve immediately.

Bettina's Fennel Soup
(Zuppa di Finocchio)

Bettina's French influence shows in this soup. She uses Ricard (anise liqueur) to enhance the delicious flavor of the fennel, but Sambuca works just as well.

Serves 6 to 8

3 large fennel bulbs, 5 to 6 cups
1/4 cup olive oil
4 to 5 cups vegetable stock
   or water
4 to 5 tablespoons Ricard
   or Sambuca
Salt and freshly ground
   black pepper to taste
1 cup croutons (recipe follows)

Cut tops off fennel bulbs and reserve. Cut bulbs in half, remove core and discard. Cut bulbs into thin slices. Mince the reserved fennel tops, spoon into a small bowl and set aside until ready to serve the soup.

In a large, non-stick pot, heat olive oil and sauté fennel until tender (do not brown). Add the stock or water and simmer until very soft. Add additional stock or water if needed.

Transfer the mixture to a large bowl or quart-sized measuring cup. Ladle 1/3 or 1/2 of the mixture, with liquid, into a blender or food processor and blend until a fine purée. Pour into the large pot and continue with the remaining mixture.

Over medium heat, bring to a simmer, add Ricard and salt and pepper to taste. Just before serving bring to a simmer, mixing occasionally until hot.

To serve, ladle into heated serving bowls. Garnish with the croutons and minced fennel tops. Serve immediately.

Croutons
(Crostino)

4 tablespoons unsalted butter
1 clove garlic, minced, optional
3 (3/4-inch thick) slices Tuscan
   or French bread cut into cubes

Preheat the oven to 350°F. In a large sauté pan, melt butter over medium heat and stir in garlic, cook and stir for 1 minute. Add bread cubes, and toss to coat. Spread on a baking sheet and bake for 15 minutes, or until crisp and dry. Check frequently to prevent burning.

Yellow Pepper Soup
(Passato di Peperoni Gialli)

The first time we were served this soup we were lunching with Wolf Rogosky at Cibreo Ristorante in Florence, where chef Fabio Picchi prepares Tuscan food with a contemporary slant. My version of this appealing soup should be creamy but not too thick.

Serves 8 to 10

6 tablespoons olive oil
1 red onion, finely chopped

In a large pot, heat 3 tablespoons of olive oil and slowly sauté the onions, carrot, celery until they begin to turn golden.

1 medium carrot, finely chopped
1 stalk celery, finely chopped
3 large yellow bell peppers,
    roasted (see recipe page 21)
3 medium Yukon Gold potatoes,
    boiled, peeled and
    cut in chunks
4 - 5 cups vegetable broth or water
1 bay leaf
Salt and freshly ground
    black pepper, to taste
Croutons, for garnish
    (see recipe page 147)
1/2 cup tablespoons grated
    Parmesan cheese

Add peppers and potatoes and sauté until soft, mixing well to combine all the vegetables. Add broth, bring to a boil and simmer 10 to 15 minutes.

Transfer the mixture to a large bowl or measuring cup. Ladle 1/3 or half of the mixture, with liquid, into a blender or food processor and blend until a fine purée. Pour into the large pot and continue with the remaining mixture. Add bayleaf. Season to taste with salt and pepper and simmer for 5 minutes. Do not boil soup: to reheat simmer on very low heat until heated through.

Remove bay leaf before serving. Ladle into soup bowls and garnish with croutons, drizzle remaining olive oil on top and sprinkle with the Parmesan.

Bettina's Tagliatelle with Baked Cherry Tomato Sauce
(*Tagliatelle al Sugo di Pomodoro Cigliegino al Forno*)

Bettina picks cherry tomatoes from her garden and bakes them in a low oven with onions and garlic for a couple of hours. Pasta is boiled, drained and tossed directly into the baked sauce, brought to the table and served.

1/4 cup olive oil
1 large onion, diced
6 garlic cloves, minced
2 to 3 cups whole cherry
    tomatoes
Salt
Freshly ground black pepper
1 pound tagliatelle or spaghetti
Freshly grated Parmesan

Serves 6 to 8

Preheat the oven to 250°F.

In a large roasting pot, add olive oil, onion, garlic, tomatoes and sprinkle with salt and pepper. Cover and bake for 2 hours.

Bring a pot of salted water to a boil, add the pasta and boil until tender. Drain and spoon into tomato mixture and toss well. Serve with grated Parmesan cheese.

Bettina's Rosemary Risotto
(*Risotto al Rosmarino*)

Bettina talked about this special way of preparing *risotto*, as we sat in her kitchen in Tuscany. This is the only way to prepare a real *risotto*, she explained. The rice is not boiled in water but is cooked in broth, which is added gradually and must be watched constantly. So, invite guests into your kitchen while you prepare *risotto* for dinner. It's served as a separate course in heated shallow soup bowls—the authentic Italian way.

6 tablespoons unsalted butter
1 onion, finely chopped
2-1/2 cups Arborio rice
6 to 8 cups hot vegetable stock

Serves 8 to 10

In a large heavy skillet, melt 4 tablespoons of the butter until foamy. Add the onion and sauté over medium heat until soft. Add the rice and mix well with a wooden spoon. Add 1 or 2 ladles of stock or enough to cover the rice. Cook, stirring constantly, as the stock is

1/2 cup minced fresh rosemary
1/4 cup minced parsley
1/2 to 1 cup cream
1 cup freshly grated
 Parmesan cheese
Salt
Freshly ground black pepper

absorbed. Continue adding stock a little at a time, until the rice is just tender, 10 to 15 minutes. Then toss in the rosemary, parsley, cream and 1/4 cup at a time of Parmesan cheese until it is creamy. Season with salt and pepper to taste.

Bettina's Rosemary Roasted Potatoes
(Patate Arrosto al Rosmarino)

Everyone loves potatoes and they go well with any main course—seafood, chicken or meat—especially when a pasta course is omitted.

Serves 4 to 6

16 small new potatoes, uniform
 in size and well scrubbed
4 tablespoons olive oil
4 garlic cloves, finely chopped
 (optional)
2 tablespoons snipped
 fresh rosemary
Salt
Freshly ground black pepper

Preheat the oven to 450°F.
 Cut potatoes in half crosswise and place in a large bowl. Toss with olive oil, garlic and rosemary. Sprinkle with salt and pepper, to taste. Arrange on a foil-lined baking sheet and bake until golden brown and crisp, shaking the pan every 10 minutes.

Bettina's Chocolate Mousse
(Mousse di Cioccolato)

You can make this *mousse* up to two days ahead of time. To turn this rich chocolate *mousse* into chocolate filled truffles, just follow the variation at the end of the recipe.

Makes 12 (2-ounce), or 6 (4-ounce) servings

1 cup semi-sweet chocolate
5 egg whites

For Truffle Variation:
1 cup additional semi-sweet
 chocolate, melted

Melt chocolate in a double boiler over simmering water. You may also use a microwave. Transfer to a large bowl and cool. Beat egg whites until stiff peaks form and fold into melted chocolate. Spoon into espresso or cappuccino cups. Refrigerate at least 1 hour before serving.

Variation: Season the chocolate *mousse* with almond, vanilla, coffee or orange extract and refrigerate. Shape teaspoons of *mousse* into small balls, dip in additional semi-sweet chocolate, place on wax paper and refrigerate.

FOLLONICA
Contessa Romana Bicocchi-Pichi at Numero Uno
A Birthday Party Italian Style

The first time we met Contessa Romana Bicocchi-Pichi was in Los Angeles, where she was promoting her wonderful unfiltered olive oil, Numero Uno. A tall statuesque redhead with a strong face and a forelock of snow-white hair, she told us that the olive oil is made in Follonica, a city in southwest Tuscany where the trees almost touch the Mediterranean. This location near the coast is unusual for olive trees, and the oil is surprisingly full-bodied and fruity—one of our favorites.

We invited Romana and Rolando Beramendi, who was her distributor at the time, to our home for dinner the next evening, and before she left she suggested we visit and stay with her at her villa in Tuscany. When we told her our next trip to Italy would be in April, the month of Marvino's birthday, she immediately offered to have a *festa* in his honor. Delighted, we invited some friends from Los Angeles and Italy to join in the celebration.

On April 24, we arrived at Romana's villa, a charming old house filled with superb antique furniture. We entered through a large foyer. Our hostess gave us a tour of the spacious interior. On the ground level, she showed us an enormous living room, a dining room, the kitchen and servants' quarters. Upstairs were eight bedroom suites, each connecting to a central sitting room. Our hostess showed us around the grounds, including the olive groves and the mill where the olives are crushed into oil and bottled.

Marvino's birthday lunch was held in the garden overlooking the Mediterranean Sea. A long table was set for twelve, under a big oak tree. Romana's staff prepared a memorable feast. We enjoyed sparkling wine with appetizers of fresh anchovies, seafood salad, sliced raw artichokes with thin slivers of Parmesan cheese, raw garden vegetables and *bruschetta*. The food was accompanied by Romana's special unfiltered olive oil, Numero Uno, made from olives grown on her estate. She has plans to open a cooking school at her Castello in Follonica, specializing in foods prepared with this olive oil.

As Marvino sat at the head of the table next to Romana, her chef prepared *risotto* over a large open wood fire, followed by succulent chicken, quail, duck, sausages, and vegetables. Dessert was a huge one-layer pinenut-custard birthday cake, *Torta della Nonna* (Grandmother's Cake), baked by Rolando and accompanied by Numero Uno's Vin Santo. The occasion, the food, the company, and Romana's unique Alice-in-Wonderland setting made the party a grand occasion for all of us.

After lunch, we drove just ten minutes to Massa Marittima, a charming hilltop village. Their specialty is a dessert known as *Panforte*: a thin, dense fruitcake that has now found its way to the States. We had remembered that the label on the package we buy in the States says, "Made in Massa Marittima." So, when we inquired about visiting the factory where the *Panforte* was made, the owner was delighted to accommodate us. We had envisioned an extensive factory, since these fruitcakes seem to be available in most Italian

Happy Birthday Marvino, from Romana!

food stores. To our amazement, we entered a small two-story building where one baker mixed, made and packaged the product. Upstairs, the owner's wife and daughter were wrapping the *Panforte* as well as special *biscotti* they make. We could hardly believe that these delicacies had such an unassuming origin.

We left with our arms full of *Panforte* and *biscotti* to enjoy for the next several weeks. Of course, we brought some back to our hostess, Romana.

That evening, we all helped Rolando prepare dinner: a salad with fresh greens from the garden, *tagliatelle* with tomatoes and basil, a veal roast, and *tiramisu* for dessert. This time we sat in the dining room, with Romana at the head of the table. We began with sparkling wine and appetizers, after which a tomato-basil pasta course was served. And that is when the strangest thing happened. As everyone was eating, we turned and saw that Romana's face had fallen right into her dish of pasta. We were in a state of shock, assuming she must be dead. But Rolando seemed to take the event in stride. "Don't worry," he said, "she is okay; this happens once in a while."

After three or four very long minutes, Romana suddenly lifted her head and carried on as if nothing unusual had happened, except that basil leaves were stuck to her nose and hair! Relieved that she seemed unfazed by the incident, we managed to continue our meal without comment. At the time, we did not think the situation was funny, and wouldn't have dared to laugh. But every time we share this story with friends, we picture Romana with the pasta and basil clinging to her face and are caught in gales of laughter.

On another April visit to Italy, we called Romana and mentioned that we were in her neighborhood. Before we could say anything further, our hospitable friend said, "We will expect you for lunch." Her daughter was also visiting, and we sat outside at a table next to the Castello. As always, the meal was wonderful; I still remember the appetizers of cherry tomatoes threaded on a wooden pick with mozzarella cheese and the orange-scented seafood *risotto*. We had a great time and promised to come back soon.

**WHEN YOU GO,
YOU SHOULD KNOW:**

Contessa Romana Bicocchi-Pichi
c/o Tenuto Numero Uno
Follonica, (GR) Italy 58022
Tel: (0566) 40036

Panforte
Le Logge
Via Goldoni 5-7
Massa Marittima, Italy
Tel: (0566) 919923
Fax: (0566) 901910

Skewered Cherry Tomatoes and Mozzarella
(*Pomodori Cigliegini e Mozzarella*)

On one trip to Italy we made a spontaneous call to Romana Bicocchi-Pichi—almost eight years after our previous meeting. She immediately invited us to lunch. That day she served an appetizer that exemplifies the Italian affinity to extend hospitality with whatever is in the pantry.

Serves 12

36 mini-cherry tomatoes
Basil leaves, cut in half
1 to 2 pounds fresh mozzarella (*bocconcini*, preferably)
36 bamboo skewers
Olive oil

Place a cherry tomato on a bamboo skewer, top with a basil leaf and a chunk of fresh mozzarella. Arrange on a platter and sprinkle with olive oil. Serve immediately, or cover with plastic wrap and refrigerate.

Romana's Orange Accented Seafood Risotto
(Risotto all' Arancio e Pesce)

While we were having lunch with Contessa Romana Bicocchi-Pichi, her daughter, Alessandra, explained that she is compiling a collection of her mother's recipes. In preparing this *risotto*, Romana adds a cube of powdered broth (*brodo*) directly into the rice at the beginning of the process instead of dissolving the powdered *brodo* in water. This enables her to adjust the flavor, in case all the water is not added to the rice during the cooking.

Serves 8 to 10

1/4 cup olive oil
1 onion, finely chopped
1/2 cup finely diced orange peel
2-1/2 cups Arborio
  or Cannaroli rice
1/4 cup dry white wine
1 vegetable bouillon cube
8 cups simmering water
1 cup fresh squeezed orange juice
1/2 pound halibut, cut in chunks

Heat the olive oil and sauté onion and 1/4 cup of the orange peel. Add rice and mix with a wooden spoon, stir for 1 minute to coat grains. Add wine; it will sizzle. Add bouillion cube and begin adding 1/2 cup at a time of the simmering water, stirring frequently.

Wait until each addition of water is almost completely absorbed before adding the next 1/2 cup. Stir frequently to prevent sticking. After about 18 minutes, when rice is tender but still firm, add the orange juice and stir vigorously to combine with rice. Just before serving, add halibut and cook until opaque. Garnish with the remaining orange peel. Serve immediately.

Italian Fruit Cake
(Panforte)

This spicy, chewy Italian fruit and nut confection is a wonderful holiday treat. Because the cake is so dense and rich, you'll want to serve small slices.

Makes 1 cake

1-1/2 cups flour
3 teaspoons unsweetened
  cocoa powder
1/4 teaspoon each ground
  cloves, nutmeg and ginger
2 tablespoons ground
  cinnamon
1-1/4 cups hazelnuts, toasted
  and skinned
1 cup unblanched almonds,
  toasted
3/4 cup chopped candied
  grapefruit peel
1/2 cup chopped dried
  apricots
1/2 cup golden seedless raisins
8 dried figs, chopped
3/4 cup honey
1 cup sugar
Confectioners' sugar, for garnish

Preheat the oven to 300°F.

In a large bowl combine flour, cocoa powder, cloves, nutmeg, ginger, and cinnamon. Add hazelnuts, almonds, grapefruit peel, apricots, raisins and figs.

In a saucepan, combine the honey and sugar and bring to a boil over high heat. Cook until the mixture thickens, about 5 minutes. Add the flour mixture, mixing with a wooden spoon until cool enough to handle. The dough will be very stiff. Mix with dampened hands, blending thoroughly.

Oil an 11-inch springform cake pan and place on a well-oiled parchment-lined baking sheet. With wet hands, press the fruit mixture into the ring, spreading evenly. Bake for 1 hour, or until the edges look set and the top is slightly puffed. Cool completely in the pan.

Run a knife around the edges of the pan and remove the sides. Store at room temperature. Before serving, dust with confectioners' sugar and slice into thin wedges.

Note: If the fruit is dry and hard, pour on boiling water to cover and let soften about 5 minutes. Drain before using.

TODI
Piero and Giulianna Dorazio
A Vacation at an Artist's Villa

In 1985, my publisher at William Morrow, Ann Bramson, told me about an artist and his wife, Piero and Giulianna Dorazio, who had renovated a villa on their property just outside the hilltop village of Todi. Having decided that we would stay in Italy for five months that year, we called Giulianna and rented the place sight unseen. Far from being disappointed when we saw it, we were ecstatic. Much larger than we expected, it had five bedrooms, five bathrooms and a kitchen twice the size of the one in our Los Angeles home, with a large rustic wooden table in the center. We invited all our friends to come and visit, and a lot of them did.

Piero, a tall, slender, balding man, had his art studio on the property, next to their house, where he worked, and he and Giulianna often invited us to lunch. A tall, beautiful redhead, she has her own art gallery in Todi. Every day the Dorazios' cook prepared delicious meals, from pasta to seafood or roasts, with outstanding desserts. It was easily the best food we had in all of Umbria.

One afternoon Beverly Pepper, a world-famous sculptor who was a friend of the Dorazios, invited us to her home, a mini castle. In the midst of planning a wedding for her son, she asked Marvino to help her choose the wines. Her husband, Bill, a

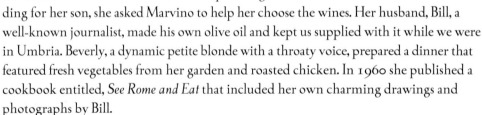

well-known journalist, made his own olive oil and kept us supplied with it while we were in Umbria. Beverly, a dynamic petite blonde with a throaty voice, prepared a dinner that featured fresh vegetables from her garden and roasted chicken. In 1960 she published a cookbook entitled, *See Rome and Eat* that included her own charming drawings and photographs by Bill.

Every morning we picked vegetables from the Dorazios' garden for our lunch. I will never forget the time Piero knocked on our door holding a huge basket filled with truffles. When we asked if we could have one, he said no, we could have the whole basket. For weeks, we ate scrambled eggs with truffles, *risotto* with truffles, and pastas with truffles. That was the year we discovered wild asparagus growing out of the rocks in the wall close to our house. We prepared a dish of sautéed wild asparagus tossed with spaghetti and truffles–a delectable combination of flavors.

During our stay at the Dorazios', Piero was getting ready for his exhibition at the art Biennale in Venice. He was painting day and night and drying his paintings with the giant heater in his studio. Watching him at work, we noticed that the tremor that was visible in his hands mostly disappeared when he was drawing. When we commented on his devotion to his work he gave us a signed lithograph with a personal dedication. He also made ceramic bowls and plates decorated with his painted designs that we were able to acquire and take home.

On our visit the following year we were invited for lunch, and Piero was excited to show us his latest project: he had re-designed their swimming pool, whose entire surface was now lined with mosaic tiles that recreated one of his paintings.

Unfortunately this great artist passed away just a few years ago. We think of him often, and we cherish in our home many of the beautiful artworks he made.

Left: Piero proudly shows off a just-finished painting, bound for the Venice Biennale. Right: Our own work of art gets a personalized signature.

Oven Baked Tomatoes
(*Pomodori al Forno*)

Tomatoes were growing in abundance in the Dorazios' garden, and of course they encouraged us to enjoy them. Prepared this way, they make a perfect topping for toasted slices of bread, known in Italy as *bruschetta*; or add them to a tomato sauce or a pizza for more intense flavor.

Makes 24

24 small tomatoes
2 heads garlic (not peeled, smashed with the side of a sharp knife)
Salt
Freshly ground black pepper
3 tablespoons sugar
16 sprigs of fresh rosemary
3 tablespoons olive oil

Preheat the oven to 300°F.

Using a sharp knife, cut a shallow "X" in the bottom of each tomato. Drop the tomatoes, 2 or 3 at a time, into boiling water until skin breaks (about 10-20 seconds). Lift them out with a slotted spoon and plunge them into a bowl filled with ice and water. The skins will slip off easily. Peel the tomatoes and cut them in half horizontally (not through the stem end). Gently squeeze the juice and seeds out of each half over a bowl. Use your fingers or a small spoon to clean out any remaining seeds (reserve juice and seeds for sauce).

Place the tomato halves side by side, cut side down on, on a well-oiled jelly roll pan (baking sheet with sides). Scatter with the garlic cloves and sprinkle with salt, pepper, sugar, rosemary and drizzle with olive oil. Bake for 2 to 3 hours, shaking the pan occasionally so the tomatoes do not stick, until all the liquid in the tomatoes has evaporated. The tomatoes will become very brown around the edges. Immediately transfer them with a spatula to a glass dish to cool in a single layer. Cover with plastic wrap and refrigerate. If keeping for more than 2 to 3 hours, cover them with additional olive oil.

Twice Boiled Soup
(*Ribollita*)

Once the Dorazios' cook served us this hearty soup, we became fans of *Ribollita*, which literally translates as "re-boiled." The Dorazios' vegetable and herb garden made it easy to prepare large amounts of this classic Tuscan dish for ourselves while we were staying at their villa. Whenever we were ready to eat it, we would simply reheat it. We purchased fresh bread daily, so we always had day-old bread available for this soup.

Serves 8 to 10

1 to 1-1/2 cups dried cannellini
  beans, or 2 (15 ounce) cans
  cannellini beans
2 large leeks, white and green
  parts separated and washed
  thoroughly in cold water
1/4 cup olive oil
10 large leaves *cavolo nero,*
  kale or chard, discard center
  stems and coarsely chop
1/2 red cabbage, thinly sliced
1 large tomato, diced
1 teaspoon dried thyme
Salt
Freshly ground black pepper
4 slices toasted day-old
  Italian bread, cubed
Olive oil for garnish
Grated Parmesan cheese

If using dried beans, soak them in cold water for at least two hours or overnight. Drain the beans and put in a stockpot, along with 4 cups of cold water. Bring to a boil, lower heat and simmer until beans are tender (at least 1 hour, depending on freshness of the beans), adding additional water as needed (about 4 more cups in all).

In a large-size pot, bring 8 cups of water to a boil; add sliced green part of leeks and boil until tender. Using a slotted spoon, transfer boiled leeks with a little of their liquid to a blender and blend until smooth and set aside. Reserve the remaining liquid.

In another large pot heat olive oil, add thinly sliced white part of leeks and sauté over low heat until tender, about 5 minutes. Add liquid from boiled green leek tops and cook for 5 minutes. Add *cavolo nero*, red cabbage, diced tomato, thyme and leek purée. Bring to a simmer and add beans and salt and pepper to taste; bring to a boil. Add additional liquid if needed. Cook uncovered until vegetables are tender and flavors are blended, about 20 minutes. Add bread cubes and cook for 30 minutes.

To serve, ladle soup into bowls, top with a splash of fresh olive oil, and sprinkle with grated Parmesan cheese.

Chickpea Soup
(*Zuppa di Ceci*)

We picked chickpeas from plants growing in a field near the Dorazios' villa. Fresh chickpeas were new to us, and we were excited about making soup with them. However, they do take a long time to boil. At home, we use canned chickpeas—their flavor is close to that of dried ones and they need less time to cook.

Serves 6 to 8

2 (15.5-ounce) cans chickpeas
1/4 cup olive oil
2 garlic cloves, minced
1 onion, finely diced
1 carrot, finely diced
1 celery rib, finely diced
2 teaspoons fresh rosemary or
  1 teaspoon dried, minced

Drain chickpeas, reserving liquid. Place chickpeas in a food processor with a little of the reserved liquid, and purée them. Transfer the purée to a bowl and set aside.

In a large pot, heat oil over medium heat and sauté garlic, onion, carrot and celery, stirring occasionally until vegetables begin to soften, about 3 to 4 minutes. Add rosemary, red pepper flakes, chickpea purée, salt and pepper and 3 cups reserved chickpea liquid and water.

Pinch red pepper flakes
1 to 2 teaspoons salt
Freshly ground black pepper
**3 to 4 cups reserved chickpea
cooking liquid and water**

Bring to a boil and simmer 30 minutes. Season with additional salt to taste. Serve soup in heated bowls and drizzle additional oil on top.

Fresh Corn Polenta with Mushroom *Ragout*
(Polenta Frescha con Ragu di Funghi)

The standard American way of serving corn is to boil freshly picked ears and serve them with butter. But with just a little more effort, fresh corn can be turned into a special version of *polenta*. Why settle for ordinary ground cornmeal when you can use tender, sweet corn kernels to make this delicious and healthy variation?

Serves 8

**Mushroom Ragout
  (recipe follows)**
8 ears of corn
1/4 cup olive oil
Pinch of sugar, or to taste
**3/4 cup grated Parmesan
  cheese**
**Salt and freshly ground
  black pepper**

Prepare the Mushroom Ragout and keep warm.

Remove the corn husks by trimming off both ends of the cobs.

Run the point of a sharp knife down the center of each row of corn kernels. To remove the corn from the cob, use a corn fork or a spoon, working over a shallow bowl, and scrape with the back of a spoon or the fork to remove the juice and pulp.

In a large nonstick skillet, heat the olive oil over medium heat. Add corn mixture stirring with a wooden spoon until heated through and tender. Add sugar, salt and pepper to taste and 1/2 cup of the Parmesan cheese. Continue to mix until the mixture thickens, about 5 minutes.

To serve, spoon onto heated serving plates and top with mushroom ragout and remaining Parmesan cheese.

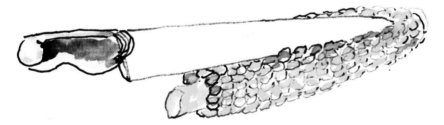

Mushroom Ragout
(Ragu di Funghi)

Makes about 1-1/2 cups

**1 pound mushrooms: shiitake
  caps or an assortment of
  fresh mushrooms**
14 cup olive oil
1/2 cup vegetable broth
Salt
Freshly ground black pepper

Gently brush dirt from mushrooms. Slice the mushrooms 1/8 to 1/4 inch thick.

In a medium saucepan, heat olive oil and sauté mushrooms until soft, adding vegetable broth and salt and pepper to taste. Sauté until mushrooms are tender and broth thickens. Keep warm.

DERUTA
Ubaldo Grazia
Ceramics, Food and Wine

The first time we met Ubaldo Grazia, Marvino and I were renting a villa from Piero Dorazio and his wife Giulianna just outside of Todi, about fifteen minutes' drive from Deruta, where Ubaldo manages his family's ceramic factory. When we walked into the factory, Ubaldo greeted us in Italian. Assuming that his only language was Italian, Marvino spoke it back to him as best he could. After watching Marvino struggle for nearly half an hour, Ubaldo let slip that he spoke perfect English—and we all began to laugh. Ubaldo said, with a twinkle in his eye, that Marvino seemed to be having such a good time trying to communicate in Italian he didn't have the heart to stop him.

Ubaldo gave us a tour of his factory that included an instructive demonstration. His potter took a sizeable ball of clay, shaped it on a wheel into a large vase, then finished it by hand—only to smash it down afterward to make sure we understood that this was only a demonstration.

Our second meeting with Ubaldo was in Los Angeles, when we attended a reception given for him by the owner of a gift store in Beverly Hills to present his latest collection of ceramics. As we were chatting with him, he told us that he had been booked into the Hollywood-Roosevelt Hotel, but was concerned that there was really no place for him to walk, because of all the "wild people" who filled the sidewalks of Hollywood Boulevard. I said, "On your next visit, why not stay with us?" That very evening he moved out of the hotel and into our guest room. Since then, when he returns to Los Angeles each year to show his ceramics and do business—usually around Thanksgiving—he always stays with us.

With most Italians, hospitality is reciprocated in a delightful way. Now, whenever we are in Italy, we are invited to stay in Ubaldo's country house, located in a small hilltop village above Deruta.

The first time we arrived at his house Ubaldo was heating up a gigantic pot of *risotto* with all sorts of delicious looking vegetables in it. We assumed this was for our dinner. But then, to our surprise, he produced his dog dishes and began spooning the food into them. Another of his pranks? With Ubaldo, it was hard to be sure. Probably just as well that we never mentioned we thought the dogs' dinner was meant for us, since he took us to a wonderful country restaurant that evening.

As you drive up to the ceramic factory, you pass through an iron gate to a large building whose exterior is covered with the traditional Deruta gold-and-blue majolica tiles. On the street level are several rooms filled with classic dishes, cups, saucers, vases and platters.

Ubaldo often gives visitors a personal tour, beginning with a demonstration like the one we had from one of his senior artisans, who may be forming the clay into anything from a vase to wash basin. After you've seen how clay is sculpted into a work of art, you

Ubaldo and Marvino, in front of his family's famed ceramic factory.

continue on to a room where the ceramics are painted and fired; on the way there you see the ancient wood-burning oven where Ubaldo's great, great grandfather fired ceramics. The next rooms are spectacular. They display not only the traditional majolica designs, but also the contemporary ceramics that Ubaldo has commissioned from artists all over the world.

The Grazie factory has been in operation since the 15th century. Ubaldo's wife, Rita, is a schoolteacher, and his daughter, Chiara, now helps manage the factory. Her love and enthusiasm for the family ceramic business is as contagious as her father's, and it's likely that she will be the next generation to take over.

Each time we visit we bring home a dozen or more colorful new ceramic dishes. When we invite friends for dinner we love serving each course on a different artist's creation. We have encouraged Los Angeles artists John Okulak and Peter Shire to work in Ubaldo's factory and design ceramics, and they always return relaxed and inspired. When friends are traveling to Umbria we always suggest they visit the factory, and Ubaldo always gives them a VIP tour. He also organizes ceramics classes during the tourist season, and you can find information about these on his website.

Ubaldo has introduced us to a treasure trove of restaurants in the area that tourists rarely find. Some of these places are regional and creative; others are country-rustic *trattorias*. When we ask why he never brought us to a particular establishment before, his smiling answer is invariably, "Oh, I thought I told you about that one." Since he always knows the owners, he and his guests get special treatment.

On one occasion, a restaurant was closed when we arrived, but Ubaldo persuaded them to open just for us. Entering through the kitchen, we were greeted by an elderly woman who was in the process of preparing dinner for her husband. She explained that she was cooking with some ingredients he had just brought in from the woods, and she described the origin of each dish.

I still remember eating from a large wooden board containing hot *polenta* that had a sausage placed in its center as she told us about the tradition that whoever finished the *polenta* first got the sausage–a practical solution in the days when families had more limited food resources.

Ubaldo introduced us to the dishes from which the recipes that follow are based upon.

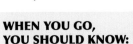

WHEN YOU GO, YOU SHOULD KNOW:

Ubaldo Grazia Maioliche
Majolica Plates and Ceramics
ubaldograzia@ubaldograzia.com
Via Tiberina, 181 – Deruta
Tel: (075) 9710201
email: ubaldograzia@ubaldograzia.com
website: www.ubaldograzia.com

Trattoria Cernacchie (near Cintoia)
Tel: (055) 856968

Taverna Sel Gusto
Ristorante Con Cucina Tipica Umbra
Centro Storico
Deruta (Pg)
Tel: (075) 9724120

Spinach with Pine Nuts and Raisins
(*Spinaci con Pinoli e Uvetta*)

This is a dish that I remember being served at the little restaurant that Ubaldo Grazia took us to. We love spinach and often enjoy it for lunch, so I was happy to discover a way in which to enhance it.

Serves 4

2 tablespoons raisins
1/4 cup dry red wine
3 tablespoons olive oil
1/2 onion, chopped
2 garlic cloves, thinly sliced
3 to 4 bunches spinach,
    trimmed and washed
3 tablespoons toasted pine nuts
1 tablespoon fresh lemon juice
8 thin strips lemon zest
Salt
Freshly ground black pepper
2 tablespoons grated lemon peel

In a small bowl, plump raisins in red wine to cover for 30 minutes or overnight in the refrigerator. Drain and squeeze lightly.

In a large skillet, heat olive oil over medium heat. Add onion and garlic cloves and cook until soft, about 3 minutes. Add spinach and cook, stirring, about 1 minute. Cover pan and cook, stirring occasionally, until spinach is wilted, about 3 minutes. Add pine nuts, lemon juice, lemon zest, and raisins. Season with salt and pepper to taste. Sprinkle with grated lemon peel.

Tomato and Roasted Garlic Risotto
(*Risotto al Pomodoro e Aglio Arrostito*)

In Italy *risotto* is generally served as a pasta course followed by a main course of fish, chicken or meat. But it could stand on its own, preceded by a salad of roasted peppers and followed by assorted *biscotti* with *macedonia* and *gelato*.

Serves 6

5 garlic cloves, unpeeled
2-1/2 tablespoons olive oil
3 cups vegetable broth
1/2 cup dry white wine
1 cup Arborio rice
2 cups chopped, seeded
    tomatoes
2/3 cup sliced fresh basil
1/3 cup grated Parmesan
    cheese

Preheat the oven to 450°F.

Place garlic on small sheet of foil. Drizzle garlic with 1/2 tablespoon olive oil and enclose in foil. Roast until soft, about 20 minutes.

In a heavy medium saucepan, bring broth and wine to a simmer. In a medium saucepan, heat remaining 2 tablespoons olive oil over medium heat. Add rice to oil and stir until translucent, about 2 minutes. Gradually add all but 1/4 cup broth mixture to rice, stirring to incorporate each addition fully before adding more. Cook until rice is tender but still slightly firm to bite and mixture is creamy, about 20 minutes.

Squeeze roasted garlic out of skins onto foil and mash with fork, incorporating oil. Add garlic to rice. Stir in remaining 1/4 cup broth if *risotto* seems dry; cook 1 minute. Add tomatoes, basil and cheese, and stir until cheese melts.

Above: Massimo showing off his sense of humor. Below: Massimo showing off his beautiful family: wife, Lara; daughter, Alexa and son, Charlie.

MODENA
Massimo Bottura
Osteria Francescana: Making Magic with Balsamic Vinegar

When in Italy, we often drive through or stay in Modena, the birthplace of balsamic vinegar. It was in the 70s, when we first discovered this magical elixir. We were told that the best version was to be found at an old pharmacy. The owner of this particular *farmacia* had made his own balsamic for many years. When we visited and asked for some, he went to the back of his store and emerged with a small dark brown bottle for sale. We still have this old-fashioned bottle and keep it re-filled with balsamic both as a memento of our experiences with this precious liquid, and to enhance the flavor of the new additions.

On one trip from Parma to Firenze we decided to put on a little extra speed to get to the Modena *farmacia* before noon, when the shops closed. We parked and rushed to the *farmacia*, only to find it had closed down the previous year. We were devastated. Where, we wondered, would we ever find such delicious vinegar again?

Years later, when it was still new, we were taken as guests to Osteria Francescana. This fine restaurant currently has two stars in the *Michelin Guide*. Chef/owner Massimo Bottura's culinary talents were inspired by his work for famed Chef Ferrán Adrià at El Bulli in Spain. Massimo has also been recipient of numerous awards, including Osteria Francescana having placed in the top 10 of the World's 50 Best Restaurants for the past two years.

From our first visit, it was clear that this would become one of our favorite restaurants. The food is as exciting as it is contemporary and delicious. While dining, we met Massimo; his American wife, Lara, a curator of contemporary art; and their two children. Before we left, they promised to come visit us in Los Angeles. Since Lara's sister lives in Los Angeles, they have been able to keep that promise.

WHEN YOU GO, YOU SHOULD KNOW:

Osteria Francescana
Via Stella, 22
41121 (MO)
Tel: (059) 210118
Fax: (059) 220286
email: info@francescana.it
website: www.osteriafrancescana.it

Franceschetta Wine and Food
Via Vignolese 58
41100 (MO)
Tel: (059) 3091008
email: info@franceschetta.it
website: www.franceschetta.it

On one of our return visits, chef Massimo invited us to a *Balsamico Gusto*, a special dinner in Villa Cavazza, home of the oldest balsamic. French Chef Michel Troisgros, and chef Massimo prepared every dish in this amazing feast with the finest balsamic. Massimo created a dish for the dinner that was as amusing as it was delicious: a *foie gras* parfait on a stick, with a surprise center of extra old *Aceto Balsamico di Modena*. Shaped as though an ice cream bar, it was coated with roasted hazelnuts. Massimo insisted no silverware be used to enjoy it! My grandchildren are especially delighted with my simpler rendition of this dish, made with chicken livers, since they can pick it up by hand and eat it right off the stick.

Designer Breadsticks
(*Grissini*)

M assimo's long, crispy breadsticks inspired me to make them in different shapes. You could, for example, top them with a cane-like handle or a heart or cylinder shape. Or you could create an edible napkin ring by twisting several strands of the dough into a two-inch circle. A large glass or two filled with these whimsically-shaped breadsticks can add a festive atmosphere to a dinner party.

Baked breadsticks can be stored in plastic bags in the freezer. Reheated in the oven, they taste as fresh as the day they were made.

Makes 3 to 4 dozen

1 package active dry yeast
Pinch of sugar
1 cup warm water
   (110°F to 115°F)
3 tablespoons olive oil
3 to 4 cups flour
1 teaspoon salt
3 egg whites
Kosher salt
Sesame seeds, caraway seeds,
   or poppy seeds

Dissolve the yeast and sugar in 1/2 cup of the water until foamy. In the large bowl of an electric mixer, combine the oil and the remaining 1/2 cup warm water. Blend in the yeast mixture and 1 cup of the flour and beat until smooth.

In a large mixing bowl, beat 2 of the egg whites until stiff but not dry. Fold the beaten egg whites into the yeast mixture. Add the remaining flour, 1 cup at a time, beating well after each addition, to make a soft dough. Knead the dough on a well-floured board for 5 minutes and place it in an oiled bowl; oil the top of the dough. Cover with a towel and let the dough rise for 15 minutes. Punch it down again and let it rise for 15 minutes more.

For hand-rolled breadsticks:
Divide the dough into quarters and roll out each quarter on a floured board into rectangles 1/3 inch thick. Cut each rectangle into 2-inch squares; roll each square up tightly and then back and forth with the palm of your hand into a long, narrow stick, as thin as a pencil and 10 to 12 inches long.
Carefully transfer each stick to a foil-lined 10x15-inch greased baking pan, placing the strips 1/4 to 1/2 inch apart. Keep the strips straight and pinch the ends down so they stick to the foil. Repeat until all the dough is used. Cover with a towel and repeat the procedure with a second baking pan.

Preheat the oven to 350°F.

Let the breadsticks rise in a warm place until round and puffy, about 15 minutes. Brush them with the remaining egg white, lightly beaten, and sprinkle with kosher salt and seeds. Bake for 15 to 20 minutes, until golden brown and crisp. Carefully remove the breadsticks to racks to cool.

For pasta machine breadsticks:
Pinch off a ball of dough 2 inches in diameter and flatten it with the palm of your hand to a 1/2-inch thickness. Lightly dust with flour. Set the pasta machine rollers as far apart as possible. Guide the dough between the rollers and roll it through. Coat it with flour and feed the sheet through the wide noodle-cutting blades, cutting it into strips about 1/4 inch wide and 10 to 15 inches long.

Let the breadsticks rise and bake them as described above.

Chicken Liver Nut Bars
(*Croccante di Fegatini*)

Your guests will probably do a double take when you serve this appetizer, which looks like an ice cream bar, coated with nuts and served on a stick. "Life is uncertain," one of them might quip. "Eat dessert first." But the first bite will make them smile as they realize this is an elegant *pâté* dressed up as a child's treat.

Makes about 2 dozen bars

1/4 cup olive oil
2 medium onions, thinly sliced
1-1/2 pounds chicken livers
2 tablespoons balsamic vinegar, plus more to serve
2 hard-boiled eggs, peeled
Salt, to taste
Freshly ground black pepper, to taste
Roasted chopped hazelnuts
2 dozen wooden popsicle sticks for assembling

In a large, heavy skillet, heat olive oil and sauté the onions until lightly browned. Transfer to a bowl and set aside. Add the livers to the skillet with additional olive oil if needed, and sauté, cooking the livers on both sides until lightly browned (do not overcook). Add the balsamic vinegar and simmer 3 to 4 minutes.

Spoon the chicken livers with the onions and eggs into a meat grinder and grind into a large bowl or chop in a wooden bowl. Add salt and pepper to taste and mix well. Cover with plastic wrap and refrigerate until firm. Shape into 3x2-inch bars, about 1/2-inch thick. Insert a wooden stick in the bottom and dip in hazelnuts. Garnish with additional balsamic vinegar.

BOLOGNA
Guido Paulato
A Personal Tour of the Best in Bologna

During our years in the clothing business, we visited Bologna twice yearly so that Marvino could shop at the *Fiera di Scarpi* (The International Shoe Show). I took advantage of this opportunity to walk around Bologna on my own, browsing through the many food shops and restaurants.

My first inkling of the culinary delights in store for us came with our introduction to Guido Paulato made by our Italian banker, Antonio Pironte. Antonio exclaimed, "You're going to Italy? You must meet my dear friend Guido,"

Always game, we called immediately to arrange a *rendezvous*. And so, while Marvino worked, I was introduced to an aspect of Bologna that a casual a tourist might never discover. Guido, a boyish man with a mop of curly hair and a winning smile, began by taking me to the great-granddaddy of all Italian delis, commonly known as "*gastronomies*." As we entered, a tantalizing aroma and carnival of sights stopped me in my tracks. I saw a large pig turning on a spit. It was hard to see the man selling cheeses, sausages and salads,

**WHEN YOU GO,
YOU SHOULD KNOW:**

Osteria Il Sole
Via Lame, 67
40013 Trebbo di Reno, Bologna, Italy
Tel: (051) 700102
Fax (051) 700290

Cantina/Osteria Bentivoglio
Via Mascarella 4/b
40126 Bologna, Italy
Tel: (051) 265416
Fax: (051) 225811
email: jazz@cantinabentivoglio.it
website: cantinabentivoglio.it

so heavily draped was his stall with an assortment of meats. Guido and I then headed for the bakery and then the open-air market, where we shopped for lunch.

We stopped to have a glass of wine at Guido's favorite bar and he introduced me to the "locals." They sat at wooden tables and benches, taking time off from work to enjoy each other's company and gossip about local affairs as they ordered wine to drink with the *panini* they had brought from home or bought at the bar. Though I was the lone woman in a bar full of men, they made me feel completely welcome.

So enthusiastic was Guido about sharing his home city with me, that he attempted to show me everything on that first day. Wherever we went we were accompanied by his well-trained dog, a boxer, who trotted alongside Guido without a leash. He waited outside each shop in anticipation of the treat his master would give him upon our return.

When we finally returned to Guido's apartment with our shopping haul, he set to work preparing lunch for his girlfriend and me. It included a platter of cheeses and handmade pasta from the *pastaio* (macaroni vendor) swimming in a sauce of tomatoes and peppers.

Guido told me he would be working at his new wine bar that evening and urged Marvino and I to drop by. Following his directions, we arrived at the designated street, only to find that we could barely make our way through the crowd. Humble to a fault, Guido had neglected to mention that his place was the hottest spot in town. The tiny restaurant façade opened into a very deep building. We followed Guido through room after room, each packed with people, until he motioned us to take a seat at a wooden table.

A few years later, we discovered that Guido had opened Osteria Il Sole, in Trebbo di Reno just outside of Bologna. He had restored an old hotel, updated the rooms and created a fantastic restaurant.

On our first visit, we stayed overnight and had dinner. There were three young chefs in the kitchen and our food was deliciously fresh and contemporary in style. Thanks to Guido's interest in wine, the list is outstanding.

We always stop there for lunch on our way from Milan to Venice or Florence. We still joke about a dinner there, in which the chef served us lamb chops as an *antipasto*. It seems this cook was a pioneer: it's now stylish at catered cocktail parties in the States to pass a tray with small rib lamb chops for the guests to enjoy. Soon after, the restaurant earned its first Michelin star. Guido and his chef have been invited to showcase their cuisine at food fairs such as "*Salone*," the Slow Food expo in Torino.

Always interested in developing new projects, Guido recently rented Il Sole to Marcello, the chef who is reportedly continuing the restaurant's tradition of "*nouvelle cuisine.*"

Guido is now managing an *osteria* in the center of Bologna called Bentivoglio, which features a large room dedicated to jazz concerts and attracts an enthusiastic young crowd.

Lamb Chops
(*Costolette D'Agnello*)

When Guido's chef served us two lamb chops as an appetizer, we wondered if this was meant to be our main course. Nowadays in Los Angeles, we often see these small chops passed on a tray as an appetizer at fashionable cocktail parties. Personally, I still prefer to eat them as a main course while sitting at a table.

Serves 6 as appetizers

Basil pesto (recipe follows)
3 (1-1/2 pounds each) racks of lamb, trimmed and French cut
Salt and freshly ground pepper, to taste
1/2 cup olive oil

Preheat the oven to 400°F.

Prepare basil *pesto*.

Sprinkle lamb racks with salt and pepper. Heat 2-3 tablespoons of the olive oil in a grill pan or a large heavy skillet over high heat. Place lamb rack in the skillet and cook just until brown, about 3 minutes per side. Transfer lamb rack, meat side up, to a large, heavy baking sheet. Repeat with the remaining 2 lamb racks.

Roast the lamb in the oven until cooked to desired doneness, about 20 minutes for medium rare. Transfer lamb racks to a work surface. Set aside for 10 minutes. Cut the lamb between the bones into single chops. Spread *pesto* over 1 cut side of each chop. Arrange chops, *pesto* side up, on plates or a platter and serve.

Basil Pesto

1 1/2 cups lightly packed fresh basil leaves
1/2 cup walnuts, toasted
2 tablespoons freshly grated Parmesan
2 tablespoons fresh lemon juice
2 garlic cloves
Salt to taste
Freshly ground black pepper, to taste
1/3 cup olive oil

In a food processor, blend the basil, walnuts, cheese, lemon juice, garlic, salt and pepper until the basil is finely chopped. With machine running, gradually blend in 1/3 cup olive oil until smooth and creamy. Set aside until ready to use.

ARGELATO
Jessica Martelli, Deborah Martelli and Alesandro Formaggi: *Ristorante L'800 – An Impromptu Pasta Lesson*

While Marvino and I were renting a house in Panzano, in the Chianti area just outside of Florence, we decided to take a two-day excursion to Venice. On such jaunts we usually stay in Mestre at the Hotel Bologne to avoid having to carry our luggage through the waterways. Every morning we would cross the street from the hotel to the train station and take the train directly into Venice: a perfect arrangement.

Above: Marvino and I pose in front of L'800. Below: Two chefs and a *sommelier*.

On this trip, when we checked out of our hotel, we took a long walk into town and found the daily open-air fish market. The fish looked pristinely fresh, as if they had been caught that morning and the variety was amazing.

On our way back to Florence, after viewing the Art Biennale in Venice, Marvino suggested that we stop for lunch at a restaurant he had read about in the Michelin Guide. He was fascinated by its specialties: mushrooms, snails, frogs' legs. The restaurant, "L'800" (*L'Ottocento*), just north of Bologna, was a little difficult to find on our first visit. Close to the *Autostrada* when you are driving from Venice to Bologna, it is certainly worth a detour.

Arriving late, we were greeted in the large entry area by Deborah, a voluptuous red-head. Speaking to us in English, she showed us to a table and gave us the menu. It turned out that she was also the *sommelier*, and when she suggested wines to go with our lunch we became aware of her expertise as she paired the food and wine perfectly. She also described the selection of pastas, which are handmade in the restaurant. Under my breath, I said I would love to watch the pasta being made. She heard me, smiled and said, "no problem." Before we quite knew what was happening, the table behind us was emptied of wine glasses and place settings. As if by magic, a lovely tall blonde woman appeared, her cheeks as red as if freshly painted. This was Deborah's sister, Jessica, who arrived from the kitchen carrying a large wooden board, a long rolling pin, flour, eggs and olive oil. Before our amazed eyes, she proceeded to mix, knead and roll out pasta in many shapes and sizes–narrow and wide, plump and thin.

Lunch was fabulous. Before we left, we met the sisters' mother and father. Deborah's husband is also a chef in the restaurant, and Luca–then boyfriend and now husband of Jessica–helps run the front of the house.

It was Jessica's dream to come to California, and six months later she, Deborah and their soon-to-be husbands, Alesandro and Luca, came to visit us at our home in Los Angeles.

When they arrived, they drove to their hotel in downtown Los Angeles. Italian

Above: Alesandro and Deborah. Right: Jessica, giving a private and impromptu pasta-making demonstration.

travel agents always seem to book their clients there, mistakenly assuming that it is the center of the city. We quickly rebooked them at a hotel in Santa Monica. Our first stop was the Santa Monica Wednesday farmers' market. Later we took them to our restaurant, Capo, and introduced them to our partner, Chef Bruce Marder. Jessica gave the chefs a lesson on making pasta and *ravioli*. When the pastry chef asked her to check out his *gnocchi*, she shared with him her secret for making them lighter. Chef Bruce prepared lunch for us, even though the restaurant was closed and we all had a great time.

That night we returned to Capo for dinner and found Jessica's *ravioli* on the menu. Tomatoes were in season, and Chef Bruce served two colorful platters of local heirloom varieties from his garden. The main course was char-grilled slices of rare steak, which they loved. We had homemade apple pie for dessert.

After leaving Los Angeles, they took a whirlwind tour of the rest of California. When we are in Italy, we never miss an opportunity to visit them at L'800. The last time we were there they served us homemade sausages, accompanied by Lambrusco, a dry red sparkling wine. That was when they told us that Deborah was expecting a baby. We later received the announcement with a photo of roly-poly baby Federico. A few months later, when we again visited the restaurant, "Freddy" joined us for lunch, sitting in his highchair. Given the usual tradition of the Italian family restaurant business, the next time we see him, he may be in the kitchen of L'800 creating recipes!

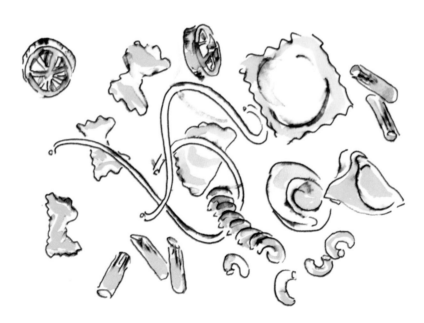

Jessica's Pasta Dough (2 ways)
(Jessica's Pasta Base)

Thisrecipe is adapted from Chef Jessica's handmade pasta that is prepared daily at her restaurant, L'800. The following directions are for her handmade pasta as well as for a more simple food processor method.

Hand Method

4 cups flour
1/2 teaspoon salt
4 eggs
2 tablespoons olive oil

Makes 2 pounds

Place the flour and salt on a wooden pastry board and make a well in the center. Break the eggs into the well and add the oil. With a fork, beat the eggs and oil, gradually drawing the flour from the edge of the well and incorporating it into the egg mixture to form a dough that can be gathered into a ball.

Knead the dough for 5 to 10 minutes, working in extra flour as necessary, until it is no longer sticky. With a pastry scraper, clean off the board; transfer the remaining flour to a fine-mesh strainer and sift, discarding the dry and sticky scraps. (Follow the directions using the pasta cutter.)

Processor Method

3 cups flour
1/2 teaspoon salt
4 large eggs
2 tablespoons olive oil
2 tablespoons water

Makes 2 pounds

The quantities and directions for the food processor method require a large capacity food processor. If your processor has a more limited capacity, make the dough in two or more batches.

Place the flour and salt in the processor fitted with the steel blade. Turn the machine on and off once. With the machine running drop in one egg and, the instant it is blended in, turn off the machine. Repeat with the remaining eggs until the dough is crumbly or resembles a coarse meal. Add the olive oil and water and process just until the dough begins to come away from the side of the bowl.

Remove the dough to a floured wooden board and knead until just smooth.

Rolling Out Pasta Dough, Manual Method

Divide the dough into 3 or 4 parts for easier handling. When rolling out the first piece, cover the remainder with a large bowl so the dough does not dry out.

To Roll Out Pasta With A Pasta Machine

Set the rollers at the widest opening. Divide the dough into 4 parts for easier handling. Working with one part at a time, flatten the dough with the palm of your hand into a thick strip no wider than the machine. Dust it lightly with flour and crank it through the machine. Fold it in half or thirds, pressing it down with your finger tips, dust with flour, turn it 90 degrees (a quarter-turn) and run it through the machine again. Repeat this process 3 or 4 more times, dusting with flour each time, until the dough is smooth, elastic and no longer sticky. Now the dough is ready to stretch into a long sheet.

Set the machine to the next opening, bringing the rollers closer together, and run the dough through. This time, do not fold or turn the dough. Set the rollers another notch closer and run the dough through again. Continue rolling the dough with a smaller opening each time, stopping just before the next-to-narrowest setting. (The dough strip will become very long, so allow ample work space, or cut the dough in shorter sheets as it gets longer.)

For stuffed pasta, follow the directions in the recipe, using the pasta sheets while they are still moist. For noodles, let the pasta dry for about 15 minutes (so that the noodles don't stick together), depending on the temperature and humidity of the kitchen. If the kitchen is hot, the pasta will dry quickly.

Options Available With A Pasta Machine

Attachments are available for cutting the pasta into a variety of shapes and widths with plain or scalloped edges. These sizes have special names, such as *tagliatelle*, *lasagna*, and *cappellini* (angel hair), to name but a few. Sprinkle the cut pasta generously with flour and continue to dry on towel-lined baking sheets.

Chocolate Pasta with Sweet or Savory Sauces
(*Pasta al Cioccolato con Salsa Dolce oppure Saporito*)

I will never forget looking into the window of a store that sold dried pasta, marveling at the assortment of pastas displayed there. When I saw dark brown pasta for the first time I wondered if it really contained chocolate. I later learned that chocolate pasta is made the same way as traditional pasta, but with sugar and unsweetened cocoa in the dough. This unusual variation goes well with a variety of sauces, limited only by your imagination—from a hearty meat sauce to a rich vanilla sauce.

1-1/4 to 1-1/2 cups flour
2 tablespoons (unsweetened) cocoa
2 tablespoons sugar
2 eggs
1 tablespoon olive oil
Classic Tomato Sauce (see recipe page 111) or
Cream Sauce (*Salsa di Panna*) (recipe follows)

Makes 6 servings

In a bowl, sift flour, cocoa and sugar together. Place on work surface and make a well in the center. In a small bowl, beat the eggs with oil and pour into the well. Gradually work flour mixture into the liquids until dough is firm. With pastry scraper or spatula pick up all the dough and knead until smooth and pliable. Follow a method for rolling out pasta dough, page 169. Cut into noodles and let dry.

When ready to serve bring a large pot of water to a rapid boil. Add pasta and cook until *al dente* (5 minutes). Drain. Spoon pasta into individual bowls and serve with Classic Marinara Sauce or Cream Sauce, garnished with strawberries.

Cream Sauce
(*Salsa di Panna*)

Makes 1-1/2 cups

1 cup whipping cream
2 eggs, beaten
1 teaspoon vanilla
1 tablespoon sugar
Strawberries, plumped dried
   apricots halves or other
   fruit, for garnish

In the top of a double boiler combine cream, eggs, vanilla and sugar. Whisk to mix well. Place over simmering water and cook, stirring frequently, until thickened. Serve immediately.

Potato Dumplings
(*Gnocchi*)

I watched Jessica as she gave the chefs at Capo restaurant, in Santa Monica, California, a demonstration on the art of making *gnocchi*. They were thrilled with the results of her technique, and have been preparing *gnocchi* her way ever since.

Serves 6 to 8

2 pounds russet potatoes,
   scrubbed
1-1/2 cups all-purpose flour
3 egg yolks
Salt and freshly ground black
   pepper to taste
1-1/2 tablespoons olive oil
1 tablespoon unsalted butter
2 tablespoons grated Parmesan

Boil the potatoes in a large pot over medium heat until soft. Peel and pass through a potato ricer into a large mixing bowl. While still warm, add the flour, egg yolks, salt and pepper. Mix well. Spoon the potato mixture into a pastry bag fitted with a #8 plain tip and pipe the mixture into long ropes on a floured surface. Cut into 3/4-inch pieces and roll the *gnocchi*, one by one, over the tines of a fork to produce a ribbed effect. Blanch the gnocchi in boiling salted water until they rise to the surface. Use a slotted spoon to transfer to ice water. Drain and pat dry.

   In a large pan, heat olive oil and butter. Add the *gnocchi*. Cook for 1 minute. Sprinkle with the Parmesan and serve.

Baked White Fish with Raisins and Pine Nuts
(*Pesce Bianco con Uva Passa e Pinoli*)

If we don't want to stay overnight in Venice, we always stay at Hotel Bologne in Mestre. We just cross the street and take the 30-minute train ride to Venice for the day. There is an amazing daily open-air fish market in Mestre. Before leaving, we purchase the freshest of fish and have the vendors wrap them with ice. We then drive back to our Florence accommodations.

Serves 10

1 (4 pound) whole white fish,
   center bone removed
Salt and freshly ground
   black pepper
Juice of 1/2 lemon

Season fish inside and out with salt, pepper and lemon juice. Arrange lemon slices inside the fish. Seal fish closed with long wood picks.
   Preheat the oven to 375°F.
   In a large roaster or fish poacher, heat olive oil and sauté onion, carrots, and celery until soft, about 5 minutes. Add tomatoes with

1/2 lemon, thinly sliced
3 tablespoons olive oil
1 large onion, thinly sliced
2 large carrots, diced
2 celery stalks, diced
1 (1 pound, 12-ounce) can
   chopped or diced tomatoes
1/2 cup golden raisins, plumped
   in white wine
1 cup dry white wine
1/2 cup toasted pine nuts,
   for garnish
Parsley, for garnish
1 lemon, sliced thinly for garnish

liquid, raisins, wine, salt and pepper and bring to a boil. Arrange the white fish on top of the sauce, spooning the sauce over the fish. Bring to a boil. Cover and bake until fish is tender and cooked through, about 30 minutes. Garnish with pine nuts, parsley and lemon slices.

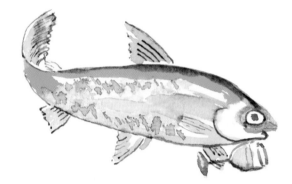

ON THE AUTOSTRADA

AUTOGRILL

ON THE AUTOSTRADA
Autogrill Sandwiches

The first time I had *panini* in Italy we were on the Autostrada at lunchtime, hours from our destination. We stopped for gas at one of the rest areas located every 30 to 50 kilometers along the Autostrada. It was then that we spotted an Autogrill. Part of a well-known chain in Italy, this particular Autogrill had an extensive buffet bar. Their *panini* looked so good that we decided to have several for lunch.

I soon realized that the best assortment of these grilled sandwiches is often available at service station snack bars. In the glass display cases, you can often find ten or more different combinations of the sandwiches, using a variety of breads and rolls. The basic components are simple; bread, cheese, vegetables and meat. You will find assorted meats, a variety of cheeses and even chopped cherry peppers for a spicy zing. My favorite *panini* combines sliced eggplant, roasted peppers, and Pecorino cheese.

When a selection is made, a server will ask if you want it toasted. Our answer is always, "yes." Told that it will take a few minutes, we watch as our sandwich of choice is placed in a *panini* oven: a portable two-sided grill that resembles a waffle iron. In just a few moments, we are handed a hot *panini* with grill marks, wrapped in parchment-like paper, with melted cheese oozing out the sides.

Not all of the auto stops have large Autogrills, but almost all of them have an espresso bar and *panini* waiting to be grilled and enjoyed.

The best way to grill *panini* yourself is with a home-style *panini* machine, similar to the ones used in the Autogrills. They are now available at most cookware stores. The heavy metal grill applies pressure and heat to both sides of the bread at once. No flipping is necessary and there is no need to apply any extra pressure as the sandwiches grill. As soon as I purchased my own *panini* press, I began experimenting with all sorts of combinations, from savory to sweet.

It's easy to prepare these Italian-style sandwiches at home, but remember that the surface of the grill must reach a high temperature to produce the desired crisp, golden-brown crust. Most of the machines have non-stick cooking surfaces, making cleanup simple.

If you don't have a *panini* press, you can create the same effect using a heavy-bottomed pan or cast-iron skillet. Place a weight on the sandwich (as I used to do with the melted cheese sandwiches I made for our kids to enjoy when they were young).

For a party, it's fun to have platters of breads, assorted cheeses or meats, and one of vegetables. Let your guests create their own *panini*.

These sandwiches make a great main course for lunch or an appetizer before dinner. For dessert, prepare chocolate filled *panini* and serve them with *gelato*.

On one of our recent trips to Italy, we stopped for a cappuccino, on our way to Il Sole di Ranco near Lago Maggiore, at a bar that was part of a service station on the Autostrada.

After I took a couple of photos of the *panini*, to get a record of the assortment of fillings available, I walked outside. I didn't notice until we got into our car, that a woman, dressed in an Autogrill uniform had followed us. She gave us a hard time, asking in Italian why I had just taken photos of their sandwiches. She planted herself behind our car and would not let us drive away until I gave her the roll of film in my camera! When I finally handed it to her, she gave me a new roll. We drove away in complete shock, wondering what secret about their *panini* they imagined I was trying to steal. If I had asked permission before I took the photos, would they have allowed it? Probably not.

My Favorite Autogrill Sandwich
(*Panini Autogrill*)

The great thing about this *panini* recipe is that the eggplant, peppers and/or cheese are interchangeable with your own favorite veggies.

Makes 4

8 slices eggplant, thinly sliced
1/4 cup olive oil
4 (4-inch square) *focaccia*
4 tablespoons unsalted butter
8 slices roasted peppers
  (see recipe page 21)
8 slices Pecorino cheese

Brush both sides of the eggplant slices with olive oil and season with salt and pepper. Arrange the eggplant slices on the grill pan, set a small baking sheet on top and weight evenly with 2 bricks. Cook until dark grill marks appear, 2 minutes, then turn and cook second side 30 seconds (follow instructions for your *panini* press if using one).

Slice through the center of each *focaccia*. Spread with butter and set half of the slices buttered side down, and cover them with half of the eggplant and roasted peppers. Cover these with the cheese slices, folding them back in toward the middle if they extend past the edges of the *focaccia*.

As you layer vegetables and cheese be sure to not only cover the *focaccia* but also to allow some of the vegetables to extend just beyond the edge of the bread so they become crisp while grilling. Put the remaining slice of *focaccia* on top, buttered side up. Grill the *panini* until the bread is golden brown and the filling is steaming hot and bubbly.

Niçoise Salad Sandwich
(*Nizzarda Pan Bagna*)

Pan Bagna translates as "bathed bread." This upgraded tuna sandwich is sold on the streets of Nice much as pizza is sold in Rome. The bread is sprinkled with olive oil and vinegar and filled with tuna, anchovies, vegetables, and herbs. The sandwich is then topped for a few minutes with a heavy plate to compress it and to ensure that the bread soaks up the good flavors of the filling.

Makes 1 sandwich

1 clove garlic
1 large Kaiser roll or French roll

Cut garlic clove in half and rub crust of roll with cut ends. Slice the roll in half crosswise and scoop out some of the inside of both halves to make room for the filling.

1 tablespoon olive oil
1 teaspoon red wine vinegar
Salt
Freshly ground black pepper
4 thin slices firm tomato
4 thin slices red onion
2 tablespoons drained canned
   tuna (packed in oil or water)
2 anchovy fillets
4 pitted black olives, sliced
2 fresh basil leaves
1 large lettuce leaf

Sprinkle roll slices with olive oil and vinegar and season with salt and pepper to taste. On bottom half, arrange tomato and onion slices, tuna, anchovy fillets, olives, basil leaves, and lettuce. Cover with the remaining half of roll and weigh down with a heavy plate for 2 minutes to compress the filling (alternatively, follow instructions for your *panini* press if using one). Serve immediately.

Lorenza's Vegetable Sandwich Loaf
(*Sfilatini con Verdure Grigliate*)

In this unusual and delicious sandwich the filling is baked right into the bread. Culinary instructor and author Lorenza de Medici, who prepares this loaf for her cooking school at Badia a Coltibuono in Tuscany, graciously allowed me to include it in this book. Just add a salad for a balanced lunch or brunch. Although this yeast dough requires several hours for rising and baking, it is well worth the time and effort.

Makes 1 large, round loaf. Serves 8

1 package active dry yeast
1 tablespoon sugar
3/4 cup lukewarm water
2 tablespoons olive oil,
   plus more for baking sheet
1 teaspoon salt
2 cups plus unbleached
   all-purpose flour, plus
   1/2 cup flour for board
Vegetable filling
   (recipe follows)

Dissolve yeast with a pinch of the sugar in 1/2 cup of the lukewarm water and set aside until foamy, about 2 minutes.

In a large bowl, using a heavy-duty mixer, blend 1 tablespoon of the olive oil, the remaining sugar, salt, and the remaining 1/4 cup lukewarm water. Blend in yeast mixture. Add 2 cups of the flour gradually until the dough comes together. Turn out onto a floured board and knead until dough is smooth and elastic, about 3 minutes. Form into a ball, brush top of dough with the remaining tablespoon olive oil, cover with a towel, and let rise in a warm place 30 minutes. Punch down, shape into a ball, and let rise an additional hour.

Prepare Vegetable Filling and set aside. Line a baking sheet with aluminum foil and brush with oil.

Punch the dough down to flatten and roll out on a floured board into a 12x16-inch rectangle. Cover with Vegetable Filling and roll rectangle lengthwise, jelly-roll fashion, to enclose the filling. Form roll into a ring; pinch ends to seal and place on prepared baking sheet. For second rising, cover with a towel and let rise in a warm place until doubled, about 30 minutes.

Meanwhile preheat the oven to 375°F. When loaf has risen, bake until golden brown, about 20 minutes. Cool on a wire rack.

Vegetable Filling

Makes about 2 cups

2 tablespoons olive oil
1 cup diced onions

In a nonstick skillet, heat olive oil over medium heat and sauté onion, bell pepper, and zucchini until tender, about 5 minutes.

1 cup seeded and diced
   red bell peppers
1 cup diced zucchini
Salt
Freshly ground black pepper

Season with salt and pepper to taste. Transfer to a bowl and cool. Makes about 2 cups.

Tomato, Mozzarella and Basil Sandwiches
(Panini Mozzarella Pomodoro e Basilico)

The red, white, and green colors of the Italian flag are represented in this delicious Italian sandwich. Marinate the tomatoes in a little balsamic vinegar, if you like, to bring out their garden-fresh flavor.

Makes 2 sandwiches

1/4 cup Mustard Vinaigrette
Dressing (recipe follows)
10 slices Roma tomatoes
10 slices soft mozzarella cheese
10 small fresh basil leaves
2 long French baguettes
   (6 to 7 inches)
Salt
Freshly ground black pepper

Prepare Mustard Vinaigrette, cover with plastic wrap, and chill. On a large plate, arrange tomato slices in a single layer. Top each tomato slice with a slice of cheese and a basil leaf.

Slice baguettes in half lengthwise (without cutting all the way through). Drizzle vinaigrette on each of the cut sides.

Arrange 5 of the tomato stacks overlapping slightly, lengthwise, along the center of each baguette. Season with salt and pepper to taste.

Mustard Vinaigrette

Makes about 3/4 cup

1 tablespoon minced onion
1 garlic clove, minced
1/2 teaspoon prepared
   mustard
1/4 cup white wine vinegar
1/2 teaspoon dried basil
1/2 cup olive oil
Pinch of sugar
Salt
Freshly ground black pepper

In a processor, blender, or mixing bowl, combine the onion, garlic, mustard, vinegar, and basil. Add olive oil and blend well. Add sugar, salt, and pepper to taste.

Grilled Eggplant, Arugula and Mozzarella Sandwich
(Panini con Melanzane Grigliate Rucola e Mozzarella)

Arugula, often referred to as rocket, has a peppery bite to it that can be refreshing and bold. The eggplant and mozzarella in this sandwich help to balance it. We have arugula growing in our garden in Los Angeles, and it is widely available in Italy.

Serves 4

4 slices eggplant, each
   1/2-inch thick

Heat a grill pan over high heat, or heat an electric panini grill on the highest setting according to the manufacturer's instructions.

Olive oil
Salt
Freshly ground black pepper
**8 slices country-style bread,
each 1/2-inch thick**
**2 cups loosely packed
arugula leaves**
**8 ounces thinly sliced
fresh mozzarella**

Brush both sides of the eggplant slices with olive oil and season with salt and pepper. Arrange the eggplant slices on the grill pan, set a small baking sheet on top and weight evenly with 2 bricks. Cook until dark grill marks appear, 2 minutes, then turn and cook second side 30 seconds.

Brush one side of each slice of bread with olive oil. With oiled sides of bread down, arrange eggplant, arugula, and mozzarella on 4 of the slices and add salt and pepper to taste. Top each sandwich with another slice of bread, oiled side up. Reduce heat to medium-high and place 2 sandwiches on grill pan; cover them with baking sheet and weight it with bricks (or follow manufacturer's instructions for your *panini* press). Cook until dark grill marks appear, 2 minutes, remove bricks and baking sheet, and turn sandwiches carefully. Weight down again and cook 30 seconds. Transfer *panini* to a cutting board and cut in half. Serve immediately and repeat with remaining 2 sandwiches.

Smoked Salmon and Cheese Sandwich
(*Panini di Salmone Affumicato e Formaggio*)

This sandwich, cut into quarters, makes an elegant appetizer before dinner, as well as a simple and delicious lunch.

Makes 6

**1/2 cup Mustard-Dill Sauce
(recipe follows)**
6 slices smoked salmon
6 slices mozzarella cheese
12 slices sandwich bread

Prepare Mustard-Dill Sauce, cover with plastic wrap and chill.

Place sliced bread on a work board and spread dill sauce on 6 slices of bread. Top each with a slice of smoked salmon and a slice of cheese to cover. Cover with 6 remaining slices of bread.

Preheat your panini press or grill to medium-heat.

Place the sandwiches in the panini press and close the lid. Grill the sandwich until the bread is toasty (golden brown) and the cheese is melted. Slice in quarters and serve immediately.

Mustard Dill Sauce

Makes about 1 cup

**3 tablespoons Dijon-style
mustard**
**1 teaspoon powdered
mustard**
2 tablespoons sugar
**1 tablespoon red or
white vinegar**
1/3 cup olive oil
**3 tablespoons fresh chopped
(or snipped) dill**

In a small, deep bowl, combine the mustard, powdered mustard, sugar and vinegar and blend well. With a wire whisk, slowly beat in the oil until it forms a thick mayonnaise. Stir in the chopped dill. Cover with plastic wrap and refrigerate until ready to serve.

Autogrill Roasted Vegetable Sandwich with Anchovies
(Panini Autogrill con Verdure Grigliate e Acciughe)

In Italy this delicious auto-grill sandwich is known as *pan bagna*. It features a mixture of baked vegetables, herbs and garlic, all spooned over crusty rolls and topped with anchovy fillets and arugula.

Serves 4

2 large tomatoes, seeded
  and halved
1 red onion, halved vertically,
  cut crosswise into
  1/2-inch-thick slices
1 red bell pepper, cored,
  quartered
1 zucchini, trimmed, cut
  lengthwise into 1/2-inch-
  thick slices
2 medium eggplant, cut into
  1/4-inch thick half rounds
  (about 12 ounces)
4 whole garlic cloves, peeled
3 tablespoons olive oil
1/4 cup minced fresh parsley
1 teaspoon dried rosemary,
  crumbled
Salt and freshly ground
  black pepper
4 long Italian rolls
1 (2-ounce) can anchovy fillets,
  drained
2 cups arugula or watercress
  leaves (about 2 large bunches)

Preheat the oven to 400° F.

In a large bowl combine tomatoes, onion, pepper, zucchini, eggplant, garlic cloves and toss with olive oil. Transfer to a large roasting pan. Bake vegetables for 20 minutes, stirring frequently. Stir in parsley and rosemary and bake until vegetables are tender, about 10 minutes longer. Remove garlic cloves from pan and slice thinly. Return garlic to pan. Season with salt and pepper, to taste.

Preheat broiler. Cut rolls in half horizontally. Open rolls and toast under broiler until golden, about 45 seconds. Divide vegetables among bottom half of rolls. Top each with 3 anchovy fillets. Arrange a layer of arugula on top of filling. Close top half of each roll over filling. Cut (rolls) sandwiches in half and serve.

Open-Face Mushroom Sandwich
(Bruschetta con Cappelle di Funghe)

The subtle, delicious flavor of the mushrooms is brought out by the open-face grilling. A perfect appetizer with sparkling wine. For a flavorful variation, brush bread with *pesto* (see recipe page 37) before topping with mushrooms.

Serves 4

16 mushrooms (white,
  Portobello, or shiitake)
4 slices whole wheat bread
1/4 cup olive oil

Place mushrooms on wooden surface cap side down. Using a mandolin or very sharp knife, cut mushrooms into paper thin slices, making sure to keep the stem section attached.

Brush one side of each slice of bread lightly with oil. Place mushrooms in a row on the dry side of bread, slightly overlapping, making

Salt
Freshly ground black pepper

3 or 4 rows to cover surface. Brush mushrooms with olive oil and sprinkle with salt and pepper.

Place bread, mushroom side up, in *panini*-style grill (follow manufacturer's instructions for your own *panini* press). Grill about 4 to 5 minutes until bread is golden brown and mushrooms are sizzling and cooked through.

Bittersweet Chocolate Sandwich
(Panini al Cioccolato Fondente)

No one can resist the delicious pairing of bread and chocolate. It is a perfect breakfast treat on raisin/nut bread. Serve it for dessert as an accompaniment to *gelato*. For an interesting variation, crumble an ounce of Gorgonzola and put on bread before adding chocolate.

Serves 4

8 small slices raisin/nut bread
8 ounce bar bittersweet chocolate, thinly sliced

Arrange the chocolate on 4 slices of bread, stopping short of the edges by 1/2 inch. Cover with the remaining 4 slices of bread. Place on hot *panini* grill or heavy frying pan, cover with the heavy lid and grill until chocolate is melted. Makes 4 servings.

Note: Use a potato peeler to thinly slice a bar of chocolate.

Ice Cream Sandwich
(Panini al Gelato)

In a hilltop village just outside of Panzano we attended a *festa* where the specialty was a hot croissant filled with ice cream. We joined the line of locals waiting to order it from a young woman. She would take a hot croissant that had been sliced open in advance, arrange a large scoop of ice cream in the center of the bottom half, close the top half around this filling, and wrap the whole thing in parchment paper. Unlike the assortment at the usual *gelateria*, there were only three choices of ice cream here—vanilla, chocolate or strawberry—but no one seemed to care. For us, the combination of the hot croissant and the ice cream was a fabulous new taste sensation.

Serves 4

4 croissants, heated until crisp
1 pint Vanilla chocolate chip ice cream (see recipe page 99)
Parchment or wax paper for wrapping

Preheat oven to 300°.

Heat croissants until crisp.

Split the hot croissants without cutting all the way through. Using a large spoon or ice cream scoop, gently pack the croissant with ice cream. Press the sides of the croissant together to enclose the ice cream and wrap with parchment paper. Serve immediately.

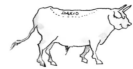

INDEX

INDEX

INDEX

NOTES

NOTES